# NOT THAT

# KIND OF GIRL

# Not

# That

# Kind

# of Girl

A MEMOIR BY *Carlene Bauer*

HARPER

*An Imprint of* HarperCollins*Publishers*
www.harpercollins.com

An extension of the copyright page appears on page 275.

FIRST EDITION

*Designed by Eric Butler*

Library of Congress Cataloging-in-Publication Data is available upon request.

ISBN: 978-0-06-084054-9

09 10 11 12 13   OV/RRD   10 9 8 7 6 5 4 3 2 1

For my mother and father
and
Dan and Ilona

# CONTENTS

# WISE AND FOOLISH

In the Gospel of Matthew, Jesus tells the parable of the wise and foolish virgins—five wise, five foolish, all waiting with torches to light the way of a bridegroom to his wedding feast. The wise virgins have enough oil for their lamps, the foolish ones don't, but they all fall asleep while they're waiting. Soon enough, the bridegroom is spotted in the distance, they scramble to their feet, and the foolish virgins realize how foolish they've been. Please, they say to the wise virgins, lend us some oil! We'd love to, say the wise ones, but if we do that there won't be enough for everyone. Go out into the city and see if there's anyone selling oil at this hour. So the foolish hurry off. And, of course, they're not there when the bridegroom arrives. Of course.

The wise virgins enter the wedding feast, and the door is shut. Here is how Matthew tells it. "Later the others also came. 'Sir! Sir!' they said. 'Open the door for us!' But he replied, 'I tell you the truth, I don't know you.'" And then Jesus provides the moral to his disciples, which is that his second coming could occur at any time: "Therefore keep watch, because you do not know the day or the hour."

As a child, whenever I heard that story, I thought the foolish virgins deserved what they got. Later, the wise virgins read as haughty prudes. You could imagine them swanning into the wedding feast and the door slamming shut—even the door's slam sounding pitiless and proud. But you wouldn't want to be foolish, either, lolling about, too busy doing—what was it you were doing again when you should have been filling that jar with oil so your lamp wouldn't go out?—to miss the party. Or would you? The party, after all, being a metaphor for heaven, which had never been the point of believing to me.

Perhaps there was another story hidden in the parable, one that the church would never tell. One of the virgins might have showed up prepared, followed the bridegroom into the wedding party, and then said to herself, *I'm glad I planned ahead, but now that I've been here a while, I'm bored. And that bridegroom seems like an insufferable boor—who does he think he is, to say he wants nothing to do with those girls when tonight he has everything in the world he could want, and can afford to give them the gift of his pardon! Where are those foolish virgins? Are they keeping each other company? Making jokes, linking arms? That might be its own party.* This young woman would be a curious virgin, let's say, in both senses of the word, in that she was genuinely curious about the life she was not living but was also something of an anomaly, an anachronism, okay, a freak. She could see the value of prudence—it was a prophylactic against most of life's pain—but she would want to see what life was like in the dark, when, her lamp sputtering, she would have nothing but her wits to guide her. She would shut the door quietly, leaving a room swelling with hope and safety behind her, and take the lamp out into the street, wondering where to begin. She would stand in the streets of the city, wondering when she'd catch up to those girls. How long would it take?

# NOT THAT
# KIND OF GIRL

# CHAPTER 1

## SHE WHO HAS AN EAR, LET HER HEAR

My mother says she can't listen to love songs anymore. Whatever men and women have to say about love is meaningless, she says, when she thinks about all that God has done for us.

But when you go to a Goodwill and see all the Andy Williams records, and think "Who could have possibly owned these?" picture my mother: Mila Ann Phifer of Haviland Avenue, Camden, New Jersey, Audubon High School, class of 1965. My mother owned more than one record by Andy Williams— and more than one record by his lady friend, Claudine Longet. She also owned records by the Association, the Turtles, Chad and Jeremy, and Sergio Mendes and Brasil '66. French girls in minidresses surrounded by daisies. Suave, smiling Brazilians holding paper parasols and cocktails. Bespectacled, turtlenecked young men with guitars looking pensively at a lake in a glade, coming to call on your secretly sad daughters. The green record case that was the reliquary of her girlhood contained records by the Supremes, Smokey Robinson, Dionne Warwick, the Mamas and the Papas, and the Beatles. "Before they started to do drugs," she always made a point of telling me and my younger sister. After that she switched her allegiances to Motown.

The first thing my sister and I knew about her life before us was that it was filled with music. We did not know who she'd fallen in love with before she met our father or what she wanted to be when she grew up, but we knew the names of her favorite bands. She told us that she gave my sister the middle name Justine because it was the name of one of the *American Bandstand* regulars, and she liked the sound of it. She told us that she used to dance with our Aunt Carol—Audubon High School, class of 1968—and Aunt Susan—Haddon Heights High School, class of 1976—in the kitchen to the radio while they washed dishes. That our grandmother's favorite song was "Misty," as sung by Johnny Mathis. That our grandfather had taken her and Carol to see the Supremes at the Latin Casino in Camden, where they gave you small wooden mallets—she still had one, in a shoe box in the top of her closet—to drum on the table instead of applaud. And when she worked at Woolworth's and the Beatles released *A Hard Day's Night*, one shift, while stationed in the record department, she commandeered the store stereo and played the album three times in a row.

To live, my mother was teaching us, was to love music, and I learned very quickly. When I was six, riding around in the car with her on errands, I heard on the radio that some planet or other was on course to collide with Earth. My stomach pitched, but when the radio went on to say that we'd passed out of danger, I announced to my mother from the back seat that I was glad we were still alive because that meant I could still listen to her Beatles records. Although I had a flair for the dramatic—"All right, Sarah Bernhardt," my mother would say to me when I took to the stairs in a huff or sighed too loudly—this wasn't something I said for effect. I was addicted to their jubilance. It drove me to corral my sister and the girl across the street into forming a band that played badminton rackets on our front porch.

Our mother told us that Mama Cass died by choking on a sandwich, but she did not tell us much about God, at least not when we were very young. We did not know that my mother had earned an enameled pin for perfect Sunday school attendance in junior high, or that the workbooks from her Sunday school lessons, pictures carefully colored with crayons, also resided in a box at the top of her closet. She and her sisters had been raised largely Baptist but occasionally Methodist in rented houses and apartments with Warner Sallman's *Christ Knocking at Heart's Door* hanging in the living room, and, since they were granddaughters of Spiritualists, sometimes swore there was someone in the room with them when there was no one at all. As a result, my sister and I were familiar with Jesus, but not overly so. Our mother sometimes took us to church with Aunt Carol and our cousins, and my grandmother taught us to sing "Jesus Loves the Little Children," but we had not yet heard that we needed to formally ask Jesus into our heart for him to recognize us as his own.

My mother had longing and hope as a young woman, and it was not exactly for Jesus. She did believe that all you needed was love— love, however, as it was depicted in *Funny Girl* and *Dr. Zhivago*. A bell and then shots rang out at Kent State, and bombs were dropping on Cambodia, but for my mother 1970 sounded like "Come Saturday Morning." Saturday was what she longed for, because that was my father's day off and their day to spend together. When we asked her how it went, she sang a few lines for us, lines about traveling aimlessly, contentedly, with a friend, sang them and smiled, making fun of the song's sweetness just a little. When she married my father— John Anton Bauer, Camden Catholic High School, class of 1959, who brought no records into the union, and no stories—her faith was such that she did not mind being married in his boyhood parish, or having us christened there by a priest, if that's what my father wanted. She would never again be so uninterested in who owned our souls.

Unlike our parents, my sister and I would never live in rented houses or in towns with bus lines and sidewalks. My father took to the woods for the same reason his father moved his family out of Philadelphia and over the river to Jersey: he wanted to come home to trees, as many of them as possible. He'd made more money than his father had, and so could buy a new house, free of stories and smells, and if you wanted a new house in the early 1980s, you had to go into the woods, because that's where they were being built. When you drove out to our house from the crowded towns our parents had been raised in, the roads grew longer and darker, and peeling houses stood lonely as lighthouses on acres of farmland.

Unlike our parents, my sister and I would never know a desultory, perfunctory love of God. Soon after my father took to the woods, my mother, who had been baptized in her teens, became born again—again—through a church that a neighborhood friend had started attending. My father did not go to church with us. He worked long hours managing a Pontiac dealership, and on Sundays he had a standing appointment with a Löwenbräu mug full of Heineken and a wheelbarrow full of mulch. Although my father did often say grace, one that was different from the one our mother had taught us. He mumbled the words, and it would take us a few years before we made out what he was saying. *Bless us our Lord, for these thy gifts, which we are about to receive, from thy bounty, through Christ, our Lord, amen.* Then he'd cross himself while we watched. *In the name of the Father, the Son, and the Holy Ghost.* Thin-lipped, head bowed, shirtsleeves rustling with swift certainty, the way he might have thrown footballs in high school.

In the parking lot of the church in which we learned what God required of us, the bumper stickers said, "God Said It, I Believe It, and That Settles It for Me." In the sanctuary—padded pews and an altar flanked by lilies in foil-covered pots—we sang the doxology, praising God from whom all blessings flow, and hymns that once billowed through revival tents and anchored radio hours, hymns that conjured up a God who was massive and benign, like Lincoln in his memorial. Our pastor, a stout, smiling man with oiled black hair and heavy black brows, was not a thumper of pulpits; his girth and ample, soothing voice were authority enough.

This was where, at seven years old, even before I had a self, I learned that you had to get rid of it. " 'In the same way,' " our pastor said, reading from Romans one Sunday, " 'count yourselves dead to sin but alive to God in Christ Jesus. Therefore do not let sin reign in your mortal body so that you obey its evil desires. Do not offer the parts of your body to sin, as instruments of wickedness, but rather offer your-selves to God, as those who have been brought from death to life; and offer the parts of your body to him as instruments of righteousness.' " He described this process as dying to self. I turned to my mother and whispered, "What does that mean?" My mother was never at a loss for explanations to my questions—my grandmother always said that my middle name should have been "How come?"—and she bent her head to mine and whispered that dying to self meant that we needed to put our desires aside in order to do what God wanted.

The women who taught us Sunday school showed me what it might look like if you had, like the hymn said, surrendered all to Jesus. In the basement, ready to bind us to Him with glue and yarn, waited the Misses Hull, a mother and daughter twinset with cat-eyed glasses, brightly pinked lips, and bouffant hairdos covered by green chiffon scarves. There waited Miss Clark and Miss Johnson, two women who seemed forty to me at the time but were more likely twenty-five, whose knowledge that they walked under the shading parasol of God's grace drew them up tall and straight-backed. Miss

Clark, who had long brown hair and dark circles under her sallow skin, would sometimes bring out a guitar and gather us around her long skirts to play us songs. Miss Johnson, who pulled her lank black bob back to the left side with one gold-plated drugstore barrette, was the church pianist; during my piano lessons, she bore down so heavily on chords that her hair swung forward and back against her pockmarked olive cheeks. It was said that Satan had appeared to Miss Johnson at the foot of her bed and that she shooed him away by saying, "In the name of Jesus Christ, I command you to leave!" I carried that story around like a pocketknife for years, should Satan ever show up one night at the foot of my bed to prove that he did in fact exist. But the Misses Hull, Clark, and Johnson spooked me even more. I looked at them and wondered if their lives, because there were no husbands, fathers, or gentleman friends escorting them to church, were in some way too stubborn, or too stunted. Why did the Misses Hull have to take refuge under chiffon headscarves and lipstick the color of all the dead cold lipsticks from the sixties rolling around in my grandmother's dresser drawers? Did Satan come after Miss Johnson because she pounded the piano with a fierce and unshakable devotion to Jesus that made him jealous?

Once, after a service, my mother told her how much she enjoyed her playing, and Miss Johnson said to her, eyes wide, "Oh, no! It's all Jesus!"

"Well, whoever it is," my mother said, "it's lovely."

My mother could not let Miss Johnson die to self over a compliment, but when the church decided to operate a school out of its basement, offering its congregants the opportunity to protect their children from other children who didn't know Jesus, or that he had a rule about loving one another or else, she enrolled us. The church sold the curriculum as "accelerated Christian education," and my mother thought we would speed ahead if we were allowed to work at our own pace. We wore uniforms, and sat at cubicles filling out workbooks that were color-coded for subject matter—yellow for math, blue for science, red for English, green for social studies—with moralizing comics running across the bottom of the pages that starred Archie, Jughead, and Betty types. We had monitors, not teachers, who were outfitted like waitresses at an IHOP, in dark green polyester vests with brass buttons and green checked pleated skirts. When we needed their help we placed a Christian flag in a gold plastic stand at the top of our desk to let them know; when we wanted to go to the bathroom or get a drink of water, we replaced it with an American flag. We graded our workbooks ourselves, at tables in the middle of the room, using red ballpoint pens chained to the tables and answer keys filed in banker's boxes.

Whenever I finished my work, I would ask if I could read at my desk, and what I read most often was the Bible. Alone with a King James Version that had belonged to my mother as a girl, its desiccated black leather flaking off into my lap, I befriended God. Every week we were asked to memorize scripture, and the verses tumbled down into me like coins in a bank. *The fruit of the spirit is love, joy, peace, patience, kindness, goodness, faithfulness, gentleness, self-control; against such things there is no law. Be anxious for nothing, but in everything by prayer and supplication with thanksgiving let your requests be known to God. And we know that God causes all things to work together for good to those who love God, to those who are called according to his purpose. Though I speak with the tongues of men and of angels, and have not love, I am a resounding cymbal. Look at the birds of the air; they do not sow or reap or store away in barns, and yet your heavenly Father feeds them. Are you not much more valuable than they? Who of you by worrying can add a single hour to your life?*

God's words became my words, the words that I used to talk to myself. In my cubicle I read the Christmas story in Luke over and over, and I saw that God was a God who herded shepherds and teenage mothers as they wandered under stars. I loved the book of Esther, because it told the story of a young woman proving her fitness to live in a palace—in it a beautiful Jewish girl is chosen to be queen by a Persian king who decrees her people dead, but her grace and courage deliver the Jews from danger. "For if you remain silent at this time," the uncle who raised her tells her when she is not sure she can ask her husband to change his plans, "relief and deliverance for the Jews will arise from another place, but you and your father's family will perish. And who knows but that you have come to royal position for such a time as this?" I thought about how, when I was learning how to walk, I'd pulled myself up on our ironwork dining room chairs, and, according to my mother, nearly poked my eye out. Now that wasn't just a story, it was a clue: if my sight had been saved, maybe that meant that God wanted me to work with the blind when I grew up! Like Annie Sullivan.

I looked into the future, squinting. And then returned to the book in my lap. I went hunting for more women's names in the concordance, and when I found them I pored over the details, wondering what it was like to live in tents and walk through palaces, trailing hair and veils. I hunted down anything else that resembled a love story: Abraham and Hagar, Jacob and Rebecca, David and Bathsheba, David and Saul's daughter Michel. I got a crush on David—redheaded, joyful, cunning, and doomed. I read the Song of Solomon, because I'd heard that that was a love story, too, and was not too shocked by what were supposedly the dirty parts. Not even C. S. Lewis was as enthralling as the Old Testament. They'd read to us from the Narnia books, but I wasn't interested. Too many princes and horses. Not enough thwarted passion.

I filled out my workbooks, read through the Bible, and learned hardly anything of academic worth during my year and a half at this first Christian school. Laura Ingalls Wilder and a set of Story of America cards that my mother ordered off the television—yellow journalism, plantation life, Paul Revere's pewter business, Civil War battles, the Mexican Revolution, Pocahontas, rituals of Aztec sacrifice, Boss Tweed and Tammany Hall—taught me more about the natural world and American history than those color-coded workbooks did. What they really meant to teach us at this school was that the world was a poxed and pustuled old thing, diseased by our pride and greed, headed for destruction.

On Sunday the hymns we sang were lullabies. *This is my Father's world*, we sang—

> *and to my listening ears*
> *all nature sings, and round me rings*
> *the music of the spheres.*
> *This is my Father's world:*
> *I rest me in the thought*
> *of rocks and trees, of skies and seas;*
> *his hand the wonders wrought.*

But at school they were intent on waking us up to our imminent doom. One afternoon, we were all taken up to the sanctuary and shown a film called *A Thief in the Night*. The film warbled and stuttered into life, and we were introduced to a young woman named Patty, a long-haired blonde who wakes up one sunny seventies day to some strange news on the radio: crowds of people are disappearing everywhere. She eventually learns that those people didn't just disappear—they were raptured. Patty had fallen in with a group of young Christians who had been warning her of the end times, but she was also dating a shiftless hippie who sneered at those squares, and since she couldn't decide who was right, she'd been taking her time in asking Jesus to come into her heart. But she didn't make up her mind quickly enough, and was left behind on earth with the other unbelievers to live out the rest of her days under an international fascist regime. And because she refused to take the mark of the beast that was being administered by the new world order, she couldn't buy groceries or wrap dresses, or go to the bank. She spent the rest of the movie running through prairies and high grass pursued by vans and helicopters for her transgression against the Antichrist, shivering with the remorse of the footdragger.

After the film, we were led back down into the basement, seated in folding chairs around a conference table in a room with no windows, and Miss Clark set forth all the terrors that would attend the end of the world. Jesus, she said, had a nemesis called the Antichrist who, in the last days, would set up a one-world government and require us all to take the mark of the beast on our forehead. If you didn't, you'd be tortured. The Romans, she told us by way of illustration, loved to tie Christians' limbs to four different horses and then send them running. And this wasn't going to happen in a time far, far away. It could happen, like, now. The book of Revelation, we were told, contained signs of the end that closely corresponded to current events—specifically to current events in the Middle East and Russia. This would be a sign unto us: that there would be movements to rebuild the Temple on the site of the Dome of the Rock in Jerusalem. Also, said Miss Clark, we would not know the seasons, so look out for warmth in winter and snow in summer. The one-world government in the film? We already had one, in the form of the United Nations. The mark of the beast? It would probably end up being a bar code that people would have to carry on credit cards—or on their foreheads or the backs of their hands. Pregnant women and nursing mothers, Miss Clark said Jesus said, would be especially at risk. I would later realize that she must have been telling us about what would happen if you asked Jesus into your heart *after* the rapture, but I lost the facts, such as they were, in Miss Clark's litany of terrors, which suggested that Jesus might not really love the little children.

When she had finished, the boy beside me raised his hand. "Can't we just lie and take the mark of the beast?" he asked. "God would know we still really loved him, right?" I'd thought the same thing. If God knew everything, he'd know we were lying to live, and would not count the lie as a sin or a betrayal. Wouldn't he? The upshot was no. You could have your own thoughts about who God was and what he would tolerate, Miss Clark was saying, but what you thought mattered not one bit. Forget about cooking up some clever bit of reasoning to outsmart his will.

I was an incredibly anxious child, an eight-year-old who, when not charmed by the saucer eyes and British accent of Hayley Mills, was given to imagining that she might die of a slow, silent heart attack or a splinter that had found its way into a vein. If you told me something was coming to get me, whether it was tetanus or the Jersey Devil, I'd believe you. Before that day in the basement, the Jersey Devil had been my greatest childhood fear. The Jersey Devil was the infamous thirteenth child of a Mother Leeds who, because she cursed aloud at having yet another child, was said to have given birth to a creature who slipped out of her eighteenth-century womb, sprouted wings, and flew out of her window to spend the rest of his days soaring through the Pine Barrens looking in on the sleeping children of southern New Jersey, seeing if there were any fit to snatch. The possibility that my limbs and the limbs of many other Christians might be used as logs for a pyre set ablaze by the Antichrist became a much more vivid nightmare.

*The very fact that we are here and able to discuss this means that everything will be all right,* the radio in the film kept telling everyone who had been left behind, we were to see that we were lying to ourselves if we didn't believe we were living in the end times. The movie convinced me that wars, and rumors of wars, were one day going to be broadcast through the clock radio my sister and I kept on our dresser. We were going to hear the rumors first thing in the morning, or wake to them in the middle of the night, history closing in on us in our nightgowns, stubbing our very young lives out. There were rumors of war, of nuclear war, already—I had read about it in *Time*, had seen the orange and black mushroom cloud roiling on the cover, and it seemed the perfect way for God to destroy the earth if that was what he wanted. And I couldn't convince myself that he wouldn't. For most of my childhood, headlines and newscasts would sound no different from prophecy—evil empires, Great Satans, angry ayatollahs. Islamic fundamentalists holding Americans hostage in Iran. Bombings in Beirut embassies and barracks. Every time Peter Jennings or Tom Brokaw popped up on the television to deliver a special bulletin during a sitcom or soap opera, I was sure they had come to broadcast some sign of the end—has the moon turned to blood, do we not know the seasons, is there squabbling over the Temple Mount?—so I would flee the room.

After that day in the basement I would be of two minds about God: he loved us, but he might also one day unleash his wrath, no matter how much we loved him. God would be the source of panic, but also the salve. At night the room would spin with my fear of the end, and I would have to say *God*—just the one word, a reminder that he existed and, like Jesus said in John 3:16, did so love the world—to myself to make it stop. Every time I heard the words *Israel, bar code, nuclear war,* or *unseasonably warm*, my heart would flutter and whirr like a hummingbird until I said it: *God*.

Not *Mom*! but *God*. Even after taking us to church and putting us in Christian school, my mother did not speak to us about who she thought God was and what she thought he required of us. I never told her how scared I was. I assumed she knew what I knew, had probably heard about it one Sunday in a sermon while we were down in the basement making Christmas ornaments or God's eyes, and because she had lived her life, did not mind giving it over to war and pestilence for Jesus' sake.

But she still let the Top 40 soothe us to sleep, turning our clock radio on to keep us company after she kissed us goodnight, leaving us curled up around a secret: the world wasn't really a terrible place. If you went out into it, said her stories and photo albums, you could come back with pocket money, records, party dresses, champagne headaches, straw bags from Acapulco, and husbands who took you to dinner. I wanted those things. I wanted to grow up into a teenager for whom all the songs on the radio made sense. I wanted to have bottles of Love's Lemon Fresh on my dresser, like my Aunt Susan did. And have boyfriends like girls did on television. I would whisper my request to God: Could I live until I fell in love?

# CHAPTER 2

## THE AGE OF REASON

Our second Christian school was a real school, not a bunker for indoctrination. There were talent shows, gym uniforms, room mothers, book reports, recesses on blacktop, and sports teams that traveled to play away games. I longed to be forced to memorize and then disgorge whole lengths of "The Charge of the Light Brigade" or "The Rime of the Ancient Mariner" on a wood platform in front of my classmates—a result of having read too many books set in the olden days—and I thought there might be similar tests of academic mettle on offer at this new school. It made up for having to move deeper into South Jersey's rural wilds because my father had been transferred to another car dealership.

There were Mennonites attending this Christian school, and aside from going with my mother to the Reading outlets in Pennsylvania to buy cheap underwear and whoopie pies, this was the closest I would ever get to the Amish. The girls, like their mothers, wore thick-soled shoes, and skullcaps made out of white netting secured to their heads, with bobby pins; the boys had a disheveled quality to their hair and velour pullovers. From the Mennonite kids we learned that words like *darn*, *shoot*, and *heck*, words my sister and I used constantly and with gusto, were called "minced oaths" because of their close resemblance to the words they were used to avoid. My friends were girls who, although they didn't mark their separation from the world with long hair and head coverings, seemed to be just as willing as the Mennonites to live impervious to the call of the radio or the lure of TV.

"I'm not allowed to watch *The Smurfs*," our pastor's daughter said one day at lunch. Sitting with us was the pastor's daughter's best friend, a tomboy who was so blond as to be almost albino. She played the flute and never wore skirts. They both listened to Sandi Patti, a plump blond woman who sang songs of operatic inspiration. Another friend in the circle loved Keith Green, the bearded James Taylor of contemporary Christian music. Or CCM, as it was called on the AM stations that played it—it sounded just like rock music, except that the "you" in the love songs referred to God.

"Why?" I asked our pastor's daughter. I knew the answer— wizards being agents of black magic, of the dark arts, friends of Satan and enemies of the light. But I wanted to hear her say it, to know for sure that there was legalism afoot.

"Because there's a wizard as a main character."

"I can't either," said our pastor's daughter's friend. "For the same reason."

My other friend spoke up. She could not watch *The Flintstones* because Fred was always lying to Wilma.

I liked these girls very much, so I could not say what I really thought, which was: "Do you really believe that Satan is trying to tempt you through the television set?"

I couldn't tell them, either, that my sister and I had a sordid past that included weekly trysts with the writhing mass of *Solid Gold* dancers. That my mother often left us to die on the carpet in front of the television with our cousins, four thick white cutlets frying in the glow of

*The Brady Bunch*. That we had seen every *Star Wars* film and owned nightgowns and lunchboxes proving as much. That while my sister and I happily went to see Amy Grant, the Christian Linda Ronstadt, in concert, and had memorized the lyrics to songs by Randy Stonehill, the Christian Weird Al Yankovic, we were also stockpiling 45s from Stevie Nicks and the Police and conducting an after-school career as showgirls at Maxine Chapman's School of Dance, where we studied ballet but also performed routines to Phil Collins's "Easy Lover." Our mother was a room mother, yes, but she could also be accused of having thrust us, à la Gypsy Rose Lee, into the tawdry world of tap and jazz. It was my mother who said to us, one night in 1978, "Girls, *The Sound of Music* is on," and introduced us to the thrill of movie musicals. And while I read Christian romance novels set on prairies, and enjoyed them, I sensed that these fictions were counterfeit. If I confessed to any of this, I was sure there would be blank, possibly disapproving stares in return, and I needed their friendship more than I needed to make a statement.

One night, while waiting in a Christian bookstore for my mother to pick up something she'd ordered, I browsed through *Larson's Book of Rock*. "For those who listen to the words," said the cover, "and *don't like* what they hear." If you listened to the radio, Bob Larson said, your life would be arranged the wrong way. If you listened to people other than Paul Simon, Kenny Loggins, and Lionel Richie, you could die of a drug overdose or start dabbling in the occult. *The occult*—another phrase, like *the world*, rung out in school and in church to convince us of Satan's slavering over our hearts. "For teenagers who are reading this book," Bob Larson wrote of secular records, "there is one message you should get clearly. If you want God to bless you, get the cursed things out of your life." Then: "The Enemy only needs to find one area of your life uncommitted to Christ to gain access to the whole. Maybe that poster or record isn't an avenue of evil to hinder you spiritually, but what if it is? Is it worth hanging on to if it is cursed?" He also wanted me to know that Led Zeppelin and Black Sabbath and Kiss were conduits of the devil. No surprise there. But Hall and Oates were conduits as well, because Daryl Hall's father was a warlock. Hall and Oates? My mother had bought us a few Hall and Oates tapes. Bob Larson, you're wrong! I thought. And not because Satan, who you might say I have accidentally let into my heart through listening to Stevie Nicks, is making me say this! Bob Larson, I allowed myself to think, and people who sound like him, are overreacting. I shut the book and put it back on the shelf.

I stood in the corner of the bookstore thankful to have the mother and father I did. I was lucky to have parents who weren't so crazy as to think the Smurfs were really going to do a number on me, or that Hall and Oates was something sinful that would slither up to us through the grass, wrap itself around our ankles, and drag us down into depravity. My father, consumed by work and certain that my mother had us under control, wasn't concerned about what we heard or saw. He was Catholic, which also made it impossible for me to believe everything they told us in school and church. I'd heard Catholicism called a false religion, which implied that my father, grandmother, and uncle were going to hell, and I didn't think that could be right, because they believed in Jesus, too, I was sure they did, even though they never spoke of him. My uncle had even tried to become a priest. Because we had Catholic blood in us, I imagined that my sister and I would be able to resist the more stringent parts of our nondenominational Christianity—like Annabel, a girl in a book I loved whose mother was a fairy and whose father was a mortal, and whose mixed blood meant that she could fly, but would probably go on to climb stairs for the rest of her life. And my mother, because she had gone to church in a place where Baptists and Methodists didn't consider the Beatles a spiritually destructive force, would protect me and my sister from turning into the Misses Hull. I hoped.

The Israelites had their Pillar of Cloud that led them during the night as they wandered through the desert, and I saw that I would have a little cloud of skepticism, made of radio static, that would keep me from straying onto the fanatic's path. I would not mention this cloud, or the questions and objections it consisted of, to other Christians. Christianity, I could see, demanded more of you than God might really want, and I had a feeling that if I did say any of this aloud to other Christians, they would call my skepticism sin. I had never heard anything in church to make me think otherwise.

Sunday after Sunday, the pastors of the churches my mother took us to told us that Satan wanted us to fail. And we really didn't have it in us to fight him off, which is why we needed God every minute of every day to help us persevere against the dark. To let go of the Lord to find comfort or enjoyment in television, books, music, friends, family, sports, money, or work, meant that we were worshipping false idols, and courting the tragedy of life without God. Not one of these kindly, emphatic men in beige or gray suits ever said that we would be courting hell—hell was hardly ever mentioned. But they made it clear that if we rebuffed God's advances, and chose to live without his love, we would be condemned to a lost life, wandering like the nearsighted, grousing Israelites from work to bar to home, wondering why our spouse left us, our boss fired us, and our children wanted nothing to do with us. That was the threat: a life empty of meaning and purpose. Of feeling *something was missing*. Of contracting, as I'd heard this lack called, *a God-shaped hole*.

The cloud of radio static could not fully drown out the voice of church. I could never be sure that God wouldn't condemn me to a cold and lonely life if I accidentally disobeyed him by mistaking what

I thought was wise for what he thought was wise. And I did want to love and obey him. Putting pen to paper was becoming reflexive to me, so in church, when I heard scriptures such as, "God would not tempt us above that which we are able," I wrote them on the sheets in the bulletins provided for taking sermon notes—because God was always going to find a way to thump you awake through the words of your pastor, and you should be prepared to take dictation when he spoke. So I wrote things like, "Saul visited the Witch of Endor— a fortune teller—to contact the prophet Samuel, and was punished for his inability to wait for God's hand." Whatever the lives in the Bible taught about obedience, pride, and anxiety, I noted, so as not to make the same mistakes. Samuel—he helped find the Israelites a king against his better judgment because they were tired of being ruled by judges, but God said, fine, let them, and then the king turned out to be Saul, who started out promisingly but then forgot that God was the one who gave him the position of king in the first place, and because of his arrogance was replaced by David. Martha, Lazarus' sister, invited Jesus to teach at her home and tore her hair out because as she ran around hostessing, her sister Mary sat at Jesus' feet listening to him talk. Martha went up to Jesus and said, Lord, I'm dying over here, can't you tell my lazy sister to help me? but Jesus said, very gently, "Martha, Martha, you are worried and distracted by many things; there is need of only one thing. Mary has chosen the better part, which will not be taken away from her."

As Christians we were to always choose the better part—and as outlined in sermons, I learned that choosing the better part meant that we were not ever to choose fortune-tellers, first billing, good works, or golden calves, or anything that made you happy when you thought God wasn't looking, because those were quick fixes. We should have the patience to wait on the plan that God had for us. That part was easy. I believed that all things worked together for the good of those who loved the Lord, and God would not tempt me above that which I was able. He would give me peace and wisdom if I asked for it, but if I asked for something in particular, and did not receive it, I should be prepared to accept this, because what God wanted for me was far more wonderful than anything I could ever dream up for myself.

I sometimes wondered, sitting in church listening to ancient tales of obstinacy, if I had been born with original sin, because stealing and lying and saying mean things had never held an appeal. My sister might have had some original sin in her, I thought. Not me. When we were not yet five, dragging ourselves behind our mother in green and yellow parkas while she cruised the aisles of a CVS, my sister asked my mother for a caramel—just one plastic-wrapped caramel from the many filling a bin. "No, not now," my mother told her. There was no fit thrown, and we exited the store. While my mother loaded the trunk, my sister turned to me in the back seat. "Look what I got," she said, a blond ball of fluff in a yellow parka holding out a hand with a caramel in it. She knew she'd done something wrong, but she wanted me to feel her joy in getting what she wanted—wanted to show me a trick that maybe I should learn. I looked at the candy and knew exactly what I would do when my mother got in the car. "Do you know what she did?" I asked my mother, who then dragged my sister back inside to put the candy back where it came from. I was Martha, my sister was Mary, and we had been given these roles at birth. I was beginning to think, however, that if I did contain anything like original sin, it would be my skepticism.

If you asked my mother, it would be my sullenness, which surged like height or leg hair in the summer before seventh grade. Because my father was transferred back to his previous job, we returned to the town we'd left, and my sister and I started at a third and final

Christian school. I wanted all the moving around and enrolling and switching to just stop already. My mother had moved around a lot as a kid too, packing up whenever my grandparents found a better or cheaper place to rent, but she had no sympathy. "Oh, you two have it so bad," she would say to us when we complained. When I thought of my mother having to live as a teenager with two other sisters in an apartment, I thought of the five girls in *All-of-a-Kind Family* crammed into a tenement on the Lower East Side, and of Francie Nolan having to creep out on her Brooklyn fire escape to get peace and quiet, and I shut up.

My sister and I were relieved to find that at this new Christian school our classmates talked openly about listening to the radio and watching MTV. We had found our people, at last! But they did not know as immediately that we were theirs. These Christian kids—it must have been because we were no longer tucked away in the rural wilds of South Jersey—could tell if your sneakers were off-brand, which shocked us a little. My mother bought our clothes at Sears and Penney's, and because she thought that our characters would be compromised if we were indulged with entire wardrobes from Esprit, had cast us down into an acrylic and poly-cotton purgatory from which there would be no escape until we made our own money and could drive ourselves to where we wanted to spend it. Which was definitely not Fashion Bug. We hated Fashion Bug, and still our mother took us there. Girls with big hair and gold necklaces and Italian last names shopped at Fashion Bug. If you said the words *Fashion Bug* to us, we would grow narcoleptic at the depressingly familiar image of fluorescent tube lights glinting off chrome racks full of stirrup pants and Shaker knit sweaters.

A girl named Tammy seemed to not mind my plaid blouses and penny loafers, and asked me to have lunch with her in the first days of school. There was something haughty and pinched in her face and in her voice; when she talked, she set the words out as if setting out afternoon tea service on a table. But we'd read the same books, and I had no business rejecting offered company, so we spent our lunches beneath a tree in the schoolyard.

A few weeks later another girl approached me after class. Georgia had outfits from the Limited and a brother who was a sophomore, and I often saw her laughing with some of the more popular boys, raucously, making fun of them but not flirting, as if she did not know she was a girl, wiping their ridiculous mess up with "Y'all are ignorant," or "Y'all are stupid." The mix of affection and derision was impressive.

"I just thought I should tell you," she said, "that Tammy always tries to make friends with the new girls because she knows they have no idea about her."

"But what's wrong with her?" I said. I did not mention that sometimes I wondered if she washed her hair as much as she should, and maybe she smelled a little bit, but other than that—

Georgia just looked at me. "Do you want to come have lunch with us tomorrow?" *Us* consisted of two other girls named Nina and Debbie. I certainly did. While it was Christian of these girls to extend friendship to me, it was clearly unchristian to take a friend away from someone who needed one, and it was unchristian of me to ditch someone who had shown me kindness, even if it might have been self-interested kindness. But I didn't feel much guilt over this, even when I heard later that our homeroom teacher had taken Tammy aside and encouraged her to wear deodorant and bathe more because we were all at the age where our bodies needed us to pay a little more attention to them. Adolescence was on its way, and I was helpless at its approach, because I was going to have to figure out what to do with my own body, which I hated.

There were girls who, just by gliding through the hallways in pencil skirts and pumps with basketball players on their arms, their purses filled with pearlescent lip gloss and teal mascara, could make me feel like something stuffed in the bottom of a laundry hamper—something powerless to rise up and climb out of the dark. It was hard, in class, to sit upright next to their aplomb. Or when I couldn't concentrate on the teacher because of a growing conviction that my period was on its way right that very moment—one more thing that would come like a thief in the night—and I was sure that it was because it had descended upon Debbie once during a long bus ride to an arts competition, and when we got off the bus, we had to bunch up behind her stained white pants like a Secret Service detail and hustle her into a girls' room. I would sit at my desk worrying about these things, about the utter impossibility of ever becoming a carefree teenage girl, and then when all the worry knotted into stomach cramps, which would mean I was technically ill, I would ask the teacher if I could go and lie down on the tan vinyl couch under the single lightbulb with the chain hanging down above me, wondering if I should have my mother come get me, or whether I had it in me to go back to class. It never occurred to me, in the nurse's closet, to whisper God's name—*God*—to make these thoughts stop. I think I knew that in order to make junior high easier for girls who, no matter what you dangled in front of them, would rather be lying on the couch reading, God would have to overturn society as we knew it. And if he was going to do that, he was going to do it to get the Second Coming rolling. It wasn't his job to magically turn me into a proper teenager. That was why I bought *Seventeen*. Which I had started to do, despite my mother's reservations, because I thought it was appropriate and necessary reading material for a girl my age. What I knew, and she didn't, was that the sex advice they gave was about as titillating as the breakdown of active ingredients on a tube of Vagisil.

What she also didn't know was that I was too preoccupied with Reagan and Gorbachev to put whatever she thought *Seventeen* had recommended into practice. The fires of apocalypse had slipped out of view for a few years, but in 1986 it became harder than ever to discount the catechism I'd been given in the basement. Gorbachev had a mark on his forehead. A mark! On his forehead! Forget about bleeding through my pants—I'd offer myself up for that on a monthly basis if it meant 1987 would actually come to pass. That port-wine splotch on Gorbachev's forehead, which could have very well turned out to be the mark of the beast, pulsed with portent. It pulsed and pulsed and then Libya exploded, and Chernobyl exploded, and something like the high-pitched toot of the Emergency Broadcast System went off inside my mind and drowned out reason. Presidential addresses did not reassure: Reagan a big outcropping of Brylcreemed rock behind a desk in the Oval Office, his words measured and therefore ominous. There always seemed to be some strange ticking quiet between them, a silence whispering *Bombs are going to drop, sirens are going to wail, the enemy is entering your homes as I speak, they're making me say these things, that's why I sound like your grandmother reading you to sleep.* I moved between school and church afraid that I would be caught in a sermon or Bible class or chapel in which someone decided the time had come to gather us all together, pull out the Bible and a map of the world, and give us all iodine pills and gas masks.

I lived especially in dread of Mr. Horner's Bible class. Mr. Horner seemed to be the sort of adult who, with his Sansabelts and his blessed assurance, which came in the form of a bicuspid-heavy smirk and a two-handed grip of the podium, could not wait for Jesus to return. "Boys and girls," he would say to us, "I submit to you that the Old Testament reveals a jealous, jealous God. Boys and girls, I submit to you that the Psalms are a testament to God's bountiful, bountiful mercy." Every Friday we had to bring in a story from the newspaper for discussion, and when we bombed Libya, I was sure he would begin class by saying, "Boys and girls, I submit to you that Muammar Qaddafi is the Antichrist." But he didn't.

If Mr. Horner wouldn't, our pastor, even though he'd never breathed a word about the end, would soon have to. I spent services staring down at the carpet, hands under my knees, heart palpitating, making plans to creep down the aisle and into the lobby and wait out the rest of the morning in the bathroom if the bulletin said he was going to preach on Revelation. I even volunteered to help in the nursery because I thought I could avoid hearing the sermon, but they broadcast the message in there so we could listen to it while we picked Cheerios out of the hair of small children. There was nowhere to hide.

So I went to my mother, hoping she would tell me that what I had been taught about the end times was nonsense, and asked her if she thought the world was going to end soon. Alarmed at my fear, which I had somehow forgotten to let her in on, she asked our pastor what to do, and came back with the news that the world was not going to end in nuclear war, and that no one, as Jesus said, knew the day or the hour. We were in the kitchen, she was making dinner, and I stood by the stove. I looked at my mother, imagining her in a cardigan and a heart-shaped locket, her blond hair in a ponytail, and wondered how she'd lived through the Bay of Pigs. I had never heard her mention the Cuban missile crisis. I knew that *The Twilight Zone* had scared her and Kennedy's death had saddened her, but what about the threat of mass destruction?

"Also," she said, "Paul pointed out in his letter to the Ephesians that to God a day is like a thousand years. So we have no idea what the timetable is." These verses didn't explain why exactly it was that God wouldn't send the world up in radioactive flames; they only told me there was no way to calculate when Armageddon was going to happen. But my mother's voice was so calm as we stood in the kitchen, steam rising from the pots under her command as she explained all this to me, that I decided to believe her. I had to live. I wanted to see England.

I would have one more year in Christian school, and then my mother would decide that my sister and I needed to avail ourselves of the first-rate public education our taxes had been paying for. My sister and I were a little nervous to start our freshman and sophomore years at a large regional high school—would we, as we had been told, be spit upon when people discovered we did not want to drink or have sex?—but mostly we were looking forward to dances, school newspapers, musicals that needed casts of thousands, and English courses taught by people who wouldn't just up and decide at the end of a marking period that, you know what, maybe we wouldn't read *Julius Caesar* after all.

My mother had sent us to Christian school—everyone's parents had sent them to Christian school—to hide us away from peer pressure and cruelty. From sex and drugs and whatever it was Adam and Eve saw shimmering before them when they bit into that fruit. But it was in Christian school that a classmate told me a dirty joke involving a man, a woman, and a shower that illuminated in one instant what took place during sex. Going to Christian school had not stopped me from reading *The Scarlet Letter* because I thought there would be many scenes of what *Jane Eyre* had called love-making. Christian school did not prevent us from making girls like Tammy a pariah. It did not keep me from wishing I was someone else entirely.

If the point of Christian school was to keep children innocent, and in doing so keep them happy and faithful, it seemed to me that it was a waste of money and time. Though there were quite a few things I was grateful to have learned in Christian school—things that had nothing to do with God, things I might not have learned even in a public school. Nina, who was half Irish and half Filipino, always wore a yellow shirt that said "Aquino Is My Hero" in red letters to gym class, and that was how I discovered who Benigno Aquino was and why he was assassinated. Because Georgia listened to Power 99 FM's Top Nine at Nine, we knew if we listened we would hear "My Adidas" and "The Show," and if you were black on the outside but white on the inside you called yourself an Oreo— because this was what Georgia, whose father was an English professor, sometimes called herself. And I probably never would have heard *The Dark Side of the Moon* in its entirety if it hadn't been for Christian school—some upperclassmen would bring tapes to play on the school bus, and when the clocks and bells started up it jangled my nerves because it was too nightmarish a sound for the morning. I liked the other tape they played, which had Echo and the Bunnymen and the Icicle Works on it. It was on the bus to Christian school that I first heard Echo and the Bunnymen.

My Christian education taught me that you could take the tiny pliant soul out of the world, but the world would find the tiny pliant soul. Some girls would get pregnant before they graduated. Some would become alcoholics. Some would make local headlines for nearly starving their children to death. Some would get married and have affairs. Some would move to New York and give up on God. We were all a lesson in the impossibility of peace of mind and purity of heart.

# CHAPTER 3

## COUNT IT ALL GLORY

Our new high school had as many windows and as much acreage as an airport. The sun flooded the cafeteria, the hallways, the classrooms, the playing fields, the parking lots. When you looked out across the cafeteria, it seemed to go on forever, like a stretch of beach, and was as populated, hot, and noisy as the shore in mid-July.

Waiting in the cafeteria for the bell to ring on the first day of school, I saw some girls who I'd been friends with in first grade, and who were on the junior varsity field hockey team with me. Joanne and Becky. Thinking that I would find a group of friends through playing a sport, I had gone out for field hockey, practice for which began before school started, and learned of the terrible tyranny of the jock. This was something we had been spared in Christian school, since in Christian school the jocks were also the artists and the artists were also the jocks: as Paul had told the Ephesians that there was now no distinction between Jew and Greek, in Christian school there was no distinction between the jock and the artist. But the jocks in public school were boring. They did not sing their voices raw while they played acoustic guitar in front of the congregation. They did not take the lead in the school musical. These girls thought it was hilarious when they used their newly acquired Spanish to make dirty jokes. Bon Jovi blared out of their Jeeps. They tossed their long blond hair and brayed each other's last names as they whacked the balls across the grass. They were evenly tanned and deep-voiced, their athletic capability rendering them nearly sexless—they were their mothers already.

I had yet to have an actual conversation with Joanne and Becky, or anyone else on the team. The girls on the field hockey team had largely ignored me at summer practice, but I didn't mind, since it was better to be ignored than noticed. As a kid I'd been to nursing homes and apple orchards with Joanne and Becky and our Brownie troop. I had been to their birthday parties, had been in their houses, remembered the names of their sisters and brothers and pets. But I was under no illusion that they owed me any attention now, being that they were firmly ensconced in whatever social hierarchy had developed in the last decade while they'd been growing up together without me. I did not want to be a responsibility to them—someone they felt obligated to invite places, someone their mother would be after them to be nice to. But I forced myself to walk over to the long table. They were wearing casual but expensive-seeming plaid skirts and blouses, and their thick hair was cut neatly and looked like it would smell like shampoo until the end of the day.

"So where have you been?" said Joanne. "I've been meaning to ask you." She was Italian and loud. Tan. She was the goalie for the team. Somewhat husky, but in no way fat. Sort of like Rosemary Clooney in a face mask.

"We've been moving around a lot because of my dad's job." I thought that would end that question, and I would not have to explain why, even though going to Christian school made it look like my family and I were religious fanatics, we really weren't.

"How long have you been in town?" said Becky, who played right wing. She was Irish, freckled, black-haired, and caterpillar-browed. She wore penny loafers and small gold hoops.

"Well, we've been here for the last three years, but we've been going to private school." This was why I could never be a spy or an adulteress or a mystery novelist or even play chess. I could never successfully maneuver myself out of the way of someone's inquiry or intent with lies intact. In our South Jersey town, private school meant one of two Catholic high schools. Bishop Eustace—Bishop Useless—was full of Catholic preppies, and Paul the Sixth was full of the kind of Catholic girls who were always hiking up their skirts and whose special devotion to Mary seemed to take the form of servicing the neighborhood. You could go to Moorestown Friends in Moorestown, a Quaker enclave settled in the seventeenth century where even the public school resembled the University of Pennsylvania, but that was old money, like the Main Line. All the money hidden away in our woods reeked of recent coinage—like brand-new carpet fibers and fresh leather interiors of BMWs.

"Bishop Eustace? Paul the Sixth?" said Joanne.

"No, it was a Christian school."

"A Christian school?" asked Joanne. "You mean a Catholic school?" It was inconceivable to me, too, that people would need more God with their math and history than Catholic school provided. "No, it wasn't Catholic," I said. "It was like Catholic school—we had religion classes—but Protestant."

"I don't get it," she said. I didn't either.

No one cared what you did or didn't do in this high school, as long as you didn't, like one science geek did, wear white suits and a mustache to class. I had yet to find a group of friends, but my sister had fallen in with some girls she'd met in study hall. It turned out, here in the evil world, that there were plenty of kids who did not smoke or drink or backstab. Christian school had not cornered the market on them. We passed each other in the hallways, sat next to each other in art class, stood in the cafeteria line for salads together. There were plenty of nice girls who still thought that cracking each other up over Coke and potato chips and cable television was a perfectly fine way to spend a Friday evening. And: Holly, an old friend we'd been reunited with, was being courted by an upperclassman with braces and a cockatoo cut full of mousse who kept giving her stacks of Maxell tapes. Well, courted and then blown off. But it was through his pursuit of Holly that word of the Smiths, the Cure, and New Order spread to our household—our two other favorites, U2 and R.E.M., having come to us over the radio and through MTV. Holly, recently of St. Mary of the Lakes, was virginal and staunchly sober, like us, and we thought that if this guy thought enough of Holly to hang around some, it augured well for our own public high school career. If we kept close, all the virginal and staunchly sober girls, we would keep each other from thinking that we needed to be anything other than ourselves. Mostly.

I did not find a crowd that year—my childhood obsession with Betsy Ray and her studious but fun-loving friends piling into roadsters headed for homecoming left me obsessed with having a crowd—and no boys were handing me tapes. But there was English class as taught by a professional paid by the state. Mrs. Shapiro had smoker's breath and a black bob going white at the temples. She wore fuchsia lipstick and whimsical earrings—whimsical earrings being the universal symbol of Eccentric Yet Sympathetic Personage at suburban high schools. She had us write our own version of "A Modest Proposal," and she read mine aloud in class. I kept my head down while she did so, thrilled to be singled out by my teacher for my work, but embarrassed at how long it was taking. I thought about the day in kindergarten when my teacher set me down on a wooden stool in front of my class with a book to read aloud to them for story time, and the distinct feeling then of having been turned into a small furry thing in a bellhop getup who'd been asked to hoof it up for the nice people. And of waiting for tomatoes to be hurled. I kept staring down at the paper on my desk. "See me for insight into your forte," she'd written on the back of the essay.

"I just want to tell you how wonderful that essay was," she said after class. Mrs. Shapiro came up to my chin, and I came up to most people's chins myself. "You know, I teach college students composition, and I passed your essay out to them the other night so they could have an example of an assignment I gave them. If you haven't thought about writing as a career, I think that you should."

An adult had told me that I was talented, and suggested that I do something with that talent. Now I could finish out the field hockey season with the knowledge that I had something more valuable than stiff-upper-lipped benchwarming to aspire to. I'd thought about quitting the team, because we won the state championships every year, and I wasn't out for the blood of the mouth-guarded girls of the Garden State, I just liked to play, liked running around on the field and giving the ball a good, hard, satisfyingly pointed whack. But I thought my father, who revered Vince Lombardi the way my mother loved the Beatles, wouldn't like it if I quit. Although when I told him I was thinking about it—I was out back one night before dinner, hitting the ball around, and he came out on the lawn with a beer in his Löwenbräu mug—he didn't give me the hard sell.

"Well," he said, "I think you should keep on with it, but you'll figure it out."

If he thought I should, I would. Whenever he looked at me, I wanted him to see a girl who finished whatever she started. Everyone always said I was my father's daughter, which meant that I was a dogged worker with a Mr. Magoo-like neglect of detail, a propensity to wear sneakers and T-shirts until they fell to pieces, and a word-less, passionate love of the ocean. "You're just like your father," my mother would say, with affection, not annoyance, when she looked at the underwear and socks bursting out of my dresser drawers. We both knew I was a slob because I had my mind on other things. And I had my mind on other things because I was my father's daughter. I was proud of this distinction. It meant I would be protected against failure. Failure of nerve, of will, of whatever I put my mind to.

What would I put my mind to?

We were reading *Hamlet* with Mrs. Shapiro, and I had fallen in love with him—his anguish, his wit, his cruelty to Ophelia. I did not want to be seduced and abandoned, but I did want someone who would love me by taking me into his confidence and shaking me out of my naïveté. But I really fell in love with Hamlet because of this line: "There are more things in heaven and earth, Horatio, than are dreamt of in your philosophy." He had given me the words for something I had been thinking but felt I had no right to say: there was more than one way to live the Christian life.

I had Nina and her family as proof. I was lonely without Nina, who had also been taken out of Christian school and put in a high school several towns over. Neither of us had boyfriends. We knew our braces and the cat's cradle of rubber bands reinforcing our braces had something to do with it, though Nina was not afraid of boys because she had a brother, so I figured that for her it was only a matter of time. While we waited, we handed each other stacks of Maxell tapes and took sculpture classes in Philadelphia.

Her father, who took painting classes at the same school, drove us in every Saturday, letting us put *Document* in the tape deck. When we came back home Nina would make us Spam, eggs, rice, and sliced tomatoes, a dish her Filipino mother had raised her on, and I learned that Spam could be a fatty, crispy, addictive thing, although my parents, who as children had been forced to eat it festooned with stewed tomatoes as if it was a roast, had made me think it was a food to be avoided at all costs. Then we would walk around Station Avenue, her town's main street, a main street my mother had grown up on, stopping at Fastow's Five and Dime, rifling through the bins full of jacks, superballs, creepy crawlers, and water guns, marveling at the chiffon scarves and packages of pantyhose that had no doubt been on those shelves since my mother's graduation day. We'd browse the used bookstore, where one day in the back of the dusty wood-paneled room we read passages from *Forever* to each other, because we'd heard it was sexually explicit. But the girl in Judy Blume's book was just some girl obsessed with a boy. We'd grown up on the Sprigged Muslin School—see Laura Ingalls Wilder, L. M. Montgomery, and Maud Hart Lovelace—and didn't know what to do with a girl in a book who didn't have an ambition to be a writer or teacher while planning to marry some manly doctor, professor, reporter, or farmer. I already held a grudge against Judy Blume for *Are You There God? It's Me, Margaret*, which made it seem like every girl couldn't wait to get their period and grow breasts, couldn't wait for the day when her body was finally teenaged. That book told a lie about how girls were: no one I knew talked about increasing their bust, and who wanted so badly to bleed?

Though her father was a devout Christian, and Nina and her brother belonged to a youth group, Nina's house, with its lived-in minimalism, furnished largely by Ikea, seemed to me a much freer house to grow up in. There was no house like Nina's in the neighborhood—you rode by pastel Victorians and white Cape Cods and then there stood her house, wood siding stained a deep brown, a deck surrounding the front and side, modestly making its statement. Her father, who had trained to be an architect, had turned a fifties ranch house into something like Fallingwater. It might have also been because her mother sometimes slept in on Sundays, and laughed and teased us like she might have still been fifteen, too. Once, having heard us wrong while we were eating Spam in the kitchen, her mother turned around from the sink and asked, her voice singsong, like a doorbell, "Who farted?" As if she really wanted to know, even if it was someone she had never met.

It was because of Nina that I knew anything about Frank Lloyd Wright, and it was with Nina that I found out about Marcel Duchamp. My parents had taken us to the Philadelphia Museum of Art, but it was with Nina that I learned the museum the way I learned her house. The way the sun filled certain rooms, the view of the city from the steps, the walk out to the waterworks at the back, the Schuylkill Expressway and Kelly Drive trailing out behind the grand edifice like wires hanging out of a television set.

One day after art class, she walked us past the rooms dedicated to the Impressionists, to whom we had given our junior high years. "No more," said Nina, as we moved on to the back of the museum. "Look," she said, leading me into a room that contained an old wooden door with a peephole. I looked, and kept looking. I knew that my mother would think that I should be offended by scenes of naked, possibly violated women, as would everyone else at church. The burgeoning feminist in me suspected I should be offended by them, too. But I wasn't. I could look through the old door and stare at the headless white body of a woman lying in a field holding a gas lamp, a cleft where her genitalia should be, while a waterfall glistened in the distance—without fainting. There would be no way to explain to the offended why I liked images of coffee grinders placed between panes of broken glass titled *The Bride Stripped Bare by Her Bachelors, Even*. If I had to try, I'd say I liked the juxtaposition of the gilded machines and the web of cracked glass—all these objects delicate and finished and then dashed—and I liked the way the title

gave rise to many meanings, perhaps ominous and amorous meanings. I didn't know how to explain it, not exactly, but I also didn't
want to sound like a pretentious jerk, like the guy next to us, obviously on a date, telling the girl that he'd always thought of naming
his daughter Rrose Sélavy. Here we were, looking at this for a good
fifteen minutes, and here we were, still alive. God had not slathered
us with boils or turned us into pillars of salt. Or trees with arms.
Or rocks with eyes. Or two tiny plastic figures, which he would
then place in the diorama, damned for all eternity to be close to the
waterfall but not close enough to ever be able to drink from it. A
book called *The End of Reason* by Francis Schaeffer—"a penetrat-
ing analysis of trends in modern thought," by a respected Christian
thinker, said the back cover—had told me that the twentieth century gave birth to art that celebrated secret messages, and modern
art's irrational, antagonistic communications were a sign of humanity's great need of God. But what was wrong with a scene that made
no sense? What was wrong with reality dropped and shattered, jar-
ring us out of our complacency? You could stand there staring at it
and it wouldn't make you run off toward a field, lantern glowing,
your clothes hurriedly shed, looking to be split open.

That spring, I left for my last church retreat. When my mother
dropped me off, everyone was milling about loading their stuff in
the blue Ford Econoline van, and I spotted Darren, who had lately
joined our youth group. I walked across the church parking lot,
sleeping bag in hand, and wondered if it would look strange if I
turned around and started walking the two hours it would probably take me to get home. A fifteen-year-old boy named Darren,
who was somehow still golden brown from a summer spent surfing
at his parents' house in Ocean City and who threw his striped polo
shirt collar up around his neck, was always going to be a source of

fear to a girl who had become famous among her relatives for what her cousins, with love, called tard burns, and spent summers walking around with deep red streaks on the back of her shins and the front of her arms. "Oh, you," I heard my friend Melissa saying as I walked up to the van. She and Darren were laughing, her nose and eyes crinkling up.

Sitting in the van induced the pains associated with my orthodontist tightening my braces: there was happy, bantering conversation going on all around me, but I could not speak or make any movement, and all the pressure had given me a slight headache. Other people could do this to me. People who were not adults and who were not related to me could make me dissolve into a mute pile of plump, pale, freckled limbs. It seemed to me that youth group would be the one refuge for the meek, who were supposed to inherit the earth. But youth group was no different from the rest of the world: it had its popular kids, too, and they were invariably the kids who didn't take any of it seriously, who made you think their parents had cut some deal involving cars or stereos to get them to come. "Wherever two or three of you are gathered in my name, there I am in the midst of you," Jesus had told his followers, but it seemed to me that wherever a dozen or more kids got together in his name, they crowded him out and he took a hike.

I went on this retreat because it was something to do, but also because the circumstances might just let a shaft of insight break through, whether it was because they let us take walks by ourselves in the woods by a stream—I loved streams, they could be coming out of a concrete pipe on a construction site, I was like a deer that way— or because some adult would tell me something comforting about God's plan for my life. Or I would see more clearly what that plan might be, because I did think God had a plan for my life, and I was hoping he would allow me to be some sort of writer. But Darren had colonized youth group for the empire of the confident and un-blemished. He made me forget that there were a dozen other people on the retreat with me. He made me forget Tracy, and Jill, and the other older girls who were talking about *Upstairs at Eric's*, which Jill had brought along with her.

Saturday morning, before we all went out canoeing, we gathered in the wood-paneled living room. Bob, our youth pastor, stood in the middle of the brown rug. Some of us were gathered around his feet, some of us were sinking into the brown-and-yellow plaid couch. "Nice belt, Bob," said Darren. I had seen the belt before. Its bronze buckle saluted Texas as the Lone Star State. "Thanks, Darren," said Bob, paging through his Bible. Then he looked up. "Let's turn to Hebrews 13:5." And he began. *You know, when I was in high school in South Florida, I would sometimes have to take my Bible to school, because a bunch of us on the baseball team would have Bible study before practice. Some of the other players didn't get it. They thought we were sissies for caring about that Jesus stuff. I knew that getting teased by some baseball players in a South Florida high school was nothing compared to what the early Christians had to endure. But being a teenager is tough. I know it's tough. Sometimes it's gonna seem like Jesus isn't really there. Where's Jesus when you don't make the team? Where's Jesus when some guy's making fun of you because you don't want to go to first, or second, or third base? But boys and girls, I submit to you that whatever you endure in the hallways at school, you can count it all glory. He promised us that.*

I began to feel that I was the only person who was listening to Bob. Why was Bob standing up there? Why couldn't he tell that nothing he said could help us? School did not require you to put on the whole armor of God. School was a mass of bodies heaving a collective sigh every time the bell rang, every single day for eight months. I loved school, but even I would tell you that it could be hot, stifling, stale-smelling, loud, and interminable. It could put you to sleep. I had yet to hear a sermon on that.

Bob kept talking. Tracy took my Bible and started writing on the flyleaf with her pencil over the spot where I'd printed my name and address. She handed it back to me, looking straight ahead. "Beam me up Scottie," she'd written. I kept my head down and smiled. She nudged my knee. I would never have tried to use some- one's Bible to pass notes, especially notes like that. Notes that were bald-faced declarations of boredom. I always thought if I was bored during church or youth group, it was my problem. The things I feel are not of God, I thought; they need to be discounted, because they aren't in the index of my NIV Bible. Tiredness, feel- ing of. Roll eyes, desire to. Insufficiency of youth pastor sermon- izing, despair at.

I did not mind having tea with Pamela, Bob's wife, however. Having tea with Pamela was a two-by-two pursuit of faith, un- troubled by my peers. Even though her faith was extreme and or- thodox, there was something about Pamela that seemed ethereal and loopy. Pamela had long blond hair and the snipped features of picture-book elves, and she sang in church to taped backup. She had a full-throated, arabesquing laugh. Pamela had also given me *Mere Christianity*, and had written this on the title page: "This will be a deep encouragement as you consider the essence of Christianity. I love you—I'm reading this one too!"

That evening Tracy snorted as we settled down in our sleeping bags in the upstairs loft. "You know what I heard when I went back downstairs to get my pillow? I heard Pamela calling Bob her boo." They all laughed. I usually laughed at everything Tracy said, because she had a cracked and dry sense of humor, but I lay there silently, wondering if I was going to wake up with my hand in a cup of warm water and a need to pee.

Sunday morning before we left, Pamela made us all buckwheat pancakes. This was another reason I liked Pamela—she reminded me of my Aunt Susan, the only remotely hippieish person I'd ever known. Though it seemed impossible for committed Christians to have hippie tendencies, because vegetarianism or a love of health food seemed to entail a veneration of the earth that could veer dangerously close to idolatry. "Boo," said Jill as Pamela retreated into the kitchen to fill another plate for us. Snickers went up from the table. I couldn't eat anything else. I couldn't stand these girls' rejection of kindness, and I was embarrassed on Bob and Pamela's behalf. Why did they love us? They talked about how they felt that God had laid a burden on their heart for teenagers, but they knew nothing if they thought ice cream socials, acoustic guitar sing-alongs, and earnest speeches were going to go even a little way to soothe us.

It wasn't that I wanted to stop being a Christian. Peace had been promised to us, so I couldn't give up. As Paul had told the Philippians: work out your own salvation. I had to keep on believing that there were more things in heaven and earth than were dreamt of by area congregations, and that I would one day find a congregation that believed this along with me.

Until then, my teenage soul—suspicious of cheerfulness, though still reflexively respectful of authority—would feel increasingly uncomfortable in the presence of the official soul. The official soul, as transmitted through church and Christian paraphernalia, was upbeat, incurious, happy with its lot. It did not have any heroes other than the ones who appeared in the Bible, and it was content to hear the same stories about these people over and over again. It described pain and suffering in such a way that a person might think alcoholism or the loss of a child were no more inconvenient than a tussle with the flu: after it passed, you could stand in front of the congregation on Sunday and testify that it was all better, and God was

good. As far as I could tell, that was the only story told by the official soul, and the real and true sadnesses had been excised for a more
mellifluous account. Which made it seem as if there were things you
couldn't talk about in church, or with people from church—what
made you laugh, why you cried at a movie, what made you angry, or
what books you read that hadn't been written by C. S. Lewis, A. W.
Tozer, or D. L. Moody. Church was supposed to be the most important thing in life, but so much of life was left out, because so much of
its trouble was assumed to be conquered. My pastor mentioned Kierkegaard in a sermon only once, and it would be a long time before
I discovered that there was a storied Christian who suffered from,
and so in some way sanctioned, depression, rage, sarcasm, and despair—the diseases that took hold in adolescence, for which church
offered no cure.

"You girls are getting jobs this summer," said my father, and so my
sister and I ended up working at a bakery with a friend from Christian school. When we weren't unsuccessfully badgering the owner
to stop using Styrofoam coffee cups because it was bad for the en-
vironment, Stacy, the head baker's niece, was buying us Kentucky
Fried Chicken with money from the till and telling us how much
New Order sucked in concert.

Matt was the cleanup boy at the bakery. I recognized him from
the halls at school. He was skinnier and shorter than I was, with a
smudge of black hair covering his upper lip and a dark bowl of hair
hanging over wire-rimmed glasses. While he mopped the wooden
floors and I folded boxes for the morning rush, I learned that he was
a more devout Christian than I was. He and his friends belonged to
the popular charismatic church that held their services in our high
school auditorium. My mother had taken us once, and we stood still
as congregants wearing khaki and linen swayed and sang "Shine,

Jesus, shine," with their eyes shut tight, hands lifted to heaven in ad-
oration, in thanks that he was moving among us in the high school
auditorium. We didn't go again, and I was relieved to see that my
mother had her limits, at least where the public consecration of the
essentially private was concerned.

One afternoon Matt mentioned going to Creation, a big Christian rock festival held every year in a field in Pennsylvania. "Have
you ever been?" he said. "It's really amazing."

"No," I said. I had given up on thinking Christian rock would
give me anything as good as U2, the Smiths, or R.E.M. I had just
bought a tape by a band that *Campus Life*—the magazine for serious-
minded Christian teenagers, filled with ads for Christian colleges
and articles about deepening your faith, which I read mainly for the
record reviews—said approximated the kaleidoscopic guitars of
R.E.M. The band on the cover of the tape looked tantalizingly dour
and both the men and women had long tangled hair. *We come to you
earnestly*, they were saying as they looked out at me from the cover,
*earnestly trying to get you, a young serious-minded Christian with pretty
good taste, to use us to study by instead of your secular music. We understand the lure of the secular, and do not feel that we have to repel all
of it—look! we have long tangled hair like Michael Stipe and our song
titles suggest that we are familiar with the Byrds!—but we have created
this in the hopes that you might find us cool enough to hang out with and
so that we will then feel justified in our own attempts to be cool and to be
Christians Who Are Different.* I listened to the tape, and it was similar, but sorely lacking—like being handed a flat Coke when you had
been thirsting for an effervescent blast from a fountain.

The music I listened to was not at odds with Christianity. The
Smiths taught the same thing that Christianity did: that humans,
as demonstrated not just by the war and destruction raging around
us but by the masses at my high school who loved Guns N' Roses

and New Kids on the Block, were not capable of choosing the good, the higher, or true. They were always going to choose what made them feel good, what didn't tax them, what allowed them to wallow in cheap sentiment and pretend that everything was fine. Left to our own devices, I saw, and Morrissey confirmed, we would not strive to perfect ourselves, to right wrongs, or to think of others. The world was indeed a terrible place. But the Smiths came from an island that had no use for God anymore. We were fallen, said the Smiths, but there would be no grace.

If I brought any of this up to Matt, I thought he would use the word *backsliding*—a church term meaning that you were spiritually falling off the wagon—and try to convince me that I had lost ground in my walk with the Lord. He might call me a fence-sitter—a term used to describe the position of the waffler, of someone who refused to come down on either side of an issue, of someone who mistakenly believed they could have their Smiths and Jesus too. I wanted to avoid that conversation. My mother was already patrolling that beat.

One day that summer, when I dropped off one load of books at the library to pick up another, I forgot to return a novel that was overdue, and ran inside while my mother waited in the car. When I came back, I saw that she was holding *The Bonfire of the Vanities*, which I'd just checked out that day.

"I want you to take this back," she said, holding the book.

"Why? What's wrong with it?"

"It's filled with the f-word."

"Well, that's certainly not why I got it out of the library," I said. I had no idea it was filled with the f-word. I'd read it was a big social novel about New York. "Do you think I'm going to start swearing after reading one book?"

"It's not that I think you're going to start swearing," she said. "But I have to answer to God for how I raise you, which means that as long as you're in my house, I'm responsible for what you hear and see." I got out of the car and headed into the library. It was pointless for me to even think of reasoning with her. Or slamming the car door in reply. My mother, as her faith had deepened, had moved away from her original laissez-faire policy on cultural consumption, and in the summer of 1989 was in full crackdown mode —I'd also been forced to stash copies of *Sassy* under my mattress when she discovered I'd bought the magazine that she'd heard called *Playgirl* for teenagers. I thought it was my responsibility to broaden my mind, and she thought it was her responsibility to make sure I didn't corrupt it. I thought of Luke's story about Mary and Joseph losing a twelve-year-old Jesus in Jerusalem during Passover. They searched three days for him, and when they finally found him, preaching in the temple, Jesus chided them for their fretting. "Why were you searching for me?" he said to them. "Didn't you know I had to be in my father's house?" And then the next verse: "But they did not understand what he was saying to them." I liked to think of Jesus rolling his eyes at his parents, trying to make them see what was really worth getting worked up about. But there was only so much comfort to be had in Jesus the mouthy brat: Jesus was Jesus, and I was a sixteen-year-old girl who needed to get her mother to face facts and admit that after she'd lifted her ban on MTV, her daughters did not immediately start rolling around in leather minidresses on the hoods of cars. This incident made me ashamed of both my mother and myself—my mother for refusing to see that using the f-word did not make a fiction writer a pornographer, and myself for not fighting to read what I wanted. I could write term papers decrying censorship, but here I was submitting to it.

When Matt asked me out, it was another threat to my idea of myself as someone who was indeed a Christian, but did not look and sound like one. One afternoon, in his red Chucks and white apron splattered with the guts of jelly doughnuts, Matt interpreted "Young Goodman Brown" for me. We discovered we'd both be in the same English class the next year, and he said he wanted to give me a head start. "His beloved's pink ribbon symbolizes sin and innocence together in one person. Use that in class. She'll love it."

"That seems an awful lot like cheating," I said. I had a horror of doing or saying anything that I didn't come up with myself. I didn't need anyone's help to impress a teacher. That was the one thing I knew how to do.

He smiled. "No, that's just one friend helping another."

"Well, thanks."

"Hey—would you want to go to the movies?" He mentioned a summer blockbuster. I was wiping the counter. In a 10,000 Maniacs T-shirt and my father's khaki shorts. My perm was growing out, and my mouth was full of braces and rubber bands. He was asking me out, when I looked like this? What was he looking at that I couldn't see? What was he hearing that I couldn't hear?

"I already saw that," I said. And that was true.

"What about—?" That too. Which was a lie. I didn't think I could lie or say no to people, but it seemed that I could, if their attentions didn't flatter me.

Matt stood in the middle of the floor, hands atop his mop handle, feet apart. He looked at me for a few minutes. "Well, maybe another time." He rolled the bucket away into the back of the bakery, and for the rest of the night I heard nothing from him but the banging and splashing of metal trays in the huge sinks.

"He said he thinks you're too good for him," Stacy told me the next week while we were putting trays of doughnuts in their racks.

"That's crazy!" I said. *He* was too good for *me*! If he was willing to give up or ignore R.E.M. for Jesus' sake, then he was a better

Christian than I was, and I was willing to let him have that distinction. I did want someone to discuss literature with, but I wanted my conversation partner to be taller and less devout than I was, and perhaps an owner of a hooded wool toggle coat, like the boys from *Dead Poets Society.*

Something told me I'd pay for my arrogance the way I paid for it in junior high when Ruth Harvey and I played the same Bach invention at a piano competition and I was sure I would win, my confidence informed chiefly by Ruth's orthopedic oxfords and thick, watery-lensed glasses. But Ruth won, and it left me with the suspicion that God wanted me to know that appearances—my pleasure and interest in how things sounded and looked—counted for nothing. God's plan for my life might involve routine insults to my pride, and I would have to welcome them, because insults to pride would be the closest any of us would ever come to standing in the light of burning bushes.

# CHAPTER 4

## NICE PROM DRESS

When Melissa, in our first days of public school, introduced me to Heather and Jenny, they had not yet done with being good girls—they were sweet, untroubled, Benetton-sweatered. But this year, our junior year, when we returned to our usual table at the cafeteria, things had changed. Heather was no longer talking about George Michael—she was carrying Andy Warhol's diaries around school and talking about *Sid and Nancy*, which she would later screen for me and Jenny in her carpeted basement. She was studying up on the countercultural underworld so that when she finally moved to New York to work in a gallery she would be able to move in the orbit of decadent famous people with ease. Jenny had waited for her perm to deflate, and when it did had dyed her hair black. She was wearing a huge olive green parka even though it was eighty degrees, and her lips were dark red. She had been a math whiz, but now seemed to think good grades were uncool. I was still working at the bakery, but they worked after school doing data entry at a trade music magazine that somehow had offices in Medford, New Jersey, in the strip mall consisting of faux log cabins, near a bank and a laundromat—the laundromat marking it officially on the wrong side of town.

Heather was still credulous, conscientious, given to giggling. She was a tall, slender blonde who favored babydoll dresses, knee-highs, and headbands, and was obsessed with Duran Duran way after their prime. Heather's other obsession was Dave Schottky, a cross between a metalhead and Beat poet whose bangs sometimes swung down in front of his brown eyes when he filled up Heather's powder blue Buick at the Shell station across the street from the Acme and who maybe was a Satanist—and that last, because she had a mother who believed in things like the Virgin Mary's appearance to the village of Medjugorje at the late date of 1981, rattled her some. Jenny's mom, who had been born in Turkey, also had a sense of the dark powers that were moving among us girls, the dark powers that Robert Smith might have had something to do with. That fat boy with the lipstick, Jenny's mom called him. She once punished Jenny by throwing out all her black clothes and buying her an entirely pastel wardrobe from the Gap. She was always throwing her Doc Martens out, and Jenny would call Heather up and ask her to drive her around the development to go look for them.

Heather would beg me to drive her by Dave Schottky's house, which sat on a back road where tasteful new Cape Cods had recently gone up, their lawns barely grown in, and when we approached the house she would yank the seat lever, flying from vertical to horizontal with a thud, lying flat on her back so no one would see her, shouting, "Drive, just drive!" Heather alone was heaven. Whenever she came to my house she would drop to her knees to ruffle up our dog, exclaiming, "You're the doggiest dog I know!" We would laugh and laugh, she'd fall off my bed she would laugh so hard, and when Heather giggled I knew that deep down, despite her attraction to men whose hair fell into their eyes, obscuring intents that were probably evil, she must have believed what her mother did. When Heather saw someone wearing a rosary for show, it drove her crazy. "It's a prayer device," she'd say, "not an accessory!"

Heather with Jenny, however, had me stumped. Jenny was the world-weary, mercurial heavy. I learned this in gym class. We were standing around in faded T-shirts and ill-fitting shorts, all of us looking like undercooked dumplings under the fluorescent lights, waiting to perform chin-ups for the President's Physical Fitness Test. The girls from field hockey, who took gym class too seriously, went first. Whatever we played they were always thrusting their fists in the air and hooting as if every skirmish were a final for the Stanley Cup. "Well, I guess they have to have something to do when they're not vomiting up lunch or beer," I said as we watched them take turns triumphing over the bar. I hated that I had to get up there and tremble and convulse in front of people for twenty humiliating seconds.

"Bitterness isn't very attractive, Carlene," said Jenny, looking not at me but out across the floor. Heather did not defend me. I wouldn't have, either. *But I thought that bitterness was our political position!* I wanted to say. *I thought it was our defense against the unthinking normality we had to contend with every day!* I said nothing for the rest of class. I would never get the hang of Jenny. I would never get the hang of people.

We all went dark that year. I wore so much black my father kept joking about buying me something pink just to break up the monotony, and then I colored my hair what the package called Chestnut Brown so as to look a little more like Louise Brooks. My sister met a girl named Mia in her history class, and was led away from Holly into a group of demure but fashionable girls who went dancing in Philadelphia. My sister now needed clothes to be worn at night, that could get you talked to by boys. She bought things that made my father nervous—they were, he said, "invitations." There was a short A-line dress with a neckline that was too low for his taste. A Mondrian-inspired shift that bared her shoulders. And the gingham bra top that she wore with denim cutoffs and tights.

Soon there were boys everywhere. They were circling the house, making their approach. Boys in army jackets who had ridden their motorcycles all the way from Philadelphia up our leaf-shaded drive-way. Boys with spiked hair and wallet chains coming through the backyard gate. Boys in rugby shirts waiting patiently on the front step for her arrival. Usually I headed to my bedroom when they appeared, to avoid having to be polite to people I could not place, although they seemed perfectly nice—what did they want exactly, and how long would they be hanging around?

There was one boy my sister could not catch: an Eagle Scout who skated and listened to hardcore. There were several of them at my high school, tall, skinny boys who camped on the weekends and loved Seven Seconds, Fugazi, the Dead Kennedys, and the Dead Milkmen. They thrashed and burned, but also tended to girls as if it would earn them a badge. My sister's friends dated these Eagle Scouts, who were attractive for their mix of righteous aggression and reverence for nature, which girls were a part of. One of them once extended his Walkman to me in health class because he wanted to teach me about Seven Seconds, and even if that was all the attention they'd pay me, that gave me hope. They seemed to me like khaki-clad redwoods with girls curled up like ferns, or foxes, against their sturdy bark. There might be whole forests of them somewhere.

The one my sister desperately wanted had taken up with a plump, monobrowed girl named Sue—who in their loyalty my sister's friends referred to as Smoo—and my sister could not understand why she had been snubbed. She told my mother all this at dinner one night when my father was working late.

"She's so awful!" said my sister.

"They call her Smoo," I told my mother, and explained why.

My mother shook her head. "You girls can be so bitter. I hear you when you're with Holly. It's terrible, the way you talk about other people. You didn't learn that in this house." We looked at my mother. We actually had learned that in this house—no one was handier with the word *asinine* than my mother. She was right, though. It was bitterness that drove us to talk like we did. While putting away a bag of chips and a liter of Coke in the kitchen, we could stoke each other into a seething fireball of crank and disdain, fueled by someone mentioning Aqua Net, Diet Coke, dance music, or Patrick Swayze—the four great loves of Normal Girls, who were a greater foe than Satan. To describe someone as a normal girl was our lowest blow. It meant that you had no idea who Monty Python was, and did not have plans that involved art and the city. I thought about beginning a diatribe on behalf of my sister, for whom I often acted as defense lawyer at the court that was the dinner table. I could tell my mother that as far as revolt went, she was getting off easy. We could either put bombs in people's lockers to redress the social hierarchy's imbalances, or indulge in a little trash talking.

Then my mother spoke. "Well, he's probably just with her for the sex," she said. It was like the rock in Exodus suddenly splitting in two to bring forth water to the Israelites. Our mother had lowered herself to earth to help us, and her knowledge was delivered so surely that we had no choice but to believe her: Sex could make you that dumb. It could make you forget you had standards. How did she know what she knew? We wanted to know, but we didn't. Or I wanted to know, but my sister didn't. The last time I had asked my mother about sex—did it hurt? I asked, and she started right in with yes, it can, the first few times, but you—my sister put her hands over her ears and said, "Oh, stop! Please!"

Holly and I, because we did not have boyfriends, huddled together in outrage over our continuing celibacy. We wanted boyfriends. We did not want to lose our virginity. We just wanted boyfriends. Everyone we knew was a virgin, and no one felt that we had to unburden ourselves of this great shame. No one was chomping at the bit to *lose it*, or had ever uttered the phrase. Sex to me was an event not unlike the Second Coming—theoretically, it was one day going to take place, and though it was something you were supposed to look forward to, I felt indifference and dread when I thought about it, not joyous anticipation. And we had yet to hear firsthand tales of male pressure, the sort of thing that cropped up in movies like *Porky's* and *Fast Times at Ridgemont High*. We talked about music, school, movies, television, magazines, other people—but not sex. We just wanted to kiss people. We weren't asking for that much, we felt.

"Every guy who goes out with your sister adores her," said Holly. We were standing next to each other, flipping through the racks at Tower Records.

I stopped what I was doing. She looked at me. I looked at her. So I wasn't the only one frustrated by my sister's success. Holly was saying that she knew my situation—sister to someone in high demand—was a demoralizing one, and was perhaps demoralized by it herself. My sister and I lived according to an unspoken treaty: I was the smart one, and she was the pretty one. That way I didn't have to worry about her getting better grades than I did, she didn't have to worry about anyone she dated suddenly switching their affections to me, and we could each hoard our spoils without having to share. I didn't want any of the boys who wanted her—there was something of the star quarterback about them, something broad-shouldered and prowling, even if they dyed their hair black with shoe polish. So my sister and I hardly fought.

What Holly said was true. My sister put the hurt on every guy she went out with, and still they came trooping up the front steps to see if she was in. When I tried to think about what weapons she might possess other than her blond hair, her style, and her vivacity, I lost my way and sailed off into resentment. I didn't want to think about what she might be doing with them that could make them this loyal. Though it didn't seem like she had to do much of anything. She just had to show up, and they'd ask her out during her shift at a farm stand, or she'd write down their numbers on flyers at shows.

"My mother," Holly said, "says that guys are afraid of smart loose girls."

We were smart girls: no doubt about it. Here we were at Tower Records on a Friday night. Stone cold sober. Fully dressed. I had worn a black wool beret out of the house to see if it was something I could pull off, but had taken it off in the store and stuffed it in my coat pocket because it made me feel like I was wearing a sandwich board that said THIS GIRL IS WEARING A HAT.

"Mine, too," I said. Our mothers could have been feeding us a line, but it was much better to think that we had been passed over because we were intimidating, not because, as I feared, we were too unattractive or boring or aloof to encourage examination up close.

In English class I would find that our mothers were indeed feeding us a line. If you were a smart girl, said the lives of the poets we read that year, you also had a responsibility to be a seductive and dangerous girl. Art required of you not just a singular imagination, but a talent for flirtation and self-destruction.

Mrs. Schmidt, our teacher, had worn a beret in her youth, and now laughed at the thought of it. "In college," she told our class, sitting straight-backed, legs crossed, on the edge of her desk, silver bracelets slipping down her forearms, "my best friend and I would run around the Village pretending to be Beat poetesses, thinking we were the living end."

With Mrs. Schmidt, who seemed both nun and knight because of her height, sure laugh, and cap of cropped gray hair, we read Elinor Wylie, H. D., and Edna St. Vincent Millay. The biographical sketches in the Norton anthology were captivating. Ezra Pound fell in love with H. D., Freud analyzed her, and William Carlos Williams remembered her "as a tall, carelessly dressed young woman with 'a provocative indifference to rule and order which I liked.' " He wasn't talking about messy rooms. Said Norton of Wylie: "A woman of great personal beauty and magnetism, fanatically proud, she combined aristocratic *hauteur* and bohemian flair with a poetic talent that dazzled both critics and the public." Millay had to flee to Europe to "recover from a nervous breakdown" and "avoid the importunities of suitors." Men had run her out of the country, had wearied her and vexed her with their neediness.

Millay's lines leapt into my head and would not leave. *We were very tired, we were very merry. / We rode back and forth all night on the ferry.* And: *My candle burns at both ends / It will not last the night / But ah my foes, and oh, my friends, it gives a lovely light!* But then there was one we did not discuss in class, which began with the lines, *I too beneath your moon almighty Sex / Go forth at nightfall crying like a cat.* Seriously? Really? Though I liked the idea of someone sitting beside me on a ferry, wanting only my company as night turned to day. I thought about the line from Macbeth—"Murder will out"—and hoped that my charms, whatever they were, would out sometime soon. Spontaneously, like spring, when they were aged to perfection, like cheese. In college, maybe. In college, my mother also told me, I'd find a boy who liked me for my mind. In college, I imagined, I would wear what I wanted, say exactly what I thought, and make jokes when they came to me.

Like the girls who sat on the other side of the classroom next to Chris Bernard. Chris Bernard wrote poems that suggested he was willing to go wherever his mind and Kurt Vonnegut took him, and spoke in a friendly drawl that said nothing could ruffle his self-possession. Not even the acne that would occasionally break out around his mouth. To him, acne was a bunch of red freckles. His hair was a deep black, soft and thick; it curled around his temples, ears, and the back of his neck. He dressed in grays and browns and blues, in wrinkled pants and baggy wool sweaters. It was as if he were perpetually just getting up, as if he were amused by school having to interrupt his thought stream for six hours every day. He drank coffee, too. I'd seen him stash a stained plastic travel mug in his locker some mornings. He lived beyond the teenage, which was where I wanted to be.

Chris Bernard did acid and smoked pot—or so Holly had whispered to me—and was always surrounded by those girls, who wrote for the literary magazine, and whose poems to me seemed self-consciously strange. They favored floating eyeballs and things turning inexplicably ochre. If they had to choose between Dalí and Duchamp, they'd choose Dalí, and I was sure those girls found my poems descriptive and literal, if they thought about them at all. I was good at geometric proofs, and I was good at sonnets: I liked making things follow. I was not a gypsyish girl surrealist, leggings under long skirts like I'd just come from dance class, floating about the hallways trumpeting my asides, declaiming my flirtations while sitting cross-legged on desktops. They were painting a mural and rendering themselves brightly, sharply. It seemed like an exhausting amount of work to me—work that you could never be sure would pay off in the end. In the end Chris Bernard might be the type who'd leave girls like me up in a barn loft with a suitcase of unwanted Bibles and a bum leg with no way to get down.

I fixated on the ghosts of the Village and the girls in my class who they haunted, and I forgot what I'd read in the other Norton biographies—that T. S. Eliot was a bank-managing Anglican, that Wallace Stevens was a boring old insurance executive, that William Carlos Williams was a doctor. That Marianne Moore had a secretarial job and had been called a hysterical virgin by Hart Crane for deeming *Finnegans Wake* offensive. All I could see was that if you wanted to get to New York and stay in New York, you had to costume yourself with sex and drink and bravery. You had to wear whatever outrageous, possibly bogus hat your time handed to you, like Mrs. Schmidt did, like Heather and Jenny did, like even my sister did, with confidence. You had to leave the house to do more than browse the aisles of Tower Records. You had to run around town tearing down mores as if they were dust-laden curtains in drawing rooms that had been shut up for too long. You had to run around having sex with as many people as you could to experience—I didn't know what. Skin and hair and smell and character? Could men infect you with insight, or inspiration? Could sex prove that you were fearless, that you did not need anyone but yourself and your work?

Then we read Sylvia Plath, and I saw that you did not have to be a libertine to predicate a life on Art. She was, after all, the teacher's pet ne plus ultra. Also, Plath seemed disdainful of the opposite sex—a group of people I did not know what to do with yet, and so had chosen to dismiss. "Your body hurts me/as the world hurts God," she wrote. Exactly! I thought. Your man-flesh is not fit for my consumption! In her biographical sketch there was no mention of suitors to be evaded. *The Bell Jar*, said my Norton anthology, showed "a terrible gap between the tone and behavior of a gifted, modest suburban girl of the 1950s and [her] hidden turmoil." I was a gifted, modest suburban girl. Robert Lowell, said Norton, noticed in her "an air of maddening docility." I probably had loads of that, too.

I took *Letters Home* and the collected poems out of the library, and felt a great relief—here was a young woman, a young woman lauded by the world, who defined herself not through her sexuality but through refusal and discipline. Though she had no use for Christianity, which bothered me, her disgust with the world and what was commonly defined as happiness was essentially religious. Plath was a godless version of Ecclesiastes' Preacher, teaching that everything we were supposed to desire was worthless—football players, good grades, enviable jobs, middle-class respectability. And from her account of meeting—crashing into—Ted Hughes, I learned that if the men you desired didn't terrify you, didn't come at you like a bear, first heavy and low, then towering and lunging, they were worthless.

I saw that you could be a suburban teenager who had the round and bubbled handwriting of a cheerleader and still be a writer. You could be a girl who recorded the aftermath of various dates and dances in your journals and then one day spin oracular music. She could teach me how to throw my voice—how to assume and project authority when I set words down on paper. Her poems were written with a paring knife, stripped and carved until the most perfect arrangement of words emerged—I wanted to write as carefully. I would be lying if I said her suicide did not lend her glamour, but what really fascinated me was her productivity. She might as well have died at thirty because she'd written and cooked and sewed herself to death. Her mania scared and shamed me. I knew I'd never catch up to her. I couldn't even be bothered to harness my perfectionism into an eating disorder, and had been convinced for a while that my decision to remain slightly, ambivalently pudgy was a predictor of failure, artistic and otherwise. Whenever my mother came into my room at two in the morning on school nights to tell me to put my homework away and go to bed, I realized my perfectionism was a bodily function I'd better get under control if I wanted to become someone who went on dates. The Bible commanded me to use my talents, but it also told me to use them sparingly, because pride goeth before a fall, and since there was nothing in evangelical Christianity suggesting intelligence should be used as a weapon for God, I was sure that when people talked about using our gifts to glorify him, it meant that God was going to put me to work writing devotional guides for teenage girls.

I'd never catch up to Plath, but I could take a job at a magazine and not have it almost kill me. I would never be mistaken for a genius, I knew that. Or even the valedictorian. But I could try to write. And I could move to New York and work in publishing.

Mrs. Shapiro, however, would mistake me for a suicide waiting to happen. Senior year we were reunited, and one day in the library, doing research for an upcoming paper, I informed her that I was thinking of writing on *The Bell Jar*. Her eyes darkened. We stood across from each other, a bookcase between us.

"I need a word," she murmured, and then reached over, took me gently by the elbow, and led us into an unpopulated corner. "I'm not sure if it would be a good idea for you to read that book," she said. "I see a lot of similarities between you and the author." Which was exactly why I'd chosen the book—it told the story of an overly sensitive girl who wanted to make it big in New York.

"Okay," I said. I wanted to laugh. She and my mother had it in for me in the same way: with excessive, unwarranted concern. *Oh, Mrs. Shapiro*, I wanted to say. *Come on! What have you seen on my face, or read in my papers, to make you think I am this close to ending my life? I think we know who the crazy one is here.* Then I remembered the day she gathered our class for an audit of term paper footnotes, and my worry that I'd slipped up and written an inaccurate citation was so palpable that she made some crack about how she'd better get started before this one—jerking her thumb in my direction—had a heart attack.

I wanted to be thought exceptional—even if it was just Mrs. Shapiro imagining that when she looked at me, she saw a seventeen-year-old girl with an exceptional amount of frayed, trembling edges who would unravel upon contact with a book that described how to take the unraveling into her own hands. I didn't care that I'd been censored again—I'd been told that I might not be as boring as I thought I was. Maybe I had it in me to crack up in some spectacular way, my soul spilling everywhere like a tumbled glass, all the broken shards giving me an irresistible glitter.

What Mrs. Shapiro mistook for mental instability—watchful, high-strung silences—Heather and Jenny understood as prudishness. They thought I was exceptional, too—exceptionally uptight.

"Chris Bernard's sort of ugly," said Jenny. Against my better judgment, I'd mentioned that I had a crush on him. Jenny, Heather, and I had gone to the restaurant Jenny's father owned for free food before they opened for dinner. The vinyl booths were dark and cool, and Muzak drifted through the air.

"He's got all that acne around his mouth," she said. "Could you imagine kissing that?"

"I hadn't thought about it," I said. Remain indifferent, I told myself. Remain indifferent, so as not to cry.

"We have to tell you something," said Heather.

"Is someone pregnant?" I said.

"No, no—it's nothing like that!" said Heather. She looked at Jenny. "It's just that we've been meaning to tell you that—"

"On weekend nights we've been riding around getting high with Jason and Kenny and Steve and Kelly," Jenny said.

Heather drew in breath through clenched teeth. "Do you hate us?"

"I don't hate you at all. I'd never hate you, not for things like that." That was true.

Then it all came out. The night they drove at Kenny Carlin's command to Saint Mary of the Lakes, where Kenny's mom was a hard-core regular and Kenny was a groundskeeper, because Kenny was drunk and decided that he absolutely had to climb on top of the nativity out on the lawn and some cops just happened to be pulling out of the convenience store across the street and saw tiny Kenny dancing on the thatched roof and then fall to the lawn. The night that Jason wanted to borrow Heather's car to drive himself home and Heather was wary but Jenny said, Come on, what's the worst that could happen, and the worst that could happen was that Jason drove the car off the road and into some pine trees. How Jenny was seeing Mark, a long-haired senior from the next high school over, the sort of boy who was really a man, a minor deity somehow bound to earth by bell schedules.

"We didn't tell you," said Jenny. "We thought if you knew you'd be angry and disapprove."

I didn't want to know what had given them that impression. The word *party*, because of how I'd overheard them described and seen them depicted in John Hughes movies, filled me with fear. I was afraid of what people would see if I let myself go wherever my mind and alcohol and drugs might take me. I didn't want anyone to ever have to step over me while I lay openmouthed like a fish that had been knocked from its bowl onto somebody's parents' shag carpet. Or pull my face, mottled with vomit and mulch, out of some- body's parents' landscaping after I'd heaved in the bushes. I didn't ever want anyone who wasn't related to me to see my body's se- crets spilled out in strangers' ranch houses when I wasn't even sure what its secrets were. Maybe my body was what was weighing me down, not God, and if I could just learn to forget about my body, my mind could finally, finally be free. My body—ovoid and white like a peeled potato, rooted and thick—was keeping me from being a person who loved art and detested conformity, a person I knew I *should* be. I skipped lunch and went jogging around my neighborhood after school, but I would get in a dressing room with an armload of clothes, anticipating wholesale personal transformation, and my body would still betray me—my hips would roadblock a dress, my chest would shrink from a bodice. The outfit would not mean what it was intended to. Instead of saying, "Here is a sweet but sarcastic high school student who takes Morrissey very much to heart," it would say, "Here is a breastless sandbag who has never been kissed and would probably run from you if you came at her looking to try."

But I kept this all to myself around Heather and Jenny. I had made sure never to say anything about what they were doing because I knew I had no right to judge them, but they'd found me out. I thought that I had been the one watching and listening, observing teenagers being teenagers the way I used to watch jump ropes whipping before it was my turn at double Dutch: okay, okay, I want to get in there, I want to get in there, but I need to make sure I'm jumping in on just the right beat because if I don't, I'll bring the whole thing down with me, all of us laid out on the pavement tangled up in rope and all of it my fault, all of it because my timing and judgment were terrible. So I'd worked hard at not making a fool of myself. Just hold still, I told myself. Don't make a noise, make a smell, make a scene.

"When I was your age," my mother always said, "people thought I was a snob. But I was just very shy. People can mistake shyness for you thinking you're better than they are. Remember that." I had remembered that, and here it was. Just because they hadn't seen and heard much from me didn't mean I wasn't telling them anything. And I probably was a snob, because I didn't really want to hang out with these kids—I had the feeling that all the guys would end up working in the service departments of local car dealerships. I wished that someone *were* pregnant. At least that way I could perform valiant acts of discretion and falsehood on their behalf, and become a saintly, heroic figure, rather than a saintly, stony, foreboding figure—one that they might want Kenny Carlin to mow down with the rider mower.

I told my sister what they had told me on a drive home from school. "I have something to tell you, too," she said. "But I thought you would tell on me."

"Have I *ever* told on you?" There were the times in the morning before school when she'd turn the hair dryer on and leave it running in the bathroom sink to drown out our conversation and then tell me that they were all cutting class and going to New York and I said nothing. The times she said she was going to a friend's but was actually going to Philadelphia and I said nothing. The Friday nights when she left the house wearing one thing and then changed into another and I said nothing.

She started talking. Mia, she said, drove a bunch of them home and into a deer one night, and didn't tell my sister until later that when she hit the deer she'd been on acid. And she'd been to parties where she was the only one not high or drunk, and knew something was wrong but couldn't be absolutely sure and didn't want to pull her friends aside to ask, "Is everyone *completely* high but me?"

"Do you forgive me? Please forgive me," my sister said. She took my arm. I shook her off with my elbow. I thought I had at least proved how valiantly discreet I was to my sister, who seemed to think herself invincible—she had to think she was invincible if, while grounded, she was going to make her best friend cover for her while she went into the city to confront an ex who dumped her for someone who, she was just going to come right out and say it, was a slut.

But my sister could buckle under convention, too. One night, on the way into the city, we stopped at the Acme to get something to drink. Once inside, my sister grabbed my arm and yanked me into the cereal aisle, where we huddled against the shelves. "It's Mrs. Andrews!" she hissed. She had spotted a church friend of my mother's.

A cashier came over the store's PA system asking for a manager to validate a check, but what we heard was our mother's voice: *I don't care what you do when you get out of the house, but while you're under my roof I'm responsible to God for how I raise you.* All the women from church had prayed over my sister's struggles with her geometry tutor and my runaway anxiety, and we were sure that they would feel they had invested poorly if they knew that this was what we were up to. "If Mrs. Andrews sees me like this," my sister said to me, our backs against boxes of cornflakes, "she'll tell Mom, and it'll all be over." I was shocked. We could not let Mrs. Andrews see us tricked out like slatternly pixies: denim shorts over black tights, a black minidress over thigh-highs held up with garters my sister had borrowed from Mia, hoop earrings, red lipstick. We were so clearly out looking to get unequally yoked with unbelievers. What could we say if she saw us? *Mrs. Andrews, this is Kelly. She had a party last Saturday when her parents were out of town that went into the late afternoon of Sunday and she answered the door on the second day in a sheet to let in people who'd heard it was still going on. And this young lady, with the nose ring? She volunteers for Planned Parenthood over in Burlington. My sister and I will be capping our evening off with Snapples from Wawa, while some of us—the girl in the red velvet dress?—will be doing acid. But don't worry about us. We're fine.* Mrs. Andrews passed by the end of the aisle—I saw her short, neat hair, her slacks and a wool jacket, dark green, with brass buttons, over a turtleneck, purse slung over her forearm. All my mother's friends looked like this. And they all greeted us with genuine warmth after services because they knew how much our mother loved us—while my sister and I smiled weakly, idling in the aisles like guilty dogs on a leash. We were not waiting for Jesus to come back, we were waiting in cars with doughnuts before the West Coast Video opened so we could be the first in line to buy tickets to see Morrissey. We loved Morrissey and Michael Stipe, loved them for their lank purity even though we'd heard they were not celibate but gay. *Buy the sky and sell the sky and lift your arms up to the sky and ask the sky and ask the sky.* Mike Mills's harmonies coming down like rain in sun. We were stopped in our tracks by Kim Deal's voice coming out of our radios, a voice like a ten-year-old girl shouting while she stood on tiptoe—we would not ever feel moved to raise our hands to heaven in church, but we would know what it was like to hear the Pixies for the first time and feel that we had been visited in our bedroom by a freaky but companionable spirit. We were laying up treasures in the bookcases over our desks: a They Might Be Giants set list in mine, a gallon jug of spring water that Damon Albarn had emptied in my sister's. If Mrs. Andrews saw us, she would think that my mother had failed as a mother of Christian girls because our outfits would make it clear that she had failed to keep us from the darkness that was Marcel Duchamp, from the darkness that was the dance club that had been a Norwegian Seamen's church, from the darkness that was Trent Reznor.

But Mrs. Andrews never saw us. And then we were at a club in Philadelphia, black lights turning everything blue, huge speakers rendering everyone deaf and dumb. We were all in a silent film—pale faces bobbing to the surface as we jumped up and down, arms flung over our heads, dresses swinging back and forth above our knees. The melodies were digitized, pixilated, and the flickering black light made everything impermanent—you weren't really you,

you were in pieces, with your real self coming to the surface, a picture developing of what could be.

"Do not be yoked together with unbelievers," Paul told the Corinthians, who were beset by false teachers. In the churches we'd grown up in, it was a scripture considered as necessary to an understanding of the Christian life as John 3:16. "For what do righteousness and wickedness have in common?" said Paul. "Or what fellowship can light have with darkness? What does a believer have in common with an unbeliever?" Quite a bit, we thought: U2, R.E.M., the Smiths, the Cure, New Order, Depeche Mode, the Replacements, and the Pixies. Music was the reason my sister and I had unequally yoked ourselves to unbelievers. Well, not technically unbelievers. Many of our friends were Catholic girls in various stages of apostasy. My sister and I would always be too good to be truly depraved and too worldly to keep away from the sinners, but with the sinners we could pretend that the only eschatology we knew consisted of Michael Stipe singing "It's the End of the World as We Know It (and I Feel Fine)." And if one day, through pretending, we forgot that we'd ever known otherwise, the hurt feelings and occasional ambush by our conscience would be worth it.

Let's go to New York for a weekend, I told Heather and Jenny, to see more of what could be. To my surprise, especially because my parents had offered to chaperone, they agreed, and that Saturday night in the city, we took ourselves, as if on pilgrimage, to CBGBs. Heather had dyed her hair, which she'd already tinted strawberry blond, with white Manic Panic she'd bought earlier in the day. In the hotel room it looked like she'd had a run-in with a jar of gesso, but in the low light of the club her hair glowed platinum. Jenny wore jeans and a cardigan over a Jane's Addiction T-shirt and kept her parka on. I had borrowed a dress from my sister: a rust-colored, floral-patterned chiffon baby-doll number purchased at the Limited. I wasn't sure I liked it, but I didn't have a wardrobe for this sort of thing, and figured my sister knew what she was doing when she bought it.

We sat at a table in the back, mostly just looking around, not wanting to attract attention to ourselves, when three figures in various layers of oxfords and rugbys and khakis emerged out of the dark, leather-jacketed crowd.

"Hey." Was this guy wearing a yellow Ralph Lauren parka in CBGBs? It seemed that he was. We might have arrived here via bridge and tunnel, but at least we knew what was proper attire at a seminal music venue.

"Do you want to smoke a bowl?" The boys hovered. They were tall, pale, damp, floppy-haired. One of them ran his tongue across his top lip. I saw it now: this was the dark side of money. This was how Jennifer Levin happened.

"No thanks," I said.

"Do you wanna bang us?" he said.

"What did he say?" Heather hissed in my ear.

"There's three of us and three of you," he said. I looked at Jenny. She sighed and crossed her arms over her chest. "We're not interested," she said, and pulled her hood over her head.

"Bitch," the guy said, and turned and took his friends with him. Not bad: within fifteen minutes of arrival, we had already been rated attractive enough for group sex. It was offensive, yes, but also encouraging.

One of the bands started up. The lead singer, already bare-chested, flung his long dark curly hair around. Heather and Jenny scrambled up to the front of the club, but long-haired, bare-chested lead singers didn't do anything for me, so I headed to the ladies' room. On the way there some guy on his way to the bar bumped into me. He looked down at me, laughed, and said, "Nice prom dress!"

I kept my head down and kept on walking. I fumed all the way to the bathroom and all the way back and for the rest of the night. Nice prom dress? Nice *prom dress?* Fair enough, city denizen in a leather jacket who might have had one too many and so is moved to pick on a teenage girl. Yes, you're right. I may look a little too dressed up for the occasion. I *am* wearing a stupid dress—I don't even really like it, but I couldn't find one that didn't make me feel like a breastless sandbag, which my actual senior prom dress will, too. Even though my friends and I can't be bothered to do anything as childish as travel to Disney World with our classmates, we will all, a few months hence, go to the prom, which will leave me wondering, especially because a friend found me a date from another school whom I liked very much but would tell me he was really too busy when I asked him on a date weeks later, what the big deal was because it was basically a wedding reception without a bride and groom. We girls are children of developments, of towns that became flush with new money back in the seventies and eighties. We are potted plants whose parents love them, and so set them down among pines and laurels in cul-de-sacs. And not only are we from the suburbs, we are from the New Jersey suburbs. New Jersey: land of chemical refineries, Mafia families, malls, big hair, guidos, irrelevant sports teams. Not only am I from the New Jersey suburbs, which is humiliating enough, I'm from the South Jersey suburbs. That means we drive our IROCs into pine trees and crash them into cranberry bogs. Shadowed by Philadelphia, towered over by New York, there are no legends here except the Jersey Devil and Patti Smith—who left her pig-farming town for Philadelphia to make art at the Painted Bride. The last thing anyone knows about New Jersey stops at Trenton. Nothing exists below Exit 7. We are hidden in the pines, our glories have sunk down into the sandy soil or eroded from urban blight. Walt Whitman lived in Camden for a while, which is why we've named a bridge for him, and it was the home of RCA Records, where the Carter Family came to make recordings, but now it's one of the most murderous cities in the union. Our accent, the Philadelphia accent, further contributes to the impression that we are more red-neck than wise guy— in North Jersey, they talk like New Yorkers, which allows them to slip over the bridges and tunnels into the city without much trouble, and only loutish weekend revelry can get you found out. Our accent sounds southern; the vowels are nasal and drawn out. If we open our mouths, you can tell what area code we're dialing from: 6-eeeooow-9. My sister has it, though somehow I have lost it, and I didn't do it on purpose, but you'd be right to suspect me of repeatedly watching *A Room with a View* to rid myself of it if I *were* trying to lose it on purpose. And we don't even rate New Jersey Transit railway stops here in South Jersey. Only the Greyhound, fuzzy and stained and stinking like zoo, goes directly to New York. We get to Philadelphia, where we're rehearsing the rest of our lives, by the PATCO high-speed line, which is a toy train preserved in aquamarine and orange, the sixties' favorite color scheme for civic uplift. And my classmates—who, according to our popular cinema, are supposed to be vicious, status-seeking wolves—haven't even stooped to sneering at me like you just did, you near-grown man. Nothing seems like it fits—my clothes, my friends, my church. If I were truly brave and original, I know, I would have gone out and made my own reality, the way I should have made my own prom dress in a fit of inspiration and outsider resolve, but didn't, because I am sort of lazy, if I'm being honest with myself. I would have bor-rowed from the lives I'd read about in Norton's, thereby commit-ting the sin of unoriginality on the way to iconoclasm—instead of wandering around knocking into and then retreating from everyone else's facade of self-confidence. A few years from now my malaise, my reticence, my silence, will be diagnosed by Simone de Beauvoir: the adolescent girl waits in a fog, she wrote, and I know that I have spent so long in a fog of hate—hating myself, hating other people, unsure that I have been doing anything right, unsure that I am a likable person, unsure of why people like me when they try to become my friend, afraid that once people get near me they will drop me like they should. I know I am a poser. But you have to spend some time posing before you actually arrive in some comfortable, natural position, right? Oh, wait, I know *you*. You're the clerk with the blue Mohawk at Trash and Vaudeville on South Street who gives my sister and me silent hell with your evil eye while we slink around eyeing the Smiths T-shirts posted on the wall, suspecting you'd rather we shoplift than come in here fouling the store with our suburban nice-girl pieties like *bathing*. And what were *you* doing when you were my age? Doing just what I'm doing. Calling up college radio stations with requests only to have the DJs laugh at your requests, going to see bands as if your life depended on it, wearing T-shirts you're going to laugh at ten years from now but still won't toss out. Maybe you are from *Long Island*! Yes! That explains the rancor. So give me credit. I'm doing all this while still believing in Jesus. That's like swimming the Channel in a suit beaded with buckshot. The Jesus I believe in is not the friend of Oral Roberts, or the mascot for Liberty University, that citadel of closed-mindedness. He's more like the Jesus that Paul Westerberg sings about in "Can't Hardly Wait," the one who rides alongside drunk romantics on cross-country buses. That Jesus. Who I am not sure really exists, because all the people I know who know Jesus would have no idea who I'm talking about if I brought him up. But I'm going to stand sweating in the club for hours more, roasting in the orange light, accidentally tasting other people's sweaters and hair. This, I must have more of this, I'll think, sitting on the curb outside after the show, as cabs float by, letting the March air cool the sweat off my neck. I'll wait on New York, where all will be made perfect. All the things that made me a failure as a teenager will allow me to excel in college, and will allow me entrance to this city. Things are about to happen. I'm going to learn to open my mouth. And when I do, a professor, preferably of history or English, will fall in love with me.

# CHAPTER 5

## SATURDAY NIGHT

A weekend of badges, folders, pens, key chains, folding chairs, maps, all of it culminating in a dramatic presentation designed to discourage date rape. I sat next to my parents, peering down on the stage where, under bright lights, there stood a twin bed, a bottle of vodka, and two people in T-shirts and shorts representing desire and folly and the dignity you lost when you signed up to be a residential assistant. A pill had been slipped in a glass, and a girl had to wriggle away from a devious plot and her own shame and appeal to school administrators. After a day so full of bureaucracy and warnings I just wanted to curl up and die, my last words being *Oh, just throw me in, throw me to the books already, please, look, they already gave you a check and I think I'm beneath raping, anybody will tell you that, so why don't I just show up on the first day of the fall semester, and endure the real pain of getting to know people, throw me in and I'll find my way, don't force this on me.* Then my roommate for this orientation weekend told me that there was going to be some drinking over in the freshman boys' dorm.

Anne and I were going to be English majors at this small Catholic college, which must have been why they put us together. She played field hockey, but she also played the violin. I could see her one day wearing the khaki shirts and shorts of zookeepers, her reddish brown hair pinned back from her face and curling over her shoulders, handling baby kangaroos and the children who were curious about them with cheerfulness and patience. I decided that we had nothing in common.

"Do you want to come with me?" she said. "I'm meeting some of my friends from school." It was nice of her to make the offer, but I'd met her field hockey friends earlier, and I suspected they'd looked at the striped shorts I'd borrowed from my sister, something she'd worn to go dancing, and sized me up on the spot: Dork, may hang out with theater people. Or maybe they knew exactly what I thought of their tans and pearl earrings. There was that, and also some dismay at my fellow students, who couldn't seem to wait until school began to start in on the drinking.

"Oh, thanks," I told Anne. "But I'm feeling sort of beat, and I think I'll just call it a night."

I waited until she had shut the door behind her, waited a few minutes more to make sure she wouldn't come back for some lip gloss or her wallet, and then took out the biography of Queen Elizabeth I that I'd brought with me. After a while I forgot where I was; after a while I felt like myself again.

At about twelve thirty, when I had just put the lights out, there was banging on the metal door. I sat up. Three boys burst in and turned the lights on. Polo shirts, swinging arms, shouts, the smell of alcohol. Anne came in behind them, telling them to please cut it out.

"Hey," one of them said, pointing at me. "Get out of bed. It's Saturday night."

"Oh, how sweet," said another. "She's in her *nightgown*." There were no ruffles or lace, but yes, I was in a nightgown. For a moment I thought they really might jump into the bed with me, and I pulled the sheets up against my chest in an involuntary spasm of modesty. *I hate you*, I told myself.

"Anne, why doesn't your friend want to come out? Is she afraid we're going to rip her nightgown off?" said a third.

There would be no mercy for girls neatly tucked away in bed by midnight on Saturday calming themselves to sleep with a book—a book about a virgin queen, no less. I got it. I was digging my own grave here. They had come upon a scene of flagrant disregard for the imperatives of Youth. I sat there wondering what I could say to them. Nothing. If I attempted sarcasm, they would just hoot at it. I just wanted to get out of here and finish the biography so I could finish the history of the French Revolution I had back at home—I had become obsessed with Charlotte Corday—and then finish my summer.

Anne took one by the shoulders and steered him out of the room. "I told you to leave me alone. Now get out." She sent them all off like a nurse shooing loiterers out of a camp infirmary, neither outraged nor amused by their invasion. "They're boys from school," she said after she shut and locked the door and sat down on the bed across from mine. "I'm so sorry. Usually they're very nice." I had a feeling they weren't.

When I got back home, I signed up for Choice Housing, Choice Housing being the college's way of giving students shelter from drunken student life, of promising us that at least in the comfort of our residence hall, we would never have to be bothered by the sight or smell of other people's vomit. In the fall, when I arrived on campus, I discovered that Choice Housing consisted solely of me and my two roommates. We were the only freshman girls who had requested the option that year, and they stuck the three of us in a double at the end of a basement hallway on which we lived with six other girls who celebrated the arrival of each weekend with a cocktail of cigarette smoke, Smashing Pumpkins, perfume from Victoria's Secret, and wine coolers. None of us ever asked the others why we'd chosen this arrangement. I suspected Mavis, who had grown up in Baltimore City but had not let it get her, was determined to keep herself diligent so she could become an accountant and never have to put anything on layaway at Lerner's again. I figured Marianne, who seemed to have belonged to a ladies' temperance union of half a dozen girls in her fancy Catholic school, considered herself, like I did, too good for drinking. Also, she loved horses.

Late mornings I had the room to myself, and I used this time to eat muffins and drink juice in the cloudy sunlight that came in through the old basement window. One day I noticed that the juice had inspirational quotations printed inside its bottle caps, which delighted me, because I was a sucker for messages from the low-rent beyond—Magic 8-Balls, fortune cookies, and games like the one in which you twisted off apple stems while reciting the alphabet to see what the first initial of your husband's name would be. "You will do foolish things," the bottle cap said Colette said, "but do them with enthusiasm." I thought four years would be plenty of time to figure out how to be foolish. Hopefully I would get some practice at throwing myself into the unknown. Into another foreign language, another country, another hair color. I could become an atheist by the time this was all over. I might have an affair with a professor. An unmarried professor—I didn't want to be that foolish.

I thought Marianne, because she and I shared some musical loves, could start work on the assignment I'd been given by the bottle cap, but she seemed content to stay Marianne.

"I think you and I grew up the same way," said Marianne one Saturday night as we walked back from the library.

"Yes," I told her. "Slowly." We passed a group of kids outside the theater—the school's tight knot of drama and art department kids, who always hung out there. I saw a girl in an army jacket, long-legged, long-haired, shove a boy with a laugh, which made everyone else laugh too. I felt for a moment that I was in the passenger seat of a car being driven past an exit I was pretty sure we should take. As we crossed the bridge over Charles Street, students came streaming toward us, laughing and shouting, their faces illuminated by the lights. "Where's everybody going?" I asked.

"Mass," she said. "And then they're going to go down to York Road to get drunk," she added. They were going to the Swallow, they said, they were going to Gator's. I had never been in the bars, but they all looked—the sign for Swallow at the Hollow featured a bug-eyed bird in a straw boater—like holes in the wall. This was, like the Mass they were going to, a weekly ritual. *Where are you going? When will I see you there? Who will you be with?* These were the things they said to one another every week, at this hour. With more high spirits and anticipation, I imagined, than they had for the ritual they were heading toward.

"How can they do that and then go get wasted and not feel like hypocrites?" I asked Marianne.

"I don't know," she answered, in a tone that suggested that not only did she not know, she also really didn't care. "Do you feel like getting dinner?" she said. Marianne didn't waste a lot of time thinking or talking about hypocrisy or duty or betrayal. I could change her mind about music by just mentioning a band but I could not engage her in a discussion of the abstract or hypothetical. Marianne never mentioned God or Mary, just went quietly off to Mass on Sunday mornings as if she were popping out for a quart of milk, leaving me passed out in sleep in the bunk below her. Perhaps to Marianne Mass was as necessary as milk, and therefore as unremarkable, so why go around talking about it and what it did for you? But why go, Marianne? I thought. What do you feel? It's an awfully elaborate and weighty set of terms to kneel under and accept if you don't buy any of it—if it's only for the sake of upholding tradition. This was the mystery of Catholicism to me. Why did people go to Mass if they didn't seem to care about it? Why stand there if whatever was being said washed over you without consequence? But who was I to be accusing Marianne of these things? There I was, not going to church just because I didn't have a car and I didn't want to depend on the campus Christian fellowship to take me because they believed in ice cream socials. Marianne, though she loved to talk, could be impenetrable. I wondered the same things about her decision to major in English. Why books? What drove her? She never stayed up late to work on anything, and never seemed too moved by whatever she was reading. And she carried Rolaids in her purse, which further added to my impression of Marianne as beyond craving excitement.

On a weekend that fall when Marianne went home, Mavis asked me to come with her and Crystal, the other black girl on our hallway, to a dance at Morgan State College with the Black Students Association on a Saturday night. I almost demurred—could they not see the veins through my freckles?—but I remembered the bottle cap. I wore my Morrissey T-shirt and cutoff denim shorts. We met at some upperclassman's room before heading over. A number of the older girls, wearing outfits of purple, orange, and green decorated with gold jewelry, looked at me sitting on a couch with amusement— yeah, I was wondering the exact same thing, I thought. How *did* I get in here, and why on earth did I think it was acceptable to wear this T-shirt to a dance at a historically black college? But Mavis and Crystal, who were talking to some of the older guys, didn't seem troubled by their cargo.

We entered the auditorium. "She's white!" somebody shrieked.

I mainly just walked around the room, watching the dancing. I passed Mavis and Crystal. I waved. They danced out to the edge of the crowd and tried to pull me in.

"Come on, C!" said Mavis. "Get out here!"

"Oh, no," I shouted. "I'm white!"

"You're crazy," shouted Crystal. "Come on!" And so I did. And I forgot where I was and who I was, and knew only that I liked to dance, that I wasn't bad at it, and that I danced the hardest when there weren't any boys in the immediate vicinity. Shortly thereafter some man with dreadlocks tried to "freak" me and my Morrissey T-shirt during some dancehall—*freak* being a term I learned from Mavis and Crystal that night. It was from Mavis that I had also learned that songs could be called joints—as in, "Girl, this is my joint!" Sometimes she would shout this, and then go over to Crystal's room, where the song, usually "Award Tour," was coming from. Crystal lived with Nicole D'Agostino, from Goshen, Connecticut, who smoked and drank like every night was a party in the woods, and to whom the word joint meant something else entirely. I wondered if Mavis and Crystal ever bonded together over the witlessness of white girls. I liked to think that I came off as less witless than Marianne. I had not hung a poster of Sting over my bed. It was true that I had told the whole of my graduating class, through my high school yearbook, that I wanted to live and write in New York and "marry Sting's double," but that was last year. I now wanted to marry Billy Bragg's double.

The things you find yourself doing when you have to, I thought as I danced. Because you can't not. Because you have to go out. Because you don't want to disappoint people, and when you don't disappoint them, you find that you can forget yourself and astonish yourself. Remember this, I told myself. Foolish things! Enthusiasm when you do them!

In my sophomore year I met Genevieve, who taught me that if

your resolve to leave the house faltered, you could always give your-self a pep talk with vodka. Six of us—Mavis, Marianne, Genevieve, myself, and two other girls—had moved into a newly constructed campus apartment.

"Keep me company while I dress!" Genevieve called out as I passed by her room one Saturday night. I had an idea that I would put some spaghetti sauce in a leftover pot of Velveeta shells. I'd put on my white terrycloth bathrobe, which I loved to wear to bed because it was like sleeping under a mound of snow. I was in for the night. Me and some poems. She was sitting on her bed in a rayon paisley robe colored in navy, burgundy, and gold—a dressing gown, nothing she was going to spend time in, it was an almost diaphanous way sta-tion between day and night, perfect for knocking back shots before putting her stockings on. She was going to some formal dance and I wasn't, because everyone was going to drink and get red-faced and sweaty. From the pictures she'd shown me, the parties Genevieve went to seemed more like rugby scrums than the acid-witted salons I thought we'd all be hosting when we got to college.

I came in and saw that Genevieve had a full shot glass in one hand and a bottle of vodka in the other, the bottle resting between her knees, which were still tan from summer. She tilted her head back and took the shot. "Goddammit!" she said, giving her curls a shake. I think she saw my eyes go wide because she said, "I'm ner-vous. A shot helps calm me down."

"Seriously?" I got anxious just thinking about all that fire run-ning down the back of my throat.

"Seriously. You want one?" She laughed, because we knew what the answer to that was. Later that night I would lose the Velveeta shells, but I would rather throw up from poor food budgeting than convulsive vodka swallowing. "Come sit by me and tell me why I shouldn't be nervous."

I took my place. I ticked off the three boys on campus she had flirtations going with in addition to the steady at West Point and the local hero who was angling for a spot on the Nassau County police force when he wasn't out dancing to Depeche Mode. "Right," she said, and poured herself another shot. "Right." And another.

Genevieve would take me to my first and last frat party—at a Hopkins frat house, since we did not have Greek life at our college—and would show me what Saturday night should be.

"Of course I'll go!" I told Genevieve when she asked me and Marianne if we wanted to go. "It'll be fascinating research." She rolled her eyes.

That night I girded myself with what Genevieve and I would later refer to as the bra of sin, which was a pink-and-black rose-patterned item from Victoria's Secret. I was throwing a coin in a fountain. The frat house was a fine old house on Canterbury Road right around the corner from what we'd heard was John Waters's place. There was a couch, as to be expected, on the lawn. We stood in an old wood-paneled room, its walls covered with group shots of brothers gone by, and I spent some time imagining which ones had turned into dentists or engineers. It was early, but it was crowded and loud, and we were viewing the evening through a smudged lens, as if we'd forgotten to clean our glasses and they'd been jostled and fingerprinted and put on crookedly in the crush.

A boy came up to us. He had thick brown hair, wore a plaid shirt and shorts, and seemed pleasant and funny. Oh look, I thought. We must seem like an attractive proposition. But I knew that chiefly it was Genevieve, who carried what was popularly known as a rack, who was the attractive proposition, and it was just that Marianne and I looked better because of her. People had to tell me when girls had what was popularly known as a rack. It was nothing I went around noticing. I had small breasts, but I didn't care about that.

Fat could happen if I wasn't careful. It ran in my family. If someone married me, thirty years from now I might have turned into the
Venus of Willendorf, my eyes forced to a slit because of the cheeks
pushing up, my forearms wearing wattles, my chin not a chin but a
steppe of skin that started at my collarbone and stopped short of my
mouth. My breasts had given me a reprieve. I always wanted long,
thin legs—that's what I noticed, that's what I envied. I had a set
of floor exercises, courtesy of *Seventeen*, that I performed throughout junior high and high school on my bedroom carpet to try to
whittle my legs down, no matter that my mother told me that I was
born with thunder thighs, and would never be able to change them.
That's what made me envy other girls—the ease with which they
strode through life because they had long, slender legs. Your chest
got you other things, things I didn't want. If you were a man who
lusted after chests, then I knew you did not really love women, you
loved what you imagined to be their mystical ability to maybe return
you to the womb, and I was having none of that, mister, you're on
your own for finding a port in a storm, and if I give it to you, it's not
going to be because your head's buried in my bosom.

But here was Brett, a freshman from New Jersey. A psychology
major. Somehow I'd gotten the idea that psychology majors weren't
that bright or interesting. The best, most interesting thing you could
be was an English major—you could do anything with it, it was the
queen of the humanities, even though it was a discipline developed
after World War II—but I didn't hold his limited mind against him.

He disappeared, and we descended to the basement—black light,
kids on torn-out van seats, plastic cups, and a band, a pretty good
band that was pleasing the crowd with some Black Crowes, who
I had to admit I sort of liked. The three of us stood next to each
other, laughing and talking. I sipped my Coke. Then someone was
kissing my neck. Or was it that someone was playing with my hair

and I thought it was Marianne or Genevieve, but then someone was kissing my neck, and I gasped and turned around. It was the boy from upstairs. He was smiling. It was me he wanted. Which I found hilarious. I wanted to scream. *You're kidding me! Get out of here! Are you sure? Are you too drunk to realize that I'm not my friend over there, who's singing along to "Hard to Handle" with her cup held high? Let us be frank and admit to one another that she will provide you with the better sexual experience.* He pulled me back to him and returned to kissing my neck. Genevieve smiled at me. The noise of the band made me feel like there was a curtain around us—and weren't people too distracted by the music to notice us? Not really.

"Let's get out of here," I said, taking his hand, amazed that I was taking control, could take control, that I was saying these words. We stumbled in the black light, over the kids on the van seats, he took me by the hand, and we ran through the big cavernous house and I thought of paintings of Adam and Eve running out from under the eye of God, we were stomping up stairs past blond girls, we actually walked in on a couple like John Hughes said you did at things like this, and then we were running downstairs, and then he threw open a door. There was a stairwell, gray, suddenly everything echoed, and he pushed me up against a wall, under a beveled window, and his lips were big, rubbery, slippery, he was eating my mouth as if it were pie. He was eating my mouth and neck as if I were pie, but I wanted him to kiss me like he did before, it was so tender, he was telling me secrets, I dreamed of boys kissing my neck like that. Now my face was nothing more to him than an aluminum pie plate that needed emptying.

Someone opened the door. "Sorry!" they said. He took my hand again and we descended a few more floors, he threw open another door and there was the backyard, stretching out in front of us. "Come on," he said, and then we were in front of an overturned

boat covered in blue tarp. We sat down, more sloppy kisses, I noticed that beer breath could taste like garlic breath, and then he drew
my hand to his crotch, but I moved it away. I could not say to him
that I had never done this, and that while I wanted research, and
here I was getting it, I thought there would also be romance, but
no, this was just research. Then I heard the clank of a belt buckle
on the top of the boat and a lightning *zip* and he was putting my
hand on the smooth cartilage. There was nothing to do but start
sawing away, quick, what'll I do, I know, I thought of the gesture
I'd seen Genevieve use to signal "Give me a break," which I knew
was some souvenir from her Long Island upbringing. He arched his
back, tilted his head, and moaned, which was somewhat disgust-
ing but it must have meant that I was not failing this test. I couldn't
look at him, so I looked out at the yard. The moonlight was coming
down full strength; the house loomed above us like an impassive
face. What was his name? Did I hear it right? Brett? Brent? Brant?
No, Brett.

"Are you *done* yet?" I said to him. Brett? Brent? Brant? Who
cared, it was a declension of meatheadedness. He finished. There
was a splotch on the leg of my jeans. "Oh," I said. "Hmm." I didn't
know what else to do but wipe it off with a handful of leaves.

"Sorry," he said. There was the tinkling of metal as he packed
everything away. He got up and left me on the boat, started walking
to the house. He took big drunk strides, even tripped once, but I let
him right himself and move farther ahead before I got up to walk
back to the house. I couldn't remember how to reach the ground
floor, and he was gone, I'd never see or hear from him again, and
that was as it should be.

I woke up the next morning, Sunday morning, and went into the
bathroom to brush my teeth. I saw the hickey. I moaned out loud.
My parents were coming in a few hours to visit me and my sister,

who was attending a state university in the Baltimore suburbs. My mother would not miss the bruise, which looked like grape jam that had migrated to the wrong place. I cursed the warm fall weather, because it robbed me of the solution of turtlenecks, but I would wear a button-down shirt and keep the collar close. I had foundation, and I had artist's hands—I had helped Marianne cover up some chin burns from a bearded RA the week before.

It always seemed gray and Soviet on my sister's campus, the metal doors leading into stairwells, everything fireproof as if the state of Maryland thought the inmates were always just about to burn the place down, whether on purpose because of the crap food or because of an accident with a candle and a Led Zeppelin tapestry. My sister's cinder-blocked room looked out over concrete walkways and bridges that snaked through spindly forest. She liked to come up to my campus, where it was green, and she could have lasagna and soft tacos and stir-fry washed down with unlimited Diet Pepsi.

Today our parents had come to take us out for even better food downtown. I took a seat on the bed, far away from my mother and father, while we watched my sister flit about the room fetching her shoes, a sweater, her bag. She passed by me on the way to her closet.

"What's that on your neck?" There was no time to lie. "Is that a hickey?"

"Pardon?" said my mother, in a tone that made it clear she heard right the first time.

My sister leapt up and came at me, peeling away my collar and staring at my neck. "It's totally a hickey!" she said. She straightened up. "I'm so proud of you!"

"Oh jeez," said my father. My mother stood there silently, shaking her head.

"Who'd you get it from?" my sister said.

The jeans were still crusted over, lying in a heap on my floor. "Frat party. Let's not talk about it."

"Frat party! You went to a frat party? Was it some white-capped meathead? Did you let some white-capped meathead give you a hickey?"

"That's enough," said my mother. My father stood silently, shaking his head. I felt bad for my father: I'd reminded him that I was in fact a girl. But this was something that pained me more than it pained him. When I was ten I asked him whether he was upset that he had two daughters instead of sons. He didn't watch sports, having given up football because he'd been disgusted by the NFL strike of 1982, and didn't shoot or hunt or fish, preferring to pay strenuous, sweaty attention to the yard instead, but I thought surely he must have been somewhat disappointed by life with three women.

"Not at all," my father said.

I pressed him. "Don't you want someone to play catch with?"

"Nope," he said. "I play catch with you guys." My father may have sold cars, but he was no bullshitter, and it was as if the thought had never crossed his mind. He kept on offering us his flexed bicep, grinning and saying, "Give me a shot," asking us to swing as hard as we could, telling us to swing harder until he cried "Ouch!" with satisfaction. This was how I liked to think of myself—determined, unflinching, right on the mark—even though I wasn't sure it was the truth yet. I'd tried not to expose my father to the bloody, teary life I sometimes led, the life that had nothing to do with him and had nothing to do with me, really, the blood that came and went every month for no reason, and the fits that came and went when boys didn't return my interest. My sister, however, had blown her cover a long time ago, which might have been why she felt free to blow mine.

She linked our arms together as we followed my mother and father out into the hall. "So who was he?" she whispered in my ear.

# CHAPTER 6

# LET'S PLAY A GAME

Then there was Jane, who was not Genevieve. Jane was raised by Korean Buddhists and had found Jesus on her own, in high school, in suburban Maryland. She had never, she thought, met any Jewish people. "Where did *you* meet them?" she wanted to know. It made being raised in New Jersey seem utterly cosmopolitan. I met Jane in a drawing class, and since she loved French and writing and could play the guitar and flute, we became friends. She bought tulips for her dorm room and cooked dishes like Dijon mustard chicken for herself—she somehow had time to do this between classes and editing a section of the school paper. She would always ask if I had eaten when I stopped by her place in the afternoons. "I don't think you eat enough," she would say.

That year, sophomore year, Jane led me back to the Christian fellowship. It was true that the members believed in ice cream socials and acoustic guitars, and attended a church that believed in worship teams and met in a middle school auditorium. I'd had enough of these evangelical clichés. But many of the members had been raised Catholic before they turned to evangelical Christianity, which meant that their faith was serious but they had not been steeped in the attitudes and vocabulary, which meant that I heard them speaking as people, not as Christians. Which meant that their senses of humor had not been sacrificed to piety. And we were a small self-governing body of Christ—no adults coming down from the mountain, shrouded in fog and squinting, to minister to us—so I felt that I had been given a chance to see what kind of Christian I would be on my own. So far I had learned that it was probably unwise to be the sort of Christian who, when it was her turn to lead a Bible study, thought a T. S. Eliot poem would make a suitable text to discuss, unless you wanted dead air and trusting gazes.

I envied Jane because she had become a Christian of her own accord. It seemed to me that people who had to make a choice to believe in a household where no one else did had a truer faith than those who had been handed it at birth. They had been brave, they had been passionate. They had fallen in love. What surprised me was how dogmatic she could be. Her mothering could seize up and chill into something puritanical.

"I've decided that I'm not going to date until I get married," she told me one afternoon while she was going through my closet. Jane, who favored pink oxfords, thought of my wearing black as "progressive," and sometimes came over to look at my clothes, wondering what piece of black she could borrow.

"What?" I said. Jane had had a boyfriend in high school, but there'd been no one in college. "Do you know Josh McDowell?" she asked. I certainly did. I hadn't read anything by him, but at church he was often held up as proof of God's existence in a manner that made me think of revival tents and *Consumer Reports*: if an atheist lawyer could turn his heart over to God, then surely you could, too. He'd begun as an apologist but now wrote books promoting the blessings of chastity, arguing that you could be lonely for the glory of God. A scheme he'd put together with help, I bet, from Paul. I was starting to bear a grudge against Paul. "It is better to marry than to burn," he had told the Corinthians. It was Paul who had written that sighing, reluctant endorsement of marriage. It was Paul who had commanded that wives submit to their husbands. Paul! I nodded while Jane explained. Paul was a megalomaniac and a misogynist, but he had written something I wished I had heard Christians discuss more. "One man's faith allows him to eat everything," he told the Romans, "but another man, whose faith is weak, eats only vegetables. The man who eats everything must not condemn the man who does not, for God has accepted him." I wanted to tell Jane that we could eat everything. Well, most things.

Another night, when she came to pick me up for an outing with some fellow Christians, she leveled her eyes at my chest. "Are you wearing that?"

*That* was a crocheted sweater borrowed from my sister over a black shirt and tights and a wool skirt. Not even my mother had ever asked me that question. "What's wrong with it?"

"Don't you think that's a little revealing?" I looked down. Everything was covered up—the only thing exposed was my neck.

"Not at all!" I said. "What's wrong with it?"

"Well, the sweater part of it is kind of—"

I loved Jane, even as she was asking me to please not be such a harlot. I did not change the sweater, and the young Christian men we mixed with that evening remained chaste, a fact that I wanted to point out to Jane but would not. Jane was still luckier than me: her Christianity was still a platform from which she could launch radical acts of self-invention.

It was through Jane that I met Joshua. Joshua had left one of the most prestigious universities in the country—no one knew why, it was said he'd been kicked out—and had come to Baltimore, to our little Catholic college, near his hometown, to finish his undergraduate career. His black hair flopped about his face, as if he were a composer of nocturnes, and he wore a long black trench coat that came to the tops of his purple sneakers, the belt of it trailing behind him. There were also faded black T-shirts and black pinstriped pants. And then there was the cooked-food, gas-leaky smell of him, which I took to be the stale smell of bedridden genius.

Jane edited a column he wrote for the newspaper, and he asked her to introduce us. She brought him over to the apartment, and we all sat at the kitchen table, talking. He told me that he had seen that I had won the school's composition award—he took second place—and he wanted to find out who beat him. No one ever beat him in anything, and that a girl did, well, that was doubly unheard of.

"I want to have lunch with you," he told me at the table, "so I can demystify you." I looked at Jane. She was smiling.

I went to lunch with rumor ringing in my ears. *That guy? God, what a freak. He wears like the same three outfits all the time. I heard he scored 1600 on his SATs. Someone told me he actually told Dr. L he was full of shit to his face, in class. Someone told me he freebases on his hot plate. Somebody else said he got kicked out of that school because he accidentally set fire to a frat house. With a hot plate? Well, I heard that he was driving some dean's daughter home on a date and they got into an accident that left her in a coma for a month.*

One lunch with a potentially crazy person wouldn't kill me. Even if he had almost killed other people. He drove us, in his black minivan, to the Bel-Loc, where they served you open-face turkey sandwiches, drowning in yellow gravy, in booths that still had jukeboxes at the table, and the waitresses called you, as certain women did in Baltimore, hon.

"A minivan strikes me as an odd choice of vehicle for a college student," I said as we entered the restaurant.

"Well, my parents bought a new car and passed this off to me. Plus, it's going to come in handy when I shoot my movie."

"Your movie?"

"Yeah. Do you want to be in it? I'd love for you to read the script. I'm going to hold auditions next semester and shoot it over the summer. I'm thinking I can get a summer fellowship to do it— it's all about cloning and the idea of the irreplaceable. I think I might want to be a movie director. You have to commodify and commercialize yourself. That's what life's about. But then I also have this other project I'd love to get funding for—I want to rewrite *Candide*, but set it in a modern university."

"Wow." What else was there to say?

While we ate, I endured a juggernaut of opinion. *Everything's so plastic, plastic, plastic. Decadence*, he was saying. *Decadence was the only valid response to our plastic existence.* I didn't know how to step in.

"For God's sake, say something!" he was saying. "I need input!"

"Well, I do have a question. I don't mean to pry, but why did you have to leave—"

"That's a story for another time," he said, taking a fry from the pile next to my grilled cheese and tomato sandwich. "That paper— the one that got you the award. How did you write it? It was technically brilliant."

"I don't know if it was brilliant. I guess I just—"

"Oh, come on, that's completely disingenuous. My papers are always a mess. I mean, there's a surfeit of brilliant ideas—I'm never worried about that—but I don't know how to arrange them. I want perfection—I want both the ideas and the writing to be brilliant. I want you to help me. Will you help me?"

"Sure," I said. But I wasn't sure that I should see him again.

Soon after that lunch Joshua called me up and asked me to come over. I said yes. He lived off campus in the attic of one of the sagging houses on Cold Spring Lane, an old house, which explained the gas-leaky smell, owned by a little old Polish lady. I climbed the narrow sagging stairs and stood in the low-ceilinged attic, the Saturday morning light coming in through the gable window, he and I facing each other, smiling, taking off my coat, feeling that here I was on the doorstep of something. The only people I talked to about books and music were my freshman composition teacher and two other adjuncts in the writing department, all poets in their mid-to-late twenties whose offices I'd hang out in to talk about bands and writers and the poems I brought to them—things I'd thought I'd be discussing with my fellow students, had they not been too busy contracting alcohol poisoning. It made me think that I'd been a fool for falling for this place because it offered a writing major and green quiet grounds—in the middle of a city—on which to write. Our school regularly sent poets to Iowa, yes, but it was also a four-year holding pen for the well-fed Irish Catholic youth of the Northeast. I had been thinking of transferring, but maybe I wouldn't have to.

He gave me the tour. His walls were bare, but there were plants, a synthesizer, a sizable television and stereo system, and shelves full of books and videotapes. There was a mattress on the floor. He was finishing something up, he said. "Have a seat," he told me, gesturing toward the mattress. I sat down. I looked around at the place. There was a picture of a smiling redhead on his desk. Jane had mentioned a girlfriend.

"Stimulus, stimulus," he said. His right hand extended in my direction, palm up, fingers wiggling, beckoning me to chatter about my day, my life. That's how it began.

He plied me with questions whenever we met. *What kind of guys make you horny? Okay, since you object to the word horny, what sort of guys do you like? Do you secretly find those florid-faced Irish Catholic logs of manhood flooding the business school attractive? No? Really? I see you have a crush on our mutual friend Michael, the junior class poet— don't deny it, I'm right, aren't I? What is your excuse for never having gotten drunk or high? Can't you see that debauchery might actually be a tool of enlightenment? Who do you think Jesus is? What does he mean? Do you ever think you could be a lesbian or bisexual? If so, would you experiment with Genevieve, your friend and housemate? What professors do you think are absolute shit? What parts of Freud do you think are absolute shit? What do you think is more important in fiction? Character or plot? Who is your favorite Shakespeare character? Why haven't you ever seen a movie by Luis Buñuel? It's shameful! And what was this about having a quarrel with the surrealists?*

He gave me names—Carlotta, ol' blue eyes. Somehow it had come out that I admired Sylvia Plath, and so he started calling me Sylvia, too. I knew it was a dig, but I loved it. He was trying to tell me to wake up. Someone had demanded to meet me, and now was demanding to know what I thought about every last thing. Someone was looking at me, taking me in, turning me over in his palm, wondering where to put me. In diners, in cafés, in his minivan, in my room, in his room, on streets under heavy clouds.

There were so many questions—so many that I could never pose my own. What sort of crime did you commit that you have come here to finish out your schooling? Why do you talk to me for hours in the dark and never touch me? Except for my elbow. Why do you ask if you can touch my elbow? Why do you call me from the library pay phone, saying things like "I'm thinking of you and your blue, blue eyes," if you have a picture of a beautiful, voluptuous, I have seen her in person, redheaded woman not girl, on your desk?

Over Thanksgiving Joshua called the house. My mother and I had just come in from the grocery store. She pushed the button on the answering machine, starting the flood of mortification and joy. *I'm at the library pay phone*, his message said. *I'm tired of studying. So I'm wondering where you are, and what you're doing. What has Queen Carlotta been up to? And please do send my greetings and salutations to her family.*

"Mmph," my mother said, her back to me, as she unloaded the groceries.

Later that night I rewound it so I could hear it again, leaning into the kitchen wall to listen to his voice coming over me like dusk. I remembered the night he'd fallen asleep next to me while I sat and looked out his window at the cars coming down Cold Spring Lane, imagining his body a sweet load pressing down on mine, wanting his limbs tied up with my limbs, hoping that when he woke up he would speak to me not in aphorisms but whispers. The voice held a promise of a hand on my face, of his lips on my neck.

My father strolled into the kitchen. "That guy's a weasel," he said on his way into the family room.

Actually, I was thinking he might be Satan—some tempter with a sin so dark he couldn't confess it. Even though I thought I didn't believe in Satan. And what really frightened me was the fact that he'd guessed at my worry.

He was leaning back in my roommate's desk chair one night— he draped himself over every chair he found himself in—toying with my Bible. I hoped I hadn't written anything incriminating in it. Anything that showed I believed the Bible could be directly applied to my life.

"Be careful with that chair," I said from my bed. "It's not mine. Additionally, you could split your head open."

He flipped through the Bible, then looked at me. "Don't you hate being watched over by some huge eye?"

"No," I said. "I don't think of it that way. I—" I hesitated, wondering if he deserved the truth. "I think—well, that God knows best for me the way parents, ideally, know best for their children. I don't find it difficult to do what he's asked us to do."

"Pardon my French, but Jesus Christ! That's your answer? You really believe that?"

"Yes." I blushed.

He tipped back on the chair. "Is that what Jane thinks?"

"I can't speak for Jane."

"Well." He set the chair down on the floor. "What sorts of things do you say when you pray?"

"That's none of your business."

"Do you tell Jesus that you're in love with him?"

"I tell Jesus that I hope he can take time out of his busy schedule to send a plague of boils unto those who ask ridiculous questions."

He giggled. I did not think that boys giggled, but he was teaching me that they did. "Okay. Okay." He tipped himself back once more. Part of me wanted to climb in his lap, curl up in his long graceful monkey limbs, and nose his soft black hair and soft white skin—and part of me wanted him to fall over and crack his head open. "Let's play a game. Here's what we'll do. I'll read a verse from the Bible, and then make one up myself, and let's see if you can tell the difference."

"I think that's a terrible game," I said. "Because I've read every book in there more than once. I've got parts of it memorized." The part about having read every book was a lie, as I still could not bring myself to read Revelation. But I played along. And then confused his made-up verse for a passage from Hebrews.

"I think you think I'm Satan," he said. His hands were clasped behind his head, and he was grinning.

A Saturday night, all the others were out, and I was home alone, writing a paper. The phone rang. Could he come over? The doorbell sounded. I opened the door. "Is Miss Bauer in?" he asked me. He had come to call on me in our girls' parlor with the blue couch and blue easy chairs and gray industrial carpet. A few lamps were on; the room was twilit. I put the room between us, sat on the edge of my chair. We spoke superficially about some things.

"So how's the disco king?" he asked. This horrified me. He was referring to a dance I'd attended with a slight and fussy biology major who spent an impressive but inordinate amount of time on the dance floor. Jane thought it was hilarious and must have told Joshua, who now knew the sort of overly sincere knight errant I attracted. This young man had also drawn a rose, a huge red rose, ten times the size of life, in oil pastels for me. When he handed it to me, at my door, I told him he shouldn't have, in a tone that made him blink and take a step back. Thank God Jane hadn't mentioned that.

"Just fine," I said.

Joshua stood up and crossed the floor. He was still wearing his coat. He walked behind me and dropped himself into the space behind my back, curled up, lounging, waiting. I could lean back and his lips would be on my neck. How to lean back, how to let him see that I knew nothing about this, how to stop being my mother's daughter? How to say to him: Hold the lantern while we run into the forest to find a place for you to split me open. I got up and sat in the other chair.

We talked for an hour, and then he had to go. I walked him out to the lobby of my building, where we talked some more. He leaned against the cinder-block wall, hands in his coat pockets. The coat was large and black and I wanted to crawl inside it. There was something about the small space and the hush in our conversation that made me think something could quietly come forth and announce itself, the way the world shed winter for spring.

"What do you think of me?" I asked him.

"What's bringing this on?" He crossed his arms in front of his chest. Something in his voice threatened cruelty. "I think we're very good friends. Don't you?" He was looking straight at me. He was calm. There was no other story troubling his expression. And I saw that we would go by his version, because I still couldn't say what I thought: that he was lying, that he was possibly obsessed with me, that he wanted to seduce me but for some reason could not do it, that I was certainly not in love with him, I seethed at him privately too often, so I was obsessed with him, and I wanted to seduce him but for many, many reasons could not do it. Lying, obsessed, seduce. Who did I think I was, Lady Macbeth? Whatever I might say would sound weak, unimaginative—it would be a sentiment far less intricately composed than his silence.

Spring semester had just begun. Joshua, his friend Michael, and I wanted to go to a poetry reading, and on the way up to the auditorium, I walked in the middle of them, wearing a red corduroy jumper that Joshua had previously referred to, with a note in his voice that I thought I could fairly describe as lascivious, as "that little Quaker girl dress." Joshua was saying that all three of us should apply for the independent study fellowship so we could write and talk all summer long. But then he moved so that he could argue more fervently about a film with Michael. They argued all the way up to the auditorium, still arguing as Michael opened the door for me and I passed under their words. I had been escorted through campus by these boys who were on fire, escorted under a bower made by their quarrel. They were friends in the manner of van Gogh and Gauguin, rising to meet each other above us all because they were the only appropriate foil for each other, and I was thrilled that they counted me as someone with whom they could go hunting for stimulus. This evening I was their peer, though on occasion I felt like their pet. Or Joshua's lab rat. Weeks before, Joshua had asked me over to watch *Return to the Valley of the Dolls* with him and Michael, and I knew he was screening the movie to see how I would react to cartoon orgies—I'd seen him flicking his eyes toward my face, his own gone white in the light of the television.

When the reading ended, we remained in our seats. Michael mentioned a line that he liked, a line that I liked, too: "Every reader is a dying man looking for distraction." Joshua turned quickly in his seat to face Michael. "But these poems are nothing but images, it's no better than MTV!" he said. Such public force of feeling about a piece of art shocked me. Nobody at school talked this way—this was the sort of thing I wouldn't be given to saying myself until four years later. I was too reverent; when I went at a text, it was only because I approved of it in the first place. I did not really want to argue with anyone. I was more interested in tracking down patterns and telling a story to my professors about the patterns. And I could not yet explain to other people why poems worked—I knew why they worked for me, and when they resonated, and when I had written a good one, but I could not explain to Joshua why I felt he was partly wrong. Because I saw instantly why he was right. Sometimes while reading newer poets, I had a thought: Why write poems, if the poem, like so many of them did, caught on the quotidian and stumbled and fell flat into a piece of autobiographical prose? Write fiction or essays! A poem should not mean but be a taut surface you skate on, the real world black below you. But wait: What exactly was wrong with a poem being nothing but images? What about Ezra Pound? What about H. D.? But I couldn't speak, because I was sure I knew nothing and they knew everything.

Joshua loved Dr. L, and said I would love him too, so I signed up for his philosophy course, in which we would meet Nietzsche and then

Marx. I was wary, however, because I had heard that Dr. L liked, during exams, to play a tape of ocean sounds to calm the students while they took the test, and no amount of white nature noise was ever going to calm me down about tests. Or anything else. Ever.

*N. came from family of ministers*, Dr. L told us that first week, and I told my notebook. *Father and grandfather. Lived with women primarily. Misogynist.*

"This the church understood: it *corrupted* the human being, it weakened him—but it claimed to have 'improved him,' " said Nietzsche. And: "He who knows how to breathe the air of my writings knows that it is an air of the heights, a *robust* air. One has to be made for it, otherwise there is no small danger one will catch cold. The ice is near, the solitude is terrible—but how peacefully all things lie in the light! how freely one breathes! how much one feels *beneath* one!"

This was the sound of someone raised with religion and still enraged because of it. His grievance was personal. This was thunderous opinion; every line of it sounded like music, not argument. These were ravings, and tinged with so much disdain, all I heard was the disdain, and so I did not take his charges against Christianity seriously. Though I agreed with him about the herd. But Nietzsche's herd also seemed to include those who were perhaps too oppressed to have his powers of vision and reason. Those poor suckers would have to wait for Marx. So I wrote a paper refuting him.

Joshua drove us off campus to study one night. To Fells Point, in his minivan, to a coffeehouse. He wanted to read my paper, and I gave it to him. I pretended to leaf through some notes while he read.

"I wish you'd given me this before you turned it in," he said, and handed it back to me.

He was saying that I had embarrassed myself. I didn't want to know why. He must have heard me talking to myself as I talked to

Nietzsche. *I am writing this,* he must have heard as he read the paper, *as if I have no doubts, but I do. If you think long enough about Christ dying on the cross for the sins of the world, the whole thing can come to seem ridiculous the way that saying a familiar, necessary word like* pencil *over and over again turns the word into nonsense. Crosses, palms, sponges soaked in vinegar, tombs, a god sending a son to the very specific town of Bethlehem, to two very specific people, living in a very specific Roman province, a young man working with wood, with fish and fishers of men. It seems ludicrously specific and earthbound compared to Greek mythology, with its rivers and trees and pools and flowers. That is poetry, and Christianity is prose, and while it may seem that a religion articulated through prose should make faith easier, because it brings the whole proposition, literally, down to earth, I will grant you that it doesn't. So you may think I am weak. But I'm not. I am fighting temptation as we speak, and his name is Joshua. Here is a young man who is a manifestation of everything I have been warned against: one's own omnivorous mind as a god. I am not sure, but I think that his heart is not a heart but a blue-black pulsing furnace that he feeds with hallucinatory drugs and sex and industrial music and science, okay yes, sex I have no real idea about but I imagine when he has it it involves biting and grunting, which to me seems dehumanizing and evil. And I have not yet succumbed.*

Then I imagined what Joshua was thinking: *Carlene, you know nothing of the centuries of philosophy that exist supporting your belief in God, some of which you learned just last semester, and since I am friends with your previous philosophy professor, she let me look through your papers and reading quizzes, so I know how in your intro to phil class last semester you so completely and hilariously and touchingly broke down when it came to Kant, leaving whole questions blank and unanswered on your quiz, and so I know your mind is second-rate, as I have suspected, and you can't even tell me what Aquinas said about it, resorting only to personal certainty. Also, you know, really and truly, if not for the fact that you're a virgin, because I know you absolutely are, otherwise you'd be sleeping with me and none of this would be happening, I'd be sleeping with you. But you pray and go to church and read the Bible, thinking someone is actually going to tell you something, and I find that a little disconcerting. Actually, somewhat repulsive.*

"He gave me an A," I said. "He wants to submit it for a philosophy prize."

Joshua, relaxed, as always, in his chair, smiled at me. The café clattered and steamed around us. "You're such a little socialized child," he said. I said nothing. He had showed me what I knew myself to be. I was the herd, and Joshua was peering down at me as he breathed the robust air of the heights.

It was hard for me not to consider Joshua a test. But I didn't really think he was Satan. What would Joshua do to me if he were in fact Satan? Did I think he was going to date-rape me, and set me running around the grassy slope by the chapel in a nightgown, singing Joni Mitchell songs, crying at the feet of the statue of Mary, mopping her marble toes with my hair?

Joshua had come out of nowhere, strolled to his mark, and began the way he knew I would want him to begin: *So you beat me.* For the last few years I had been writing a story in my head that had a character like him in it: someone who would think I was the only thing worth trying to catch because of my mind. This character would notice me because he saw me doing something he wanted to do, and thought we should get together and write a story side by side. Joshua had been writing a story, too, he was fashioning a persona and projects, and maybe I resembled someone he'd been thinking up. *Are you for real?* I often wanted to ask him. *When does the performance end?* But I was not smart or brave enough to figure out how to make the story end with us together. If I acted, I would wreck it.

He would push me away, or do something more hurtful than just stand there forbiddingly with his arms crossed. In that way, or some way, God would punish me for refusing to deny myself something so obviously sinful.

What Joshua wanted, I was convinced, was a girl who did not consider herself beholden to God. Someone like Genevieve, with her mass of curls and huge chest, who could hold her liquor and knew how to flirt. They had a class together. One night after a professor had taken them all out to a play, they ended up in our apartment, in the room next to mine. I lay awake for a little while listening to their voices. Genevieve apologized, of course. "We were so fucking drunk," she said. "Plus, he's a terrible, terrible kisser. Believe me." I did. I had to. Or the girl that I had seen floating about him at some lectures—an aurora borealis of a girl, her white-blond hair streaked with pink and blue, wearing a silver lamé shift and heavy black boots, toting a copy of *Sexual Personae*. I heard her sharp laugh, which sounded like she knew there was nothing in the world that held truth or beauty. Or the girl who had written a play that had been staged at school, another redhead, fond of whiskey, with whom he ran off for a weekend to New Orleans. And then there was the actual girlfriend, whom I kept forgetting about, because he seemed to be forgetting about her when he murmured to me on the phone after midnight.

And when he called me for editorial direction. Joshua was writing an article for a magazine. A magazine! He would tell me what he wanted over the phone, and when I saw what he was getting at, I would interrupt and finish his sentence.

"You know," he said. "Sometimes you're very smart."

"Oh, *some*times," I said.

Now he laughed. "And sometimes you're very shy." Pause. He

continued. "We have a very bizarre relationship. I can't figure you out." He sounded genuinely perplexed. "I mean, some things I have figured out one hundred percent certain, but there are these vast huge wastelands that I can't—I have no idea what's going on."

"Well, what do you have figured out?"

"Well, I don't like to put people in these Cartesian compartmentalized planes. But. Okay. You have no self-confidence. Except for when it comes to blowing me off."

I could only laugh.

He called me up the next day. "I can't quite move from this idea, this section, to the other." He read me the passages. I thought about it for a minute.

"Maybe you could—" And I gave him two sentences that I thought solved the problem.

"That's perfect! I'd wanted to say that, you know, so it sounded more—"

"Humble?" I asked.

"Yes."

"Which is something you know precious little about," I said.

He laughed. We hung up. The phone rang again.

"Hi. Can I ask you a question?"

"Yes." My stomach turned.

"What is the nature of our relationship?"

"We're friends," I said. I couldn't say anything else. I didn't want to be tricked into changing the terms.

"That's it?"

"Well, yes. Is that okay?"

"Yes. Yes."

Soon our phone calls involved references to his friend Mandy. "My friend Mandy," he kept saying.

"Maybe," said Jane, sitting on my bed, eyeing me to make sure I wasn't going to sob uncontrollably if she said it, "God isn't giving you a boyfriend because he knows— "

"I couldn't handle it?" She nodded. I had been thinking this all along, that God was saving me from floating down a river clutching rosemary and rue.

Holly and I got jobs at Denny's for the summer. I was going to waitress. Genevieve waitressed, and it would make me tougher, like Genevieve. I was going to prove to everyone that I was a girl who could hustle and sweat and not drop or forget things. I was also thinking waitressing would be an opportunity to practice Christianity. I was going to pretend, spurred on by Zooey's bathtub sermon to Franny, that cranky old people ordering Grand Slams for dinner and midnight teenagers giving me lip while they ordered root beers and Samplers were Jesus, and so required kindness and patience. Every shift contained an opportunity to subjugate the self to love. And to remember to render decaf unto those who asked for decaf, so as not to accidentally induce a heart attack.

Joshua wanted to come visit me. Though I was terrified at the thought of him sitting at the dinner table with my mother and father, scrutinizing the psyches that gave birth to my own, I gave in to him. He came on a Thursday afternoon in July. He was winter to me, all arch and greatcoat gallantry, and his pale face and faded black clothing looked out of place in the sun, in the green yard. When I saw him coming through the gate, flanked by the clematis and rhododendrons, I think I blacked out, and it would not be clear to me what exactly transpired over the next twenty-four hours. Did I drive us to Philadelphia for something to do, to get him out of my awful ordered suburban house? And did we go to a café on Pine Street? There might have been a notion that in the city, away from my parents, away from school, he might kiss me. But it is possible that he began to hate me then, began to turn peevish because I might have let it slip over tea in the café that I did not want to be any gender other than my own, had no interest in mind control or the judicious use of controlled substances, and enjoyed the work of a poet he could not stand. Or maybe it happened when he found a James Taylor tape in the glove compartment and I lied and said it was Jane's. There might have been a conversation before bed where he pressed something he'd written on me and I was silent, wary, still convinced that he was insincere in his attentions. In the morning I think I heard him say, "Should we play a game?" in a tone that sounded like boredom. "What should we do?" he said. "Should we do something other than sit in the yard?" After that, he might have shouted "Fuck!" in front of my mother—we were on the front steps waiting for the afternoon to end, he was telling a story, playing the role of the friend of his who *had* set fire to a frat house, and she caught it just as she was coming up the walk. But I wasn't sure because I had blacked out, and did not come to until three o' clock Friday afternoon, when I saw that his car was backing out of my driveway.

I couldn't wait to get to work and wait tables that day. To move between the steam of the cook's window and the cold fog of the deep freeze, shouldering loads, then shunting them off, back and forth between heat and cold, all the noise and voices wiping Joshua away. He would have to pay. It took all I had to say what I said that night in December, and I wasn't about to speak up again. I had a sense of being at fault somehow, but I was too proud to see that when he asked me to define the nature of our relationship I should not have refused. I believed I was innocent. Joshua had to have known that he was dealing with a girl who needed to be led—who needed him to stop circling and hinting and come right out and confess what he felt for her. He had to have known he had all the power. If he thought I had any, he had kept that to himself.

Vacuuming the dining room was the last act of the evening. It included getting down on my hands and knees on the worn brown carpet and pulling cold French fries and napkins and straws out from under the tables. In and out from under the tables, mortifying the flesh, making a decision. I would never speak to him again.

# CHAPTER 7

# THE VOYAGE OUT

When I was a junior and my sister was a sophomore, we moved off our campuses and into an apartment on 30th Street, across from Johns Hopkins, two blocks up from 28th Street, which was the lowest numbered street it was said you should go if you were a student living in Charles Village and you wanted to keep a handle on your car, your wallet, or your life. I spent a lot of time the first day there staring out of our windows at the row homes, at the tangle of fire escapes, at the rickety porches and disorderly lawns, weeds high and feathery like carrot greens. In our living room a picture window looked out on a big yellow sorority house, and through this window we would watch the sun set in a sky needled by television antennae. We put our desk, with our word processor on top, in front of it. I knew that for many nights to come the green letters blinking on its black screen would be the only light in the room. My window, a city. A city, my window. I had always wanted a desk with a view, and now I had one. I had always wanted to live in a city, and now I did.

When classes began, I walked to school, and while I walked I wondered if I would see Joshua. He showed up in the course I was most looking forward to.

"I love Dr. O," he told me on the first day of class. He had taken the seat right behind me and was leaning forward. "We're friends."

I continued to face front. My heart quickened. I had never deliberately snubbed anyone. The deliberate snub was a move honed and perpetrated by popular girls, suitable only for slumber party intrigue. I didn't think I had the stomach to spend a whole semester ignoring him. But this was more like Jane Eyre running away from Rochester, leaving him to think about what he'd done—or, rather, hadn't. That didn't sound so bad. That could be construed as noble.

"You're not going to talk to me, are you?" he said.

"No," I said. "I'm not."

I was trying out composure. I was trying out a cool dispassionate form. Virginia Woolf, who I read for the first time that year, seconded my resolve. She ushered time and feeling into incantations. She counseled wit, not anger. Had it not been for Woolf, I might have minored that semester in Late Twentieth-Century Reenactments of Nineteenth-Century Narratives of the Jilted, Wounded Heart.

"It is one of the great advantages of being a woman that one can pass even a very fine negress without wishing to make an Englishwoman of her," she wrote in *A Room of One's Own*. And in that one sentence she skewered imperialism. This was how you wrote and argued, I thought. Like Hamlet thrusting the rapier through the arras, slaying Polonius, slaying bloated old convention and cant, who didn't even see it coming. Crafting attacks that would prompt onlookers to decide unequivocally in your favor and say, with detached approval, "A hit, a very palpable hit." Woolf's essays decreed that personal grievances had no place in art. In *A Room of One's Own*, there was this on Jane Austen: "Never, even at the emotional age of fifteen, did she round upon herself in shame, obliterate a sarcasm in a spasm of compassion, or blur an outline in a mist of rhapsody. Spasms and rhapsodies, she seems to have said, pointing with her stick, end *there*. . . . With these words her passion is neatly circumscribed, and rounded with a laugh."

Woolf took Charlotte Brontë to task for not being able to keep her injured feelings out of *Jane Eyre*. Brontë, she wrote, "had more genius in her than Jane Austen; but if one reads them over and marks that jerk in them, that indignation, one sees that she will never get her genius expressed whole and entire." It was incredible to me that Woolf could find a masterpiece wanting—a masterpiece that I loved, partly because of the indignation. Why shouldn't Charlotte Brontë transform her anger at being forced to spend her life locked up in a parsonage, at being forced into working as a governess while her brother squandered his education on drink, into art? But I saw Woolf's point. I'd heard it before: bitterness was not attractive. Giving in to emotion—betraying your emotion—would get you nowhere. It would get you labeled hysterical and typically female.

No one would ever be tempted to call me Sylvia again. My sister had recently let me use a snippet of Plath reading—"They are the last romantics, these candles"—as the outgoing message on our answering machine. That lasted all of three days, because the professor I was doing research for left a note of alarm and concern on the phone before telling me about some work he needed done. "Goodness!" he said, Mississippi still in his voice. "Is everything all right over there?" Then a Baltimorean with the wrong number, befuddled and cranky. "Who's livin' here?" A TV droned in the background. "Y'all must be a bunch of witches."

I changed the message. It was over. Plath had become the friend who was always overreacting, who all the boys think is needy and psychotic. She was the friend I had to hide because she was the truth about myself.

When it came time to write a paper on Woolf, there were full notebooks and days and nights of scratching out and rearranging, index cards stacking up in my bedroom. Writing of Lily Briscoe feeling paralyzed whenever Mr. Ramsay or his sycophant, Charles Tansley, came sniffing round her easel, bringing storm clouds of disparagement with them. Lily standing still at her easel, trying to capture the scenes before her, steeling herself to paint by repeating, "This is what I see, this is what I see." Up until four the night before, typing and proofing and smoothing out sentences, feeling weightless and elect, nothing but fingers and head.

The paper came back with news that Dr. O loved Joshua, but he also loved me. There was a long encouraging note from him on the back. *This is what I see*, I'd told him, and he liked it. "What will you do with this talent?" he wrote in conclusion. If I had talent, it meant that I didn't need Joshua to exorcise the trepidation church had instilled in me. I just had to keep studying and writing, and what I found in books, and in the encouragement of the professors who assigned them, would lead me toward becoming a formidable, free-thinking person who Joshua—and the girl who felt it was easier to pull the covers to her chin than fend off distress with an excoriating line or two—would not recognize.

I also hoped, though I would not ever say this aloud to anyone but Jane, that I would somehow serve God with that talent. But not the God I had been given. He, too, was someone I no longer wanted anything to do with.

One weekend home my sister and I went to church with my mother. It was the first time we'd been since the congregation had moved into a sprawling building that, with its vast parking lots and boxy architecture, could, if glimpsed from the air, pass for a shopping mall, or the Pentagon. The sanctuary, as usual, resembled a funeral parlor outfitted by IKEA—white walls, beige industrial carpeting, metal chairs with tweed-upholstered seats—but was about the size of a large movie theater. It put me in mind of the term used for the auditorium in junior high: the all-purpose room, otherwise known as the APR. My sister raised her eyebrows as we walked in.

We filed in to a row. "Where are the hymnals?" I asked my mother. "We don't use them anymore," she said, with disappointment in her voice, because my mother, like myself, loved a good seven-versed Fanny Crosby epic. The hymnbooks, filled with doilies crocheted out of nineteenth-century syntax by blind women and missionaries who'd lost spouses to malaria, had been replaced by "praise songs," which were beamed onto a screen behind the pulpit by an overhead projector. They were played and sung by a worship team—electric piano, drums, guitar, and bass that competently chugged and thumped like my high school's rock and jazz ensemble. The songs swooped down and then swelled; they let you talk to Jesus directly, using terms of endearment and abject gratitude.

I stood with everyone else but didn't sing, and got light-headed from all the sincerity. There was nothing solid here. The songs did not catch your tongue in a thicket like those old hymns, they did not march you along toward fortitude and contemplation. Now there was no antidote to the stock phrases I had been hearing over the years that had begun to pain me whenever they were uttered. *The Lord has really laid a burden on my heart for you. How's your walk with the Lord? She has a heart for single mothers. She has a heart for children's ministry. Let's just lift these things up to Jesus. We just pray, Lord, for your wisdom and guidance.* It all sounded like effeminate earnestness, even when men spoke. It was lingo. People picked up the phrases and passed them around like a contagion, which meant that they were perfectly happy to use what was lying about and say what everyone else was saying. There was no reflection on this habit, no idea that God deserved better than clichés. There was no art anywhere, just the utilitarian and relevant and transparent. Could everyone who came understand the songs? Could you quickly stack the chairs in the back if the sanctuary needed to be used in an hour for the junior high all-nighter? If someone dropped the tray full of grape juice during communion, would the carpet repel it? Was the sanctuary free of ornament save for some lilies in foiled pots along the front of the stage, so congregants could more quickly penetrate the word of God? The songs ended, and we all sat down. It was as I had read: this was the feminization of American culture; this was the democratization of American Christianity.

Then a man walked to the stage to give his testimony—to tell us how God was at work in his life. He had been a homosexual, he told the congregation, but had been through a rehabilitation program to purge himself of his sickness and now thanked God for the grace given to him daily that allowed him to overcome his sin. I knew that this was what Jerry Falwell, James Dobson, Ralph Reed, and Pat Robertson believed and recommended, but I had lumped them all together and put them on some not-so-closely orbiting planet of the insane and intolerant. It was unbearable to hear these words aloud, to hear a man lying to himself, and to sit in a place where these words would go unchallenged. I would not assume that all the people surrounding me agreed—many of these were people I'd grown up around, who were friends to my mother, and I wanted to give them the benefit of the doubt—but the silence in the seats sounded too much like acceptance.

As children, my sister and I had been told that the churches we attended were nondenominational—which I understood to mean that our faith was not Catholic, Presbyterian, Methodist, Baptist, or Lutheran. We were Protestant, but not mainline Protestant. When people asked, that's what I told them—we were nondenominational. I would have never said we were fundamentalist—fundamentalists went to Bob Jones University and Christian schools whose cheerleaders wore culottes instead of standard-issue pleated skirts. But if someone had been standing on the outside of the sanctuary this Sunday, or any Sunday, listening at the doors, I could not convince them that this wasn't fundamentalism.

I began to search for a pew that I would not fidget in. I lived in a city now. Something broad-minded and welcoming would have to turn up.

First I went to the Presbyterian church Jane had been going to. It was a shabby, cozy church, shaded by leaves on the outside, with wooden pews, worn red carpet, and a hymn board on the inside, and was sparsely but fervently attended by both black and white families. It was old-time religion—no praise songs here. The pastor was thin and blond with a mustache and a Baltimore accent. I went until the Sunday he preached a sermon in which he spoke about the sin of abortion. His voice was too harsh, too certain, and I did not think that we could say we knew what God thought about it. I knew for sure that it needed to be kept legal.

Next I went to the Cathedral of Mary Our Queen with a friend. It was sparsely and listlessly attended, though the congregants were well dressed, and the priest's monotone echoed throughout the vaulted space. My friend and I were just about the only people singing the hymns. This was Catholicism as I had experienced it in childhood and through my classmates: well-heeled and apathetic. Going to Mass on the rare occasion my father asked us to go with him had always unsettled me and my sister. The priests always mumbled, everyone else was mumbling too, and crossing themselves, and it all seemed like a creepy rite. My sister and I never knew when to sit or stand or kneel, the songs were minor-keyed, and we were the only girls in dresses; everyone else came in jeans, and if they weren't in jeans they were wearing soccer shorts. It ended not with a hymn but a mass exodus that occurred right after communion when everyone

fled down the aisles because they had to get out and get their kid
to the game on time, and the mass exodus caused traffic jams that
foiled the Sunday-morning motoring of everyone else. That was
how I learned that to be Catholic was to belong to an ethnic group,
not a religion. You didn't really have to believe it, or act like you
believed it, to be a Catholic. You just had to show up every week for
Mass and go to Catholic school.

While my friend took communion I sat looking up at the stone
carvings placed along the outer aisles. In one, John the Baptist stood
with Jesus in the Sea of Galilee while the Holy Spirit, in the form of
a dove, hovered overhead. Under that, the words that God had said
to John: "This is my beloved son, hear ye him." Where could I get
both stone carvings and committed singing?

What about the Episcopal Church? I had never been to an Episcopal church, though I had a suspicion it would be smugly liberal
and therefore dead. The sort of church Jesus, in Revelation, spit out
of his mouth because it was lukewarm. I had never known an Epis-
copalian, though I knew it was the faith that preppies used to mark
birth, marriage, and death, but could also tend toward the pagan—
services held to bless animals, colorful felt banners declaring that
the earth was the Lord's and the fulness thereof. I went one Sunday
by myself to a church one of my professors attended, sat in the back,
and wondered as the balding priest spoke in measured tones about
Nelson Mandela and e. e. cummings whether I had wandered into a
Unitarian church that just happened to recognize Jesus Christ as the
one true Lord and Savior.

Jane then returned to the Lutheran church she'd belonged to in
high school, and took me with her a few times. The liturgy and the
coffee hour spoke to the Old World German in me, but Immigrant
Irish laziness won out, and nine in the morning on a Sunday was,
finally, too much to tithe. Searching had worn me out. I gave up.

In high school, when I told my French teacher where I was headed for college, she smiled and said, "So, the Jesuits got their hooks into you." At the time I had no idea what she was talking about. I knew nothing about the various orders and their reputations. I knew only that the Catholics who ran the place, because they were Catholics, weren't interested in strong-arming us into pews; the chapel on campus was merely a good portent, nothing more, its spire a radio tower emitting a signal saying that I'd be watched over as I studied. But I was beginning to see what she meant. The Jesuits had created a school that required students to take theology but allowed atheists to teach philosophy, and for that they had my loyalty.

Then they provided me with a theology professor who explained that there was more than one way to read Revelation, and that the book was thought to be a revenge and escape fantasy written to soothe the early embattled Christians, and did not have any bearing on the present. In one afternoon the Jesuits' school freed me from dread. I had been given intellectual permission to finally dismiss what my childhood churches called the truth as merely *a* truth, and a shaky one at that. If that was the only freedom I'd been given by my Jesuit education, I would have been grateful to Catholicism forever. James Joyce was probably shouting at me from his grave— wee-brained girl, learned you nothing from my book?—but he hadn't been schooled by bloody-minded evangelicals entranced by their own game of Risk, feverishly speculating on the fates of the countries on the board with Revelation in one hand and the newspaper in the other.

In another theology course, taught by a convert to Catholicism, we read Flannery O'Connor, her stories as spare as the gospels, her cartoonist's hand drawing grace-starved faces with bold and heavy strokes. Any writer who had a saturnine college student chuck a book at a prattling pious hen, even if we were to understand that it wasn't entirely just, was a friend of mine: O'Connor's stories suggested you could have a little fun at the expense of people who loved God too much in the wrong way. In this class we read *The Long Loneliness*, the autobiography of Dorothy Day, who gave up a life as a socialist sympathizer and journalist, as well as her common-law husband, to convert to Catholicism. Day, I learned, founded the Catholic Worker movement, which preached pacifism and solidarity with the poor in its newspaper and communal houses, where the ministering and ministered to lived together. Her autobiography said to me that only the Catholic Church could lure a Village bohemian away from her riot of a life. Who had the Protestants lured to their side or kept in their pews? John Updike? Who had turned their lives back and toward mainline Protestantism or evangelical Christianity? Only the Catholic Church could match Day's own life for color and poetry—only the Catholic Church could give her a room in which to keep reading Tolstoy and Dostoyevsky as a devotional practice. I saw that Catholicism held open the doors for those who wanted to love God and live on the left. For those who wanted to love both the world and words while loving God.

The Catholics were sly. If a book, or something else, had stirred you, they made it very easy for you to turn vague notions into action. Working for social justice was an intramural sport at our college. An office on campus provided volunteer opportunities, and professors often required classes to do service. Unlike the evangelicals, Catholics weren't going to make you trudge up and down Florida beaches during spring break to serve college students with tracts telling them that Jesus had a plan for their life. They were going to send you into the city and out to soup kitchens, homeless shelters, women's shelters, after-school programs. This was a church, however flawed, however much the pope opposed the liberation theologians, that harbored and fostered revolution on behalf of the poor. It was out of the Catholic Church that Dorothy Day conducted an experiment that was quixotic and yet more fundamental than fundamentalism in that it insisted you do exactly what Jesus commanded: Give up everything and follow me.

Then my friend Helen, who I'd met in an English course, introduced me to Walker Percy. Helen was tall and statuesque the way I'd always imagined Jane Addams or Susan B. Anthony to be, like a suffragette in a wide-brimmed hat who had acquiesced to the hat out of practicality, not out of propriety. She also had a laugh like a maniac hyena. Helen described herself as a feminist and a charismatic Catholic—and that was news to me, that there were Catholics who believed in arm-waving and speaking in tongues, especially when I thought Catholics, at least as I was beginning to understand them at this college, knew better than that. She recommended that I read *The Moviegoer*—Percy's novel about the spiritual crisis of Binx Bolling, a New Orleans stockbroker whose religion was movies and pretty secretaries.

"Christians talk about the horror of sin but they have overlooked something," said Binx. "They keep talking as if everyone were a great sinner, when the truth is that nowadays one is hardly up to it. There is very little sin in the depths of the malaise. The highest moment of a malaisian's life can be that moment when he manages to sin like a proper human. (Look at us . . . we're sinning! We're succeeding! We're human after all!)"

What I heard in his book was that sinning could be a sort of sacrament in which you could truly measure how cold and alone you would be without God. Coining the term malaisian meant that Walker Percy knew that there was malaise, but he didn't wallow in it—he joked about it. He refused to wipe it away with the blinding ammonia of piety.

Soon after I finished reading *The Moviegoer*, a poetry teacher recommended Graham Greene's *The End of the Affair*, in which an unnamed writer has an affair with Sarah, the wife of his friend Henry. Henry never finds out, but after the writer's relationship with Sarah ends, Henry asks him to follow her because he suspects her comings and goings mean she's cheating on him. So the writer agrees, and hires a private eye to do the following, but it turns out that God is the man who has taken her from both her husband and her lover.

Greene had burned everything unnecessary away from the story. It was mean, as in small and cramped, and it smelled like a confession poured out in a dark pub during a winter in burned-out London. Hearts were broken and charred, and hardened against God. "I wrote at the start that this was a record of hate," says the writer, "and walking there besides Henry towards the evening glass of beer, I found the one prayer that seemed to serve the winter mood: O God, You've done enough, You've robbed me of enough, I'm too tired and old to learn to love, leave me alone forever."

Before Sarah fell in love with God she hated him. "I want to do something that I enjoy and that will hurt you," Sarah told her diary. "Otherwise what is it but mortification and that's like an expression of belief. And believe me God, I don't believe in you yet." I had heard many times over the years in church that it was natural to be angry at God, that it was not a sin, but no one had ever described what that anger might look or sound like, which meant that actually, you really shouldn't be.

These two men wrote for God by writing against God. Their stories contained beer, Gary Cooper, the ample laps of secretaries, redemptive sex, awkward sex. Their characters sank down into lying, jealousy, anger, viciousness, dissipation, laziness, New Orleans, London. Loneliness. Cities. They hated the world, hated its trouble, but they were not wishing for the next one to come. You had to love being in the world to write, they knew. You had to want to look long and hard at it, eavesdrop and stop and stare and pick strange things up from anywhere you could and stuff it all into the books. You had to forgive God for putting us all here on earth instead of blowing us into small glass creatures and then setting us immediately on the high-up shelf that was heaven to cool and grow fragile, to become nothing you could handle roughly. The world would not poison you, these books said. The world would not turn you against God. Only we ourselves could do that. We ourselves contained enough sin to get ourselves in trouble. Falling down and getting up, falling down and getting up. This was the Catholic narrative. In the Protestant narrative, you dragged yourself through the sludge, Satan constantly at your heels, and then upright at the altar, where you pledged to stay unwaveringly innocent forevermore. Or else. One wrong move and you'd pay and pay in guilt, you'd be gangrened with guilt. More than we all thought the Catholics were. Perhaps a Catholic God would have much more mercy on our stubborn wanderings than the God I had grown up with.

I started going to Mass. The chapel was right on the way home from the library and the computer lab. There was no excuse not to start going if it was right in front of me. On Sunday nights I began slipping into a pew in the back where I could get the hang of kneeling, standing, and speaking when we needed to speak; Helen came with me and gave me cues. The homilies were brief but pointed, sometimes given by nuns and female faculty, and this I liked, because at home women only stood in front of the church to recruit teachers for Sunday school and leaders for ladies' Bible study. To me there was a connection—tenuous I knew, but a connection— between the presence of women in the pulpit and the statue of Catherine of Alexandria I'd seen in the Met—the saint holding a book in one hand and a sword in another while her foot crushed the head of a pagan emperor, which symbolized her triumph over his court philosophers, who could not refute her arguments for God's existence. The songs were plain but robust, and carried a trace of the medieval. The singing was spirited. The liturgy, with its lines lifted from the Gospels, did not allow the colloquial to creep in. It gave you solitude in which to ponder why you might not have been worthy, why you might give God thanks and praise, and though you would hear the same words every week, that meant that each week you were given a chance to try again. And the sign of peace brought the chance to rustle about in handshakes and warm greetings.

I thought I could hear God more clearly in the cool dark, under the high ceilings. But I could not convert. When everyone filed up to the altar to take communion, I knelt on the prayer bench, one half of me asking for forgiveness for all the things I'd failed to do correctly and asking for strength and wisdom for myself and my friends. The other half reeled off the sins of the Catholic Church. The Spanish Inquisition, the silence of the church during the Holocaust, its refusal to ordain women, its ban on birth control, pedophile priests. And then transubstantiation. I could not believe that at the moment of communion the bread and the wine became Christ's flesh and blood. I kept thinking about what Flannery O'Connor said about the Eucharist—"If it's a symbol, to hell with it!"—and stayed put during communion. What was I doing here? I was a barnacle. A freeloader. A poser.

A line from the liturgy kept me coming: "Let us proclaim the mystery of faith." I took this to mean that Catholicism had room for the depressed, the doubting, the fantastic, and the ridiculous. For what could not be understood immediately. For what we did not know for sure. And if I wanted to speak up and say *This is what I see,* they would let me.

# CHAPTER 8

## IMMANENCE, ARRIVAL

That spring, I walked into my fiction class with a plan. I was going to enter *Seventeen*'s fiction contest, and the deadline would arrive just before junior year was over. I meant business, and so I could not see or hear anyone but the teacher—the teacher, and a girl with long, soft, unruly red hair who wore threadbare flannel shirts, jeans with the knees blown out, and faded purple Converse sneakers with ballpoint pen marks running around the rubber sides. Her name was Caroline.

She did not cut people down in class or carry herself with hauteur. She seemed like a wise bear cub—a slow, sure walk, white hands, white paws. A bear cub, round with joy. She seemed like someone who didn't think about what other people thought. The story she had read aloud in class seemed dreamy, in the best sense—as if she had put herself to sleep to make herself dead to the meaningless details we all yapped about that made our stories sound like tap-dancing. Caroline had submerged herself and her characters into an echoing, sorrowful reality, and her characters would speak only to say the necessary thing.

I wondered if she was the girl Jane had gone on about. Jane had taken a fiction class the year before and talked about someone with long curly red hair who had written a story that involved a girl doing ecstasy at a club and making out with another girl; the story scandalized the class, and there was a lot of astonished whispering outside of it. At the time I was slightly shocked, too—because I couldn't believe there was someone at our college who knew what ecstasy was and went to clubs to take it.

Would we have a silent competition and speak only in passing?

Then weeks into the semester our car got stolen, so I had to take the bus to school. One day we both ended up waiting for the bus together. It began to rain, and I had an umbrella and she didn't. I smiled and lifted it up. "Do you want to share?"

"Thanks," she said, as she ducked under. "You're in my fiction class, aren't you?"

We talked after class that day, standing in a doorway for almost half an hour as she told me where she'd transferred from, where she grew up, about her double English and history major, and that story she did indeed write. We made a plan to meet at a café in our neighborhood and talk some more on Saturday night.

We sat there for a few hours comparing notes on books we'd read and English professors we'd had. Soon we were sitting in her efficiency apartment on school nights, listening to records and talking until morning. And drinking coffee. I had never touched it, but Caroline lived on coffee—coffee, kimchi on ramen, double cheeseburgers from the takeout hole on St. Paul, and Marlboro Lights. The aquamarine thrift-store ashtray near the Mr. Coffee on her desk was always dangerously full of cigarette butts. "Here," she said the first night, handing me a full mug. "You gotta ease into this with a lot of milk and some sugar." It was our ceremony, hovering over dark blue mugs with spoons, sugar, and milk that was always about to go bad, before we plunged down into the sea of papers and books covering the carpet, clearing spaces away with our feet so we could sit cross-legged facing each other with the stories we'd written. We would talk until one or two in the morning, my voice hoarse from talk and need for sleep, and then I would walk down her asylum-gray linoleum hallway, hoping that no one jumped in the elevator and raped me before I got to the lobby. And then I'd run the one block between Caroline's place and mine so I wouldn't get mugged and become the subject of one of those police reports tacked up in the lobby of the bank across Charles Street. And in the morning, if my sister and I saw Caroline waiting at the bus stop on the way to school, we'd pull over and pick her up.

Helen often took me on a whitewater rafting trip down the stream of her consciousness that made me think she might have been lying about never having spoken in tongues in her charismatic Catholic church—but Caroline talked even more. Here was someone who had lived—City Gardens mosh pits, Germany, acid, pot, sex, alcohol, hair dye—and who didn't mind sharing information about the living she had done. Caroline did not judge me for what I had not done and what I would probably not ever do. She had gotten it all out of her system, she said. She had done everything that most people came to college to do and had no interest in wasting time that way again. She wanted to spend time the way I wanted to spend time—reading, writing, and talking—and had read much more than I had, having spent her television-free childhood treating the library like it was a bottomless bag of M&Ms. She could talk like I'd never heard anyone talk—sometimes I grew slack under all the words—but she listened, too. She was like a fifty-year-old woman who, having raised a family and gone through menopause, now had room and time for everyone she met. Time for endless cups of coffee, and all my questions.

"When they stop talking? That means they want to kiss you."

"Acid? Acid is awful. It can make you totally fucking paranoid. I've driven people around while they were coming off bad trips. They were scratching themselves, screaming about seeing rats in the backseat. I've seen people try to throw themselves out windows. You really need to be someone who's secure in yourself if you're going to do it. But don't do it."

"Pot? Eh. It makes me say stupid things and then want to eat a ton of Little Debbie Nutty Bars."

"Dukkha," she would say, whenever trouble had stalked her or found her, or was threatening someone else. "You know, it's the Buddhist idea that all of life involves suffering." I did not know. I did not know much about either Buddhism or suffering, but I thought Caroline might. She had a mistrust of men for reasons she alluded to but would not divulge, and I had a feeling that if or when I learned what had happened, it would make me sad and angry.

One Saturday morning, she called me at home. I was sitting on the couch, not quite awake, reading, looking out on to 30th Street, trying to decide if I should get up from the couch and start the day.

"I had a dream last night," she said. "You're the only person I can tell this to."

She'd dreamed that God was talking to her, which she said happened from time to time, and she wanted to know what I thought this particular communication meant. We had both been reared in evangelical households, which was one of the things that had brought us together, but she had given up on pursuing any formal relationship with God, so it surprised me that she still wanted to take his calls. I was glad to do something for her, even if it was just being a person to whom she could safely reveal a pocket of mysticism. But I still couldn't understand why she wanted to be my friend. She was a pirate madam sacking her way through life, standing on the prow of her ship, pistols at her side, long red hair flying in the ocean wind, and I was a tubercular Victorian housewife watching her exploits from back on the shore, on a sanitarium lawn, so overwhelmed by my own sensitivity that I had to be put in a wheelchair just to give me the illusion of backbone. And in friendships between the spine-less and worldly-wise, it was always clear what the less experienced party got out of it—secondhand smoke, a louder mouth, greater access to men and danger. I thought girls as different as we were had to circle each other with suspicion, but she came on over and pulled me to her. Why had Caroline—who, I'd learned over the course of many nights, had pushed other girls facedown into gravel drive-ways, hacked and dyed her hair to pieces in junior high, and incurred multiple suspensions in high school—done it?

"I see my friends as family," she said to me that morning. I wanted something similar. In Caroline I saw a partner in ambition—we could encourage each other in ways our families might not have been able to. It felt like blasphemy to say this aloud. I'd been raised by women who lived for their husbands, their children, and their faith—my grandmother would add the Eastern Star, the Masonic ladies' auxiliary, to that list. When I read and agreed with sentences from feminist critics like "Having denied their daughters the stabil-ity and security of a confident early symbiosis, they turned around and refused to allow them any leeway for separateness or individu-ation," their love could come find me, and scold me, as if they'd wondered where the heck I'd gotten to in Bamberger's and what did I think I was doing hiding under a dress rack? I had thrown off the God of my childhood, but I couldn't throw off the lives of the women who raised me, who wanted me to know that there was nothing more satisfying than selflessness, and individuation was just a fancy word for wanting things that would never fulfill you the way family could. Feminism was definitely one of those things.

Before school ended I went with Helen and the rest of our school's young feminists, chaperoned by our gender studies professors, in a van to Washington for a NOW rally. It was a bright green-blue day, and there was a lot of standing around on the Mall with hands shading our eyes, squinting to see—was that Patricia Ireland? Hillary Clinton? Me getting sunburned, Helen getting tan. The last time I'd been here was for a pro-life rally—I couldn't remember why I'd done such a thing, other than my mother wanted my sister and me with her on the church bus to D.C., which depressed me, but I tried to tell myself that passive complicity was behind me now.

Or so I thought. Girls from other colleges, famous colleges, were marching along the Mall—girls who, I imagined, had their own zines, who, like Caroline, actually owned Bikini Kill records, and maybe had their own bands. Girls who'd marched in Take Back the Night rallies. Here were the girls I had read about in *Rolling Stone* and *Spin*. Girls who spelled women as womyn. Girls who said things like "Suck my left one." A large group of them, wearing black bras and tank tops over denim shorts, were coming our way with a banner. I stood and watched them while Helen craned her neck to watch Joan Jett take the stage. One girl had SLUT written in marker on a white stomach; another had BITCH snaking down her forearm. And then Helen and myself: wearing striped T-shirts, shorts, and sneakers, looking like we had come to baby-sit or serve you fried clams out on the deck. Though our legs were proudly unshaven.

I tallied my public acts of feminism to date. It seemed that there were only two. There was Dr. A's class last year. I'd asked a question about Chaucer's Alison, and from then on whenever we discussed female characters—Shakespeare's Miranda, Pope's Belinda, the Wife of Bath—Dr. A would turn to me, leaning on her podium. "Miss Bauer, what do you think about the role of woman in this narrative?" There was always a little smile—smirk?—in her query, but I always answered cheerfully. I had to admire Dr. A, who drawled her opinions like she was downing a martini, braced her podium while rolling off lines from *The Canterbury Tales* in booming Old English, and couldn't give a damn about the world that had sprung up after Vatican II. Identity politics had not toppled the convictions of Dr. A, who never hesitated to remind us that she was not just Catholic, but *Roman* Catholic. With her camel coat, sturdy brown pumps, and wash-and-wear cap of faded ginger curls—crisp and dry as an autumn leaf—she was the closest I would ever get to being taught by a nun, though she was married. Inconceivable! Who would Dr. A bow to besides God and Chaucer? I was not Dr. A's favorite—she didn't seem to have any—but I thought she got a kick out of me. And thought enough of me to give me a kick in the pants. She submitted a paper of mine for an award, but the notes on the back made it clear she thought my literary criticism needed some work. *Your head is a little muddled,* I heard. *Discipline your mind! The questions are not ones of gender and history! Those questions are beside the point! The questions are about form only! Remember Cleanth Brooks—indeed, what is it to us what Keats had for breakfast?*

Public Act of Feminism #2: I'd lent a skeptical but curious classmate my heavily annotated copy of *The Beauty Myth*.

The papers I wrote couldn't count. I was angry, and I hated, but I didn't have the sort of anger that made you tear off your clothes and scrawl epithets on your body and scream into microphones and chant and organize. If these girls at the march broke into my apartment and searched it for signs that I was a sympathizer, they'd find some copies of *Chickfactor* and a few issues of *Sassy*. Records by the Spinanes, Juliana Hatfield, the Breeders, Lois, Heavenly, Tsunami, and Liz Phair. There was no Huggy Bear, no Bratmobile, no Heavens to Betsy, no Bikini Kill. Mostly I had been communing with the dead. Virginia Woolf. Mary Wollstonecraft. Simone de Beauvoir.

Because the dead, who could still chastise us, didn't resort to the playground taunt. The dead used upper-case letters. They polished their prose and didn't issue forth agitprop. Maybe if I hadn't been weaned on the Beatles, I wouldn't crave melody so much, and if I'd dated someone in high school who'd turned me on to punk so that I didn't expect everyone to handle their anger like Elvis Costello, who lashed out in tightly wound lyrics, not just firebombed chords, I'd be marching with those girls.

I considered myself, per Liz Phair, one of those girls who were "shyly brave." In my head this meant one thing—I said things in papers that I would never say out loud, said things to Helen and Caroline that I would never say to strangers—but out here on the grass I had to admit "shyly brave" meant "hesitant coward." Here they were again, those girls from high school English class, performing and parading their dissent, reminding me that if my rebellion could not be seen or heard from across the room, or fifty yards away, it was nothing, that if I hadn't renounced obedience and chastity by now, at twenty-one, I was nothing, and that Joshua would always be right about me: I was a terminally socialized child.

Females were immanent, said Simone de Beauvoir—lying there waiting for meaning, rescue, fulfillment, concerned only with themselves and trivialities. While males were transcendent—acting, doing, getting ahead, improving humanity's lot. I was determined not to be found immanent—always just almost arriving. "There is only one way to employ her liberty authentically," she wrote in *The Second Sex*, "and that is to project it through positive action into human society." I had been plugging everything into her equation, and found myself wanting.

I'd just been lying there thinking. And I might have inherited my existential lassitude. There was no transcendence in my mother's family tree. No woman in my mother's family, as far as I could tell, had ever taken up a job because she felt called to it. My grandmother, who didn't graduate from high school, had waitressed for a living; one aunt worked in hospital administration because she had to; the other wanted to stay at home and raise her kids, even though there wasn't much money; my mother was our mother because we could afford it, although when we couldn't afford it, she'd take a book-keeping job to cover some bills. All of them would tell Simone de Beauvoir that their positive action had been loving their children and husbands ferociously, mothering like lionesses, clamping their jaws around the scruffs of our necks to pluck us away from starvation, bad manners, and broken legs. I knew I was lucky—*blessed* was the word, my mother liked to tell me, and corrected me whenever she heard me begin to say *lucky*—for having been given their love, but their love was not enough. These women had given me my laugh, my relish of stories, and my quick tongue, but recognizing that was not enough, either. I longed for proof that they were as responsible as my father for my desire to take those gifts and shape them into something strangers would notice and need. Then what I hoped for would not feel like an offense against my mother, who I wasn't sure I'd ever heard say what she hoped for, whether it was what she'd wanted to be when she grew up or where she wanted to go on vacation. I'd wanted life to be larger than life before I'd heard the phrase, and in the presence of family this hunger could feel like an affliction—something to be suppressed, nothing to cultivate.

When I was seven, I got the idea, probably from *Time*, that the 1960s involved social upheaval and wild music and dress, and I thought that my mother, because she'd graduated from high school in 1965, must have protested the war or marched for civil rights, or loved Jimi Hendrix and Janis Joplin. One day I asked her whether she and my father had been hippies.

"Not everyone who lived through the sixties was a hippie," she said, in a way that made it seem that hippies were silly. I was disappointed: this meant that my mother did not have any crazy or colorful clothes in her closet, and no crazy or colorful stories to tell. Even at that age, I sensed that history had come calling, offering various modes of rebellion, and my mother had flatly turned it down. I had already decided that her wedding dress, which resembled a high-necked, long-sleeved nightgown made out of organza, did not, as I thought wedding dresses should, suggest glass slippers left on palace steps in haste. And it had been almost immediately repurposed—my Aunt Susan wore the dress to her own wedding—which further stripped it of enchantment.

I kept hunting around for my mother's secret heart, hoping that one of my questions might be a knock at the door of a forgotten wish. "Didn't you want to go to college?" I'd asked her in high school when the catalogs began piling up, and the green campuses with their stony halls called out to me like a mother country. When they first started dating, my father told her that more school would further her accounting career, so she started taking some classes at a community college, where she read Fitzgerald for the first time, and learned that she liked his books.

"I stopped taking those courses," she said, shaking her head at her youthful inability to persevere, "when I married your father." She paused. "And not everyone went to college back then like they do now. I just didn't think it was for me."

I wanted to grab my mother's arm and tell her that everything she wrote, sewed, canned, cooked, cleaned, fixed, added up, or typed was excellent and free of error, and college could certainly have been for her. But she would have only smiled absently and shrugged.

Then my sister and I wanted to know why she didn't go see the Beatles when they landed. Sure, they'd be specks on the stage;

sure, I knew all those girls had screamed so loud that John Lennon couldn't hear himself play, but how could she not go? Just to catch one chiming, blazing, radiant chord, just to watch them raising their faces to harmonize.

"New York seemed so far away," she said.

We wished that my mother had been the sort of girl who needed to drive a hundred miles to hear those sounds. It would be something we could tell our friends. She would be our sister then, not just our mother.

I stopped thinking of my mother and turned to Helen, who was standing on her toes and shading her eyes. *Helen,* I wanted to say, *do you ever feel that you're always missing the speeding train packed with believers and adherents?*

Before I opened my mouth, she took my hand. "Oh, let's get closer to the stage," she said. "The Indigo Girls just came on!"

I was not one to throw people together in expectation of a smashing party—but at the end of the year I got my courage up and invited Caroline to come meet Helen and me after six o'clock Mass on Sunday. I hoped they'd hit it off. They both stood in quarrel with the world. They lived with their ears to stereo speakers, and to God; they lived with their ears to the past and what was prophetic there.

Helen and I sat talking in a pew in the empty church, enjoying the breeze from outside, when Caroline crept up to us shyly, because she didn't know Helen and she didn't know Catholicism, and then drove us to the Rendezvous, a one-room art student bar off Howard Street where Caroline had been supervising my beginnings as a drinker.

"This woman I baby-sit for," Helen was saying as I sipped a whiskey sour, "her husband's a doctor, and they're moving, and she's eight months pregnant, and she's organizing the whole move by herself. While pregnant. Pregnant! Not going on, dude, that's what I'd say to her husband if I were her." *Not going on, dude.* Helen, I thought, I love you. You and your principled refusal, which does not unfortunately extend to the Indigo Girls and *The Bridges of Madison County*, but which I nonetheless hope rubs off on me eventually because all I have going for me is principled ambivalence.

And Caroline was laughing. "What an asshole!" she said as she stubbed out her cigarette. I beamed in pride. They'd taken to each other immediately. And one day the three of us would live in a way that would finally, finally, bring men and women around to equality, and everybody could thank us later, when another dispensation of girls found our books and believed they were words to live by, and as a result would never have to shave their legs again.

In our sisterhood, we might have recognized men as the oppressor, and raged against them in the abstract, but we could be charmed by individual cases. There was one I'd seen around campus, and I liked his red hair, his height, his glasses, and his Unrest T-shirt. He looked kind and studious. "You and the concave chests," said Caroline when I pointed him out. Suggesting that one day, I'd see, I'd grow up into a girl whose dreams were filled with rows upon rows of large penises, rows and rows dangling and twirling, the inside of my night mind like an old salumeria in the Bronx.

I mentioned him to someone who just happened to know him from high school, and she gave me his number. His name was Tom. I called him up. There was a movie, there were phone conversations during which I made him laugh. I would put the phone down and stare at it, a little astonished at how easy this all was. He would try to pay for things, but I told him we were both broke and it was ridiculous for him to do so. Since he lived outside Philadelphia, we took our arrangement into the summer.

He met my parents. We stood in the living room, and I introduced him. My father smelled his fear. "Well, sit down!" he told Tom. "You don't have to be afraid of me!" I didn't know how true that was. I hustled us out of the house.

His parents had me over to dinner, and I liked meeting them. I was good with peoples' parents. We climbed up to his room and he played me record after record until it turned dark and my head hurt with all the knowledge and enthusiasm he had unloaded on me. I thought I knew a lot about music, but Tom had me beat if we were talking grade of obsession and funds allocated to that obsession. I could not imagine unloading all I knew about the British and American novel on a person. I wasn't going to unload it all on Tom— what could he do with it? It would be impolite. It would be impolite, also, to ask if his recitation of this epic catalog was shyness, or stalling, or the mind of an electrical engineer major in flight. The stereo needle lifted away from the turntable and a memory came to me: of Joshua, and Michael, and the day they walked through campus arguing, their conversation skidding out of my reach, me trailing behind their esteem for each other in a haze of arousal and envy. A thought then occurred to me: I had unloaded what I knew about the novel on someone. Caroline.

"Do you want to go for a drive?" he said, interrupting the doubt that had started to pool.

We ended up in a spot above the Schuylkill Expressway where you could look down and watch the cars pass by in an oceanic rush. He did not kiss me, but standing next to him in the night was enough. I did not care that he had majored in something as practical as electrical engineering because someone in high school said he was that good at math and physics, and he wished he had majored in English and writing, like me. I suspected I might be the more transcendent one here, but it didn't matter, because he'd made me tapes with intricately crafted covers, annotated in small letters, all caps, with a black felt-tipped pen, as if he were engraving something. I imagined his head bent down, pushing his glasses back up his nose with a knuckle as he wrote. I imagined that if he kissed me, he would take care, and I would pass out from the care he took.

But when he tried to kiss me, I wouldn't let him. He dropped me off at home after a show, his car ticking and sighing in the driveway. We stood by the gate to my backyard. I knew it was coming. I knew I should bend toward him, but I couldn't. He took my hands, and when he leaned in, I backed up. "I can't!" I said. "Oh, I'm sorry, I can't. It's too high school!"

"What?" he said. Instead of telling him that I was worried what he would think because I had never really kissed someone, I pursued some other objections. "It's too perfect! Too suburban! The driveway, the back gate, my house, my parents inside."

He didn't laugh, or try to talk me down, or make a game of it by trying again. He would not try again for the rest of the summer, and I had no idea why.

"Of course he wouldn't try again," said Caroline, who had come for a visit. "You scared the shit out of him." She was living on St. Paul with Mike, who was friends with Tom in Baltimore, and after I lent her one record she went crazy and started soaking up music with the both of them, amassing piles of CDs and surpassing me in knowledge of bands and small labels. I was impressed. She handed me *Live Through This*, which I had been meaning to buy. "You gotta listen to this," she said on a visit. She had been listening to it constantly. She played it for me while we drove to the thrift store out by the airport circle, where we each bought a pile of shirts. I was purging my closet of the flowered.

And I bought steel-toed combat boots from J. Crew, which I knew was a corrupt way to go about trying to look less like a wallflower—ordering your armor from a place that outfitted date rapists. But they were perfectly suited to the jeans with the blown-out knee and 60-cent plaid shirts and T-shirts with band names and cardigans I would wear during senior year to class and to all the shows Caroline and I would go to. My sister and I each picked up a pair of these boots when we went to visit my aunt in Maine. I took them out of the box, put them on, and clomped around the aged New England grass, showing them off. *Go on, take everything, take everything, I dare you to. When I get what I want, I never want it again.* Thinking of that and of Elizabeth Bennet tramping through the mud to visit her sister. We had been sitting in the front yard under a big maple tree in lawn chairs, drinking iced tea. "You look," said my aunt from her lawn chair, "like the lesbians down at the Shop and Save." I took it as a compliment.

Helen and Caroline called up and each got themselves a pair. They made our ankles bleed, but we thought that was fitting. "Steel toes, motherfuckers!" said Helen over the phone. She told me she had also cut her hair short and spiked it while waiting for school to start. "We will be bringing you the pain!"

Steel-toed boots, we found when we returned to school, may have made us look less immanent, but they were no defense against literary theory and its debilitating side effects. Helen was doing an independent study on Derrida. She was going to fight it out with the last best thought anyone had, and it was putting her on edge. "Why do you still believe?" she said to me one afternoon that fall. We were eating fried rice and egg rolls in a food court. She was telling me how she couldn't believe in any of it anymore. She was bristling and worked up. Not even Joshua had been this confrontational. *Are you interrogating me about faith and doubt in a food court?* I wanted to say.

"I know this isn't going to help you," I said, "but when I read the Psalms, I think that God must exist. Those stories in the Old

Testament or the Gospels might not be true. But those songs and prayers, because they're so personal, because they're an individual expression of a relationship between God and the psalmist, seem to me a better piece of evidence for the existence of a God who moves among us and cares for us." I thought a bit more. "And I suppose it's because I haven't—personally—yet—experienced God's absence."

"But the Holocaust."

"I admit that whenever I think of it, it makes me think I can't believe, and that one of these days I probably won't because of it. I'll never be able to reconcile that or any other atrocity with the idea of a merciful omnipotent God. I can't even do that now."

Nothing I said would help her, and when we walked out I could still feel some distance between us. I would rather she'd told me she'd lost her virginity instead of her faith—it would be easier to defend my decision to hold off on sex. "I am so glad I did not have sex when I was in high school, when I think of the spazz I was at sixteen," Helen once told me, and I knew that at twenty-one I was, if not a spazz, someone who definitely did not need to be contaminated by someone else's self-loathing as expressed through physical intimacy. I had enough of my own, and if mixed with someone else's, we would both be asphyxiated by toxic gases not unlike the ones said to emanate from collisions of Lysol and Drano.

Once we got in the car, Helen brightened some. "Okay," she said, staring straight ahead at York Road. "What intellectual figures—dead or alive—would you have sex with?" Before I could answer, she reeled off a list. "I'll go first. Nietzsche, Derrida, and Jesus," she said.

"Helen!" I laughed. "Derrida? He's five times older than we are. He's a leathery gnome!"

"Now you go! Come on, you know you want to have sex with Jesus." Then she laughed her laugh: heeheeheeheeheeheehee.

"I'm assuming we're talking about the Jesus who threw the money-lenders out of the temple and said Martha's name twice because she was a stress case and just needed to come sit and hang out with him for a while," I said.

"We are!" Heeheeheeheeheeheeheehee.

"Then in fact I do," I said. In fact I did. He was Hamlet, only much less conflicted about what his father had asked him to do.

"Anybody who says they don't," Helen said as she tuned the radio, "is lying."

Jane, meanwhile, had been looking into having sex with more than one person. She had returned from a year in France, and was wearing more black. She had also been wearing a fluorescent blue wig to parties. She too had had it with God.

"How can you still believe?" she asked me. This time we were in a more fitting setting: a quad by the humanities center, lounging after class, sitting near some expensive new shrubs. "I gave my whole life to that. How could I have been so stupid? How could you have stood me?"

I would not tell Jane that I could pretty much have told her so when we met sophomore year. I could have told her that she was subscribing to some unreasonable ideology, so unreasonable that she might turn violently against it one day, and she could live the Christian life without the legalism she was tending toward. But I could not feel too superior. I would never be able to persuade others to hang on to a faith that I acknowledged made no sense. I had never bothered with apologetics because I didn't need to be convinced of God's existence, and had never felt that it was my job to convince others. There'd been so much emphasis on witnessing in church that I vowed never to speak to anyone who wasn't a Christian about religion unless asked. At the end of my college career, this now seemed unforgivably lazy.

Helen and Jane pressed on with their search for the selves they had buried under diligence. They both now knew what a hangover felt like. And they both, on separate occasions, asked me to ask Caroline if she would teach them to smoke. What had gotten into these two? And what was wrong with me, for not taking the opportunity to start chipping away at my own intractable diligence when people I had so much affection for, not people I feared, were the ones acting up? Their rebellion didn't seem like the urbane carousal I'd pictured myself being pulled into one day—it seemed like a frantic, prop-filled, dutiful spree, something I'd better stay out of the way of unless I wanted to find myself warily gyrating under a fluorescent green wig at some party they'd begged me to drive them to.

When I brought their request to Caroline one night at the Rendezvous, she blew out a stream and shook her head. I thought I knew what that meant: Did I ask her to introduce me to the Rendezvous so I could order my first drink? No I did not.

"Why do they want me to do this?" she asked. Putting the reason into words—*They look up to you and trust you to lead them into temptation gently and without making them feel ridiculous for just now getting around to rebellion*—might remind Caroline what kind of bush league dugout she'd been sitting in.

"I know," I said. "But I told them I'd ask you."

"I'll do it, but they're crazy."

And then Caroline was the only one of us left who knew what she stood for and why. The spring before we graduated she and I took a course in literary theory. It started off well. We'd discovered we were feminist New Historicists—actually, Dr. A, we did care what Keats had for breakfast, and what news he might have heard from abroad while eating it, and whether it influenced his poetry. I was making check marks in margins at every argument understood, head down, ears open, cracking a code. And our professor made it clear we were his favorites. But then we read Barthes, Foucault, and Derrida. Nietzsche I could deal with. Nietzsche was a grandstanding performance. He thought he knew the truth: that man should himself be a god. But these men spoke in a voice like that of God undoing God to say that there was no author and that there was no truth. Instead of speaking the world into being when it had been without form and void, their words rolled everything back into darkness. *We know everything now*, they murmured. *And what we know is that we can't know anything.* Lily Briscoe's refrain now seemed irredeemably naïve. How naïve to think that art was a product of a genius that transcended time, and was not determined by your sex, race, and class—and that it wouldn't be rewritten by the reader or viewer. I saw that I was only a Christian because of when I was born, where I was born, and to whom I was born. It was an accident, and I accepted this. But it was not enough to make me stop thinking I heard God's voice when I asked for him—it made me question everything I'd been told, or believed, about reading and writing. How childish I had been, to open a book and fall into it headlong.

After class one day I took a walk in the park near campus to shake some of it off. Yellow tulips and floating petals—it didn't work. A glossy Irish setter jogged by with a Frisbee in its mouth. I wished I were that dog. That dog looked happy, and for good reason: dogs didn't know about game theory. Teachers had been lying to us all these years, letting us think that language was a perfectly foolproof way to get our point across. And now they wanted us to know that it would never be pure, illuminating expression, and fiction was too diseased by its authors' prejudices to tell us anything about the human condition. Why were they springing this on us now, when people at Brown had known this from the beginning? I sat down on a bench and cried in the sun. Why write? Why read? Why live? And why was I crying in public, wiping my eyes with the back of my hand, over an English course? My father might want his money back if he knew that four years of college had made it possible for his daughter to make such an extravagant break with reality. Or was that "reality"? I was doomed, and in so very many ways.

My mind was shorting out, but Helen had regained possession of hers. "The void!" she kept saying, whenever we came across something that revealed once again the world's fundamental absurdity. In a way that suggested it was to be feared but also celebrated and leapt into. "The void!"

Through all this Caroline remained our clock. We could still trust her to tell us when we were too good for the room. We went to see a band that the *City Paper* had hyped, wanting to support local heroes, and they were terrible. "Let's get out of here," she said, so we stood up from our table and filed out, and the lead singer, a long-haired ex-hippie in a paisley button-down, heckled us and gave us the finger. We went to a party full of more freshmen than we bargained for, where one of them, dancing drunk, got himself tied up in a lamp cord and then while crashing to the floor almost landed in Helen's lap. "Let's get out of here," Caroline said while he rolled around at our feet, groaning, and we got up from the couch we were sitting on, stepped over him, and left.

Then we would speed around the city in Caroline's custard-colored Toyota Tercel—the go-kart, she called it. Baltimore had not gotten itself together and shaped itself into a college town; each of our pleasures was flung far from the next. We drove around looking for our version of the city, playing the same tape over and over again, which crescendoed in "Fuck and Run," singing along because we didn't know why the hell we were alone, either, and we were exhilarated by our loneliness because it meant we were being tested, or destined, or chosen—anything to muffle the thought that we were alone because we were too much of a not entirely good thing. We hung out on Charles near the Washington Monument, where there were vintage clothing stores and a café that sold books out front. The Rendezvous, where we occasionally spotted John Waters, with colored Christmas lights strung along the mirrors, jars of pickled eggs and onions standing behind the bar, peanut shells covering the floor. At Christmas, 34th Street in Hampden for the outrageous display of decoration on the front porches. Record stores and coffeehouses in Fells Point—most kids went to Fells Point for the bars, but we liked it for the stretches of row homes and warehouses, for the industrial, aluminum-sided anonymity, previously settled by Poles. The 8 x 10 for shows. Diners where we could get burgers late at night. Caroline always grabbed the check while we were all still drinking our last bit of coffee or stealing each other's fries. And then told everyone what they owed, took the cash we handed over, dealing the change back to us within seconds, everyone too stunned to challenge her. She had lived ten lives before we'd all found each other, and we were not about to question her judgment. "Let's get out of here," she would say, and we did.

# CHAPTER 9

# TELEGRAMS AND ANGER

Fall was turning into winter, and I was turning Russian—heavy, surly, fatalistic, staring out at my parents from knowing, narrowed eyes as I ate their food. I had been looking for a job in New York for months but had yet to land one.

"You'd better know who you are before you go up there," said my mother one night at dinner.

That was easy enough: teacher's pet and virgin. But the point of going up there was to forget who I had been. At the age of twenty-three, I had yet to have a boyfriend, drink myself sick, smoke, or take drugs. I believed there might be a God, and that God believed in me. All of which seemed incompatible with being a New Yorker as I understood it: being a New Yorker, I thought, meant that you didn't believe in anyone—landlords, lovers—or anything. I was planning on New York to crush and vanquish the pale, serious girl I had been so far. When I left, if I ever did, I wanted to be crawling out of the Holland Tunnel with my heart in my hands, a heart wrinkled and black like dried seaweed, cured of all improvident hope in humanity.

At night, in the four-poster bed that once supported a canopy— one of those indignities, like stirrup pants, that you could find yourself subjected to because you were a girl, and you had been born in 1973—I read Thomas Merton's *New Seeds of Contemplation*. The book had belonged to my uncle, who had passed away that summer. When we cleaned out his house, I'd taken that and other remnants of his time in the seminary from his shelves.

"Do everything you can to avoid the noise and the business of men," Merton wrote. "Keep as far away as you can from the places where they gather to cheat and insult one another, to exploit one another, to laugh at one another, or to mock one another with their false gestures of friendship. Be glad if you can keep beyond the reach of their radios. Do not bother with their unearthly songs." Too late.

"But if you have to live in a city," he continued, "and work among machines and ride in the subways and eat in a place where the radio makes you deaf with spurious news and where the food destroys your life and the sentiments of those around you poison your heart with boredom, do not be impatient, but accept it as the love of God and as a seed of solitude planted in your soul." I turned the pages, looking for something more reasonable. "For unless it is clear that we mean seriously to undertake a *total renunciation of all attachments*, the Holy Spirit will not lead us into the true darkness, the heart of mystical desolation, in which God Himself mysteriously liberates us from confusion, from the multiplicity of needs and desires, in order to give us unity in and with Himself."

But all I had at the moment were my desires. I did not want to be liberated from them.

I didn't want to be exploited or insulted, however. Could I fulfill my desires without being cheated and exploited? I was ready to prostrate myself before a Xerox machine, but you had to ask me nicely, or be parentally short about it.

"What would you do if you were yelled at?" a human resources woman asked me during an interview at a famous publishing concern.

"Well, I've never given an authority figure any reason to yell at me," I said.

"What if it was your *boss*?" she asked.

"I suppose I'd apologize and put my head down and keep working."

"What if they wouldn't *stop* yelling?"

Then I'd quit, lady, I thought. I realized that girls who had graduated from small Catholic colleges had no right looking down their noses at outfits like theirs, but the Catholic college taught us perhaps too well what we should be willing to use our humility for. I fussed around with some empty amplifications and then she thanked me for coming in.

On my way out to the lobby I saw a girl my age with a blond ponytail and princess carriage wheeling a cart full of bags from Dior through a doorway. Then a woman scurried and clacked out from that doorway toward the elevator bank, her bug eyes evincing impending hysteria while an assistant scurried and clacked behind her, assuring her that the car service guy would definitely, definitely be there and if he wasn't, just call her. *Call* her. The bug-eyed editor started to huff, but the assistant, whose shirtwaist and high heels were as nipped in and sharp as her voice, shoved her into the elevator and clacked back to where she'd come from. There seemed to be nothing of value—well, nothing I valued—happening in this office. It was a hive running on imperious whim. I didn't want to wear high heels and run around lording my competence over people. I didn't want to work with the snobbishly pert. I didn't want presents from Dior, and I didn't want to spend my time soothing adults who would really only appreciate me as a thing to shout at when they couldn't shout at the people who were really making their lives miserable—bosses, spouses, parents, children. I wanted to find an office that would resemble the newsroom of filmed fiction: one filled with the cast of demanding but inspiring oddballs and the orgy of coffee-fueled, camaraderie-buoyed brainstorming that had never materialized at the school papers I'd written for.

Caroline got a job first—as the assistant to an executive who oversaw medical journals at a trade publisher—so she'd laid up a working girl's trousseau of rayon and silk and knew what passed for professional. I'd thought my desperate aim to please, wrapped up in a long black dress from Contempo Casuals with a pair of Mary Janes from Macy's, would suffice. When I mentioned that during an interview someone told me, kindly, that I should probably get a suit, Caroline drove down to my house to help me find one. In a carpeted discount department store off the turnpike, she led me away from racks of dresses. She told me we had to grit our teeth and imperson-ate women who believed in capitalism. I didn't know where she'd gotten this idea, but I loved her for taking things out of my hands and putting them back on the rack.

Soon after, I landed a position as an assistant to an editor at a large commercial house in Midtown. "I'm so proud of myself for hiring you!" said my boss, an exuberant feminist in her early thirties, when I showed up that first morning. I smiled wanly, having just gotten off the Greyhound in my bus-rumpled suit. I was grateful that she had hired me, because she didn't seem at all like someone who'd need me to tell her where the town car was waiting. She was calm and straightforward, with a ready laugh. I'd turned down a maga-zine intership to work with her, because during the interview she asked me who I read and told me about her time in graduate school trying to write the last word on Thomas Pynchon, and since the interview had been a conversation, not an interrogation, I thought maybe I'd be working for an older sister who would tell me where to go and who to meet, who might even, I fantasized, have the name or two of a young man I should get to know in her Rolodex. She'd made it clear I was wanted—she had a writer she knew I admired call me at my temp job to assure me I'd done the right thing—which made me nervous. I'd never had an office job before, and I could disappoint her in many ways—all I could think of were the many ways. Lost messages, lost packages, mixed-up reservations, information accidentally leaked. Enthusiasm should be saved for later, when I'd proven to be an asset. And then she gave me a book to edit the first week there, and never disagreed with an editorial mark I made. How reckless of her to be so trusting!

Caroline and I would eventually find an apartment in Brooklyn, but for that first month I lived on the edges of Carroll Gardens, right around the corner from the BQE. A friend of a friend had renovated what used to be a tin-ceilinged butcher shop into a cavernous ground-floor apartment, and offered to let me stay there rent-free with her, her boyfriend, and her big white armful of cat. As well as an albino rabbit—a friend of the neighborhood she sometimes gave asylum to that liked to lurk in doorways, dozing in the sun, or out on the concrete patio that for some reason had cantaloupe growing up and off the laundry lines. I slept in the storefront window, on a platform covered in burlap—*Free girl! Yours for the taking!*—on cushions that I dragged there every night from the couch, and was shielded from onlookers by a pane of frosted glass and an iron gate.

When my parents came to visit, my father grinned hard and wide. "Oh jeez," he said, and chuckled in disbelief at the milk crates filled with galleys from work, the clothes I'd hung on the rod of a screen my roommates used for their work, the rabbit. Before I found the job, my father would see me looking at the classifieds in the *Times* on a Sunday and say, "I didn't see any ads for writers in there." Now I had proved to him that people would pay you for having majored in English.

I looked at my father, hands in his parka pockets, looking up at the tin ceiling, pacing the length of the place, checking it all out while my mother and sister unloaded blocks of frozen soup into the refrigerator. He returned, shaking his head.

"You must really want this," he said.

I laughed. "I do!"

"You know what my favorite story is, right?"

"I think so." I was about to demur—okay, Dad, okay—but I needed to hear it.

"The day we dropped you off at college, after we'd moved all your stuff in," he said, "we were out on the sidewalk about to get back in the car, and you had to go to some orientation thing. You waved good-bye and walked over the bridge to campus and you never looked back. I stood there and watched you go, waiting to see if you might turn around. But you never looked back!" He smiled. I knew that was his favorite part by the way he lingered on it—the part at which I left my family behind without hesitation. In telling this story he gave me permission for flight. I clung to his reassurance that I had it in me to push past whatever I might come to outgrow, to chase and snare what I wanted, because this time I was not walking off into four years at a college in Baltimore.

On the way to the F train those first weeks in January, I passed Christmas trees lying on curbs in the bitterly cold air—they were drunks thrown out of a party, stripped of all their charm and rolling about on the street, propping themselves up against iron gates. I hoped this was not an omen for my future. I too could be tossed out of the city, used up too quickly, all my greenery deemed passé before I could prune any of it off myself. I walked to the subway with a stomach clenched in apprehension of the long, harrowing day, wearing myself out from worry before I even reached my desk. I thought I was going to drown in the ceaseless torrent of details flooding in over phone, fax, and e-mail, that I would never be able to stanch the flow. While scrawling down phone messages I realized this was waitressing in marginally nicer outfits, though very often I thought I'd rather be waitressing. That was another job I'd taken because I wanted to prove something, but it hadn't taken me long to see that I was pretty good at it. It rewarded me quickly. This job wanted me to know that it was nice, what I'd done in college, that it was nice, that I was *creative*, but it was a shame that I'd never been the sort of girl who cleared her head by cleaning, and it was too bad that I'd refused typing classes, or any other acquisition of secretarial skills, because I thought it might crush my incipient Amazon spirit.

My desk was near the top of a line of cubicles and offices called editorial row, and I was flanked by two young women whose capability and efficiency cowed me. The assistant behind me, who never seemed cross or ruffled, had a plummy laugh that sounded as if it was 1939 and George Cukor had just said something hilarious to Norma Shearer. She had filled her office with a vase full of tulips, neat stacks of pastel Post-its, and paperweights containing photographs of her parents' dog. I imagined that if she could have, she would have dragged an Oriental rug in there, too. The associate in front of me seemed to revel in being cheerfully, triumphantly stressed. She would often stand facing me in her cubicle with a headset on, taking every call that came in, an air traffic controller bringing the whipping winds of crisis to calm: her mother's irrational demands, an author's financial freak-out, a showdown with the production department.

All the young women I worked with devised color-coded filing systems, arranged their manuscripts alphabetically, worked by softly glowing lamps, maintained spotless desks and empty outboxes. They had a wifeliness about them, even though they were single, and while I did not aspire to wifeliness, I did aspire to be useful, and it seemed that the two were linked. These girls could keep order, and keep their effort to a minimum: they never seemed

to be there when I was there late, or on the weekends, which were
the only times I could write rejection letters or open the mail that
had accumulated in a towering pile. Even Caroline got off on setting
her boss's desk straight—but for her it wasn't wifely, it was more
in the way some people got off on completing crosswords. I hadn't
really known this about her until we moved here, and it made me
jealous. It made me think that I wasn't all that smart. If you were
really smart you could stare at a knot of competing requests and
see instantly where to tug the string to get it unraveled. If you were
really smart you took pleasure in puzzles like that—you knew it was
another way to exercise your mind, like those logic problems on the
GRE involving only so many seats on the bus and five dozen camp-
ers needing a place to sit. But those problems had always made me
want to start gnawing on my pencil eraser, hoping that as I worked
it in frustration I accidentally swallowed it, then choked, and had to
be carried out of the test on a stretcher, causing the ETS to convene
and overhaul their definition of analytical aptitude.

   At the end of editorial row lived two young men, both from Long
Island, both with Italian last names, and when you came upon their
cubicles it was as if you'd come upon a frat house at the end of an
immaculately pruned block of landmarked mansions. It was here
that two myths of book publishing—that it was made up entirely
of women and children of privilege—exploded. Whenever I passed
them I was heartened: I was not the only slob! It was not a mark of
failure! Toys from Happy Meals sat on the ledge that divided their
desks, contents of gym bags crept out from under desks toward the
hallway, pages of manuscripts dripped off the shelves, and because
the two were weekend devotees of Saratoga and Belmont, there were
often racing forms lying about. Boisterously derisive and good-
naturedly profane, they always had time to answer my questions
about where to find certain forms and certain people. Whenever I

appeared, they moved books and sneakers off their one extra chair and told me to sit down.

"How are we?" said Vince.

"Aside from the fundamental dissatisfactions, we're doing well," said Paul. The melancholic wisecrack: it was as if they'd poured me a shot and set the bottle down between us with a sympathetic, hospitable thud.

Then I would go back to my desk and the young editor I'd been hired to replace would come over and find out that something hadn't been done out of general overwhelmedness and say, eyes widening, "Oh, you've gotta do that right now!" And then my heart would start racing again and I would sit there thinking that whenever people walked by my office, past the boxes of books and piles of manuscripts that needed rejecting, they felt sorry for my boss, for choosing so poorly.

But when I made mistakes my boss turned philosophical. "These are the things that happen," she said. She hardly ever asked me to get her coffee, and when she did, she was conspiratorial about it. "Get us some iced confections," she'd say, slipping me some bills and sending me out to Sixth Avenue. She asked to see my writing and returned it with an approving note. We shared a similar fetish for writing implements and *Spin* magazine. She wanted my opinion on eyeglasses, took me with her to meetings and lunches with authors. "Tell them where you lived when you first moved here," she'd say, smiling. "She lived in a *window*!" My boss was telling me that not only was she proud of herself for hiring me, but she was proud of me, for being willing to cram myself into whatever available corner to live here, but I could not hear her.

I remained convinced that she sat in her office thinking she'd made a mistake in passing over girls from Princeton and Cornell, and would not relax into her kindness. If there was work to be done,

I could not stop doing it, even if the work benefited megalomaniacal self-help authors. It could have been worse: I'd turned down a job that would have had me working on books about guardian angels, therefore promoting sham spirituality. I tried to remind myself that the woman I worked for did not believe in lying or manipulation, and rolled her eyes whenever anyone else tried to pull it on her, which meant that she, too, had never wasted time with the girls who practiced those feminine martial arts. She stood her ground honestly. She was not a sham. I considered myself lucky that she was the person I was killing myself to please.

One night, when I was knee-deep in padded envelopes and books that needed to be mailed out, she came over to my cubicle, looking to chat for a few minutes before she went home.

"So I hear the assistants are gathering this evening. Are you going?"

"Oh, no," I said. "I should really take care of this."

"Sometimes it's good not to burrow," she said. *I am the one who needs you to do this*, she was saying, *and I am telling you that you need to arise now, and go to Innisfree, by which I mean wherever it is in the East Village people are drinking now. You should be young*, she was telling me. But I had never known how to be young.

"So what's it like?" a professor friend asked me on a visit to Baltimore, wanting to hear all about the job. I tried to sell it as comedy, so she would see that I was fully aware of the absurdities. Words were cheap, I had learned. They were sluts. They'd go anywhere with anyone for the right price—celebrity blow jobs in glossy magazines, ghostwritten biographies, poorly written novels. Also, books seemed to be largely written by jerks. There was the white-haired pop sociologist who made much of his former career as the lover of a famous old hag of a writer and couldn't tolerate well-meaning hemming and hawing on the phone. "Is there anyone there who *does* know what they're doing?" he grumbled one morning. I left out the part of that story where I made off to the ladies' room to cry in a stall and vowed never to cry at work again. Then the husband-and-wife team of nutritionists from Massapequa, the husband half of which demanding, angrily, to know when the author photos needed to be submitted because he had to make an appointment for hair plugs. The biography of Courtney Love that had us living under constant threat of a phone call from her lawyer and ended in our crabby disillusionment as we realized she was less a Cassandric genius than a weight-obsessed floozy. The false new age prophetess who corralled me into taking her manuscript changes down over the phone from a California poolside—which turned out to be merely switching "an" to "the" and back again for two hundred pages.

"Do you do anything real?" she asked when I finished.

"Well," I said, "I guess not." The proximity to famous people allowed me to better explain to my family what I did up there in New York: if I'd met Katie Couric in a *Today* show greenroom and then purloined some Danish for later, something must be going right. But it didn't convince me of anything, and it wouldn't convince my professor, who raised me to take myself seriously as a writer and thinker. I wasn't writing or thinking much lately. I wasn't even reading. I would not repeat to her the advice the young and accomplished editor gave me to ward off the general overwhelmedness. "I know it sucks," she said, "but do what I did when I was an assistant. Just act like you're too much of an idiot to know what they're talking about or how to get it to them." I nodded, though I was horrified. Playing dumb went against everything I stood for. There would be nothing left of me if you took away my brain. There was no guile or avarice to run on.

To show my professor that I was doing what she had done for me, I could have told her about the two authors, a psychology professor and a rabbi, whose manuscripts I poured nights and weekends into, who were grateful for an editor who cared about their words as much as they did. "You need a nice Jewish boy!" the rabbi exclaimed when she found out that I was single, and even though she knew I was a Christian, told me that if I wanted she could put me in touch with a really great B'nai Brith chapter in New York; the psychologist, who did not have any daughters, liked to have me over for dinner with her obstetrician husband, and told me that I was a real old-time editor, someone who rolled up her sleeves and dug in and made house calls, and she couldn't have finished the book without me. I lapped up their motherly concern. But this didn't seem real to me, quite, either. No one I knew would ever hear of the books, let alone read them.

"It's just like in *Howards End*," I said to Caroline one night. We were having beers at our wood-paneled neighborhood bar. Here was some progress: I had acquired a taste for beer, which had previously put me off with its skunky effervescence. I'd been wondering how people got on with life after school, but it had become clear pretty quickly: they drank and fornicated. Now that I understood why tilling the soil came after the fall, I understood and now enjoyed drinking. But I was the worst sort of lightweight—one and a half bottles would lull me into thinking that my freckles were a sweeter constellation, my tongue a glinting, merciless razor. Three and a whiskey sour the size of a Big Gulp produced a show that only a select few had seen: Sad Drunk, Live from the Vomitorium.

"FedExes and bitchiness are our telegrams and anger," I said. "They're just meaningless tools of the outer life of business and money and stupid details. It's just telegrams and anger." Caroline nodded, kept drinking. She'd read numerous Latin Americans and postcolonials, but not *Howards End*, not of Margaret Schlegel taken aback by the telegrams and anger kicked up by her impetuous, idealistic sister Helen's dalliance with a young man from a money-making, sport-playing family who lived happily at the level of the unreflective, materialistic outer life. Caroline excelled at administrative assisting, and so did not need to ransack literature to work up a theory that placed office jobs in opposition to the life of the mind. Telegrams and anger, telegrams and anger. I whispered it to myself whenever I felt particularly bewildered. The inner life, personal relations—yes, Helen Schlegel was right, they *were* the real thing, for ever and ever. They had to be. I thought work was going to be the real thing—eight to ten hours a day full of events through which I writ my inner life large—but it wasn't.

Even less so after my boss informed me that she was going to start her own business because she did not want to lose her life to the absurdities. She stopped buying books, and while she focused her attention on leaving, the work dried up, the panic lifted, and for several months I took long lunches and left at six every night. I could now think about being young. Personal relations were now the matter at hand.

Joe was the other assistant who wanted to write. He knew more about Thomas Merton than I did. With Joe I talked about everything and nothing, about brothers and sisters and books. Though not about movies. Joe claimed to not like movies, and since he believed that everyone was allowed one cultural blind spot, he did not feel bad about this in the least. "No movie," he said, "could ever save a life the way a book could." Things filled him with a profound sadness. There were such things to him still as lovely evenings. Caroline made fun of me for not being over *Franny and Zooey* yet, and I knew Salinger was something I should see through by now, but he wasn't done with him either.

I was astonished to hear words I'd been keeping to myself, words I'd never shared even with Caroline, come out of another's mouth—

a young man's mouth. A young man with a girlfriend, which made me wonder what sort of spiritual exercise I had been given, because he was tall and sincere, haunted both by God and the writers he'd read. He had no time for the city's climbers and schemers, and while walking the streets with him, thinking of how he liked to take long runs, I thought he might really belong out in a field, herding animals to and fro, contemplating life and books and sheep. He was an intellectual equal and an ally, though I would frequently defer to him because his intelligence had been refined in the Ivy League. And he deferred to me—what bands should he listen to, what women novelists should he read?

Together at lunch we sat on the steps of St. Patrick's eating sandwiches out of paper wrappers, and he bought me chowder at the counter of the Oyster Bar. We slouched over the railing of the rink at Rockefeller Center exchanging barbs and encouragement.

"There seems like there's more troubling you than you're talking about," he would sometimes say. "Truth?" he would add, cocking his head, his question the gentle prodding of doctor's hands, when I told him I was doing fine, just fine. *Do you really want to know?* I wanted to ask him. *And why?*

At Bryant Park once we took a rest on some benches. "Maybe we shouldn't talk about this stuff," he said of our habit of confession. That day he was wearing a hat with a pompom on top and straps on the side—it looked like something he'd picked up outside Madison Square Garden after a Phish concert or picked off the top of one of the Andean flute players near Times Square. It made no sense with his navy pea coat and khakis, and the inexplicable accessory made me like him even more, made me think that perhaps he was capable of one day admitting that he harbored a welter of electric, undeniable fondness for me.

"No," I said, "imagine if we didn't and all of this was just festering."

"You're right," he said. I thought I was good for him. He could be unnecessarily squeamish—he once groaned in disgust when I said I had "diarrhea of the mouth"—but I could make him laugh, hard, a laugh with a geeky, giggly edge on it, as if I'd returned him to the unselfconscious provinces of eleven.

"You know, our conversations are a soothing tonic," he said. He turned to look at me. "You're one of the most alive people I know."

"Thank you," I said. I had to look away. We fell silent, staring out at the lawn, up into the yellow-gray afternoon, at the Empire State Building, the sun coming in and out, and the light seemed to me evocative of him: steady, neither garish nor dull, quietly shifting and deciding where to shine and when. I wanted to bring him out the way he'd brought me out with his questions—I wanted to be the one to get him writing his fiction on a regular basis. He said he'd been going about it in a rather recreational way, sitting down to his computer with a beer on Saturday afternoons.

When we sat together like this, I could ignore his being spoken for. I would not believe he was as attentive to the plight and conjecture of other young women who were not his girlfriend; I would not believe that after such a long time alone God would put someone like him in my way merely to advertise the one to come. *You think this is tall and intellectually scrupulous? Wait until 2015!* Years later, it would make me queasy to remember the blind faith I had in our eventual union—I thought that God's grace and the laws of Shakespeare comedies were working on our behalf, and if I kept sitting next to him in companionable reflection he would see that he needed to escape from his current plot and take a leap into mine. In reality, Caroline was our only champion, and when she wearied of that role—"Have you noticed that he can be a bit of a prick?"—I didn't listen. I was the mentalist and he was the spoon. But he wouldn't bend.

He rang me up on a Saturday night that summer. Did I want to go out? Was Caroline around too? I called into her room, threw the Chinese food I had been eating into the refrigerator, brushed my teeth, and we met him at a neighborhood bar. We made him laugh—on purpose and unintentionally. When we complained that some friends of ours had recently ditched us for boyfriends, he said, "I wish I knew some young women who could take their place, but I don't know any who would be worthy enough." Caroline blew smoke in his face as retort, and he smirked and fanned it away. Drinks and songs and faces rolled about and sparkled like marbles; nothing needed to be in place until late Sunday afternoon. Joe leaned back in his chair and smiled at us, giving us cash for our drinks, waving away our wallets. "Uncle Joe is flush tonight, ladies," he said.

After a while Caroline left us alone, and two hours later, he said we should probably get home. But he did not seem to be in a hurry to leave me. We walked slowly under streetlamps, talking, and from time to time Joe reached into the lit-up trees to pull down a leaf or two. His dawdling was voluptuous. Tall pale boy staying close to the side of short yearning girl, shining trees, a Saturday night: if anyone saw us they would assume we were in love, or on our way there. Wouldn't they?

We came upon St. Augustine's, and Joe stepped onto the wrought-iron fence and stared up at the spire. They'd lit the trumpeting angel from below. I stood looking up next to him, holding on to some spikes.

"Have you ever gone to church here?" he asked.

"No," I said.

"We should go one Sunday," he said, staring into the church-yard. It sounded as if he was saying, *Your secret confusions and desires are my secret confusions and desires*. I stood there, waiting to see if Joe did possess any secret confusions and desires. I wanted to ask him why he was standing with me in front of this church well after midnight with his girlfriend unaccounted for. But only I would construe an invitation to church as flirtation. And if I asked him to kiss me I could see where he might rear back and purse his lips. I knew Joe. He never let anything stray out of place. His desk was neat, his clothes were neat, his handwriting was neat, and he never spoke a sentence that didn't sound like it had been typed up sixty seconds beforehand. What had transpired was nothing more than idle chatter. There would be no revelation on which the rest of my life would turn. He seemed almost jolly as we continued on, while I silently accused him of lacking passion and self-awareness. Spineless! I thought. Or blind! And then took refuge in the compliment he'd paid me: I was alive. If I couldn't have him, I could at least have that compliment, which I could use to remind myself that I was changing, that I was capable of change.

Caroline and I both. We would not say this to each other—who needed to tempt fate and sound like a sap?—but we were—I could see it in her face and she in mine—happy. Unguarded, unfurled. It manifested itself first in a change of clothes. Our apartment, overrun with books, papers, and magazines, was a refutation of the feminine, as traditionally defined, but Caroline had retired her gas-station attendant shirts in favor of tops that showed her cleavage, and I now wore lipstick and painted my nails in strange, sparkling colors. We were no longer philosophically opposed to putting ourselves on display—so much so that we decided that we would throw a party with Paul, who happened to live on our street. We thought we might celebrate having been released from the convent that was Baltimore, from a life that had required nothing more than dusty, faded thrift-store selves.

Our apartment became so crowded that our bedrooms filled up with people I did not recognize, and at one point in the kitchen, Caroline and I were pushed into the pantry by the crush of guests.

We stared at each other in the middle of the crowd we'd amassed. "What the fuck!" Caroline said, laughing. The word *fuck* had never sounded so giddy and sweet, so running over with joyous disbelief. When it seemed safe to emerge from the pantry, we found a college friend in front of us. "You two are rock stars," he said, eyes shaded by a baseball cap, smiling, taking a drink of his beer. Were we? Perhaps we were. Caroline was being fought over by two men a decade older than everyone else here—a slight, plaid work-shirted alcoholic she met in a fiction class at the New School, and his friend, a carpenter shaped like Gérard Depardieu. She dragged me up to the roof with her for safety and then over to meet a young woman in overalls who she thought could replace Helen, who was in divinity school, and had refused to move to New York when she finished because the disparity between the rich and poor was too great. Suddenly Joe and Dave were coming my way. If Paul and Vince were the rat pack of two, Joe and Dave were the Oxford dons. They hovered over me, smiling back, loosened by drink. They were drinking Budweiser, which I had decided was some sort of misguided gesture of solidarity with the people who lived at the ends of subway lines, because it was the beer of my grandfather, which he liked to pour out of the can and into a glass.

"I think you're the most earnest girl I've met in New York!" said Dave, who brought up Aristotle and Wittgenstein over grilled cheese so regularly that it made me sad: it didn't matter that these thinkers had not been my friends, these were friends whose company he desperately missed, and he just had to bring them up to remind himself that they existed and had some place in his life, which had turned into a farce involving forms in triplicate. I wanted to tell him to save himself and just apply to graduate school already. Earlier in the evening he'd come out of my bedroom, gin and tonic in hand, and on the way past me into the kitchen for a refill, said, *"Feeling*

*Good*, eh?" which meant that he had looked at my bookshelf and was telling me he knew that not only was his hostess certifiable, she was also not above a little mass-market cognitive behavioral therapy.

"If you leave, it would be terrible," Dave said. I had been saying I might quit the job. "All the hope would go out of us."

"Yes," said Joe. "You're one of the only people I know who still believes in this city."

"Thank you," I said. "I think."

They lifted their beers to me. Perhaps I should have had made an effort to hide my pleasure at being in New York, and knowing people like them, so they could not see through me so easily, but I was flattered by their teasing, which I thought was really flirting. I looked around. Laughter and shouts were bursting like fireworks over every corner of the roof. "But the critique of the narrative *is* the narrative," I heard someone say. The Williamsburgh Bank clock tower said one thirty. The door to the stairs thumped open and there was Paul, hauling up a second cooler of beer. People cheered. Two hours later, all the beer had run out, and a friend came to tell me that Dave was flat on his back on the hardwood floor of my bedroom with *On Moral Fiction* tented over his face, one arm on his chest, the other flung out to his side, his hand gripping a drink. Caroline and I descended to take inventory. Someone had upended the spinach dip, causing a dish to break. The toilet was clogged. The cops had come and gone. We had arrived. We had convinced people that we were worthy to spend an evening with, and they liked us so much they brought other people, and stayed very late, and broke things. The indie rock had run out, and Paul's sentimental boomer heart felt that it was late enough in the evening to burst from beneath his dress shirt and show itself, and so there was Van Morrison on the stereo. Paul's last name was Italian, but he was drunk, and as such had turned Celtic, pink, sweaty, bearish. His black hair was falling down into his flushed face, his navy blue host's blazer was sagging down toward his knees, and he was swaying toward and away from me at the end of this night, grandly spooling forth his thanks and farewells, and I was trying to decide if I should grab him by the shoulders and kiss him, or wait for him to fall on top of me so we could begin it that way. But no, I couldn't, and he wouldn't. He was instead tripping down the stairway to the street, his slurred words coalescing into a brogue—when sober he liked to quote Beckett and Joyce—and I decided that it was better to cultivate older brothers at work rather than awkward silences.

I might have minded more about the prevalence of older brothers if Caroline and I hadn't paid a visit to Tom in Baltimore, where he lived in a row house with some boys employed by video stores, and some girls attending art school.

"Let's go out!" we said when we arrived, eager to drink in old haunts with clear eyes. But we ended up sunk for most of the weekend on a gold velour couch, watching taped episodes of *Mr. Show* through a curtain of dust motes. Caroline and I looked at each other from across the couch, and I knew that without speaking we had reached the same conclusion: postcollegiate lethargy was a country, like Luxembourg or Estonia, that we would never visit, and never have to regret skipping, because it was inessential to an understanding of the world.

Caroline took my hand and turned to me when Tom and his roommate left to get more beer. "We've got to get out of here!" she whispered. I nodded, head lolling back on the sofa. And felt a little thrill: the allergy to inertia proved that we were truly New Yorkers.

We had one more night, and that night Tom and I sat out on the porch talking, and I looked out at the street, which seemed southern and haunted, with its white-columned porches ghosts in the dusk. Earlier in the day, Caroline had told me that she'd told Tom he should try something. I sat there next to him for two hours as if he was a present on Christmas Eve, and at about midnight I decided to help us out.

"Can I kiss you?" I said. I couldn't let my body speak for me—it wouldn't know where to begin.

"I'm shaking," he said. He'd crouched down, back against the front of the house, to steady himself. "I can't stand this," he said. "I can't stand how nervous I get." I was making him this nervous, he told me, which made no sense, because I had never been able to tell what exactly he thought of me. I stood on the porch looking down at him. His red hair, cropped close and soft. His long freckled hands resting on his knees, trembling. I wanted to put my hand on his head and tell him to get up. I wasn't nervous. I needed to atone for the ridiculous things I'd said in my driveway. And for burying myself alive under Jiffy-Paks and bound manuscripts.

In his basement bedroom, we sat down on the back seat of a van. Car parts out of context—how hilarious. But there was no more time to be precious about backdrops. And then he was not as nervous; then he took control, and we were no longer as shy as we had been in daylight, as we had been that summer.

"Can I give you a tip?" he whispered in my ear. "Try breathing through your nose."

I was something let out of a cage, it was true. "I'm sorry," I said.

"It's okay. I thought—I figured—that I would have to spend some time—teaching—you if this happened."

"I'm sorry." So I had been right, to think I could tell he wanted to. I was not a bungler of signs.

He smiled. "You should stop saying you're sorry. I'm not sorry."

He kept at me, laughing and sighing. Then a thought broke through: Why hadn't someone in New York pounced on me, why had Tom—Tom who still hadn't finished the paper that would allow him to graduate from college, and I didn't think he ever would, which is why I knew that I would lie beside him whenever he let me, but probably not love him, and I didn't like that, it was just that I knew what I wanted, and it was someone who inspired me to do my own hard work, it was someone, I was so sorry to keep saying his name, like Joe—did it mean I was too sweet, did it mean I was too good, did it mean I was too childish, to want to touch him also because he knew the same highways and shore towns and supermarket chains? *Shut up*, I told myself. *Shut* up. *This is practice that you can take back up there so that you will not completely embarrass yourself in front of strangers who will not have Tom's patience and comforting suburban Philadelphia provenance.* And then the worry vanished. We did not sleep. I didn't want to. I could not get enough of his mouth.

"You've changed," he said, in the morning. "You were always running away."

Joe had noticed it, and Tom notarized it: no longer shy, possibly fearless. Possibly. When I thought of myself that summer I spent with him, I saw a girl sitting in his bedroom listening to him talk, blinking at the talk, too polite and too desirous of his affection to say what she thought, or what she knew, unsure even if she knew what she thought she knew, convinced that if she tried to speak of it, the names and dates would jam up inside her like paper in a dyspeptic fax. Now I could make snap decisions. I could not stand in lines without rolling my eyes, and I stole seats out from underneath fellow subway passengers. I no longer liked to wait. I had become selfish and speedy.

It must have been New York, what Tom saw in me. I did believe in this city. It had acted on me the way God acted on repentant sinners—set them on a new course, supplied them the courage to give up their old life. I no longer felt that I was a drag, an oddity, a laggard. No amount of prayer had ever silenced the drone of self-loathing—the sin that had no name until I'd read Kierkegaard, who had called it despair. But the city had.

Church no longer seemed necessary. I'd tried going to one on Fifth Avenue with Nina for a few months when I first moved here. I'd look down from the balcony and sense that there were many members of the financial and legal sectors below me. And, as might be expected from a church on Fifth Avenue, there were many older women with hats, which spoke of a confusion of church with social obligation, as if their souls would have been just as refreshed by attending a garden club tea. Nina and I even went to the singles meetings after services. But just because the chairs arranged in a circle on carpet were chairs on a carpet in New York City did not keep it from being as dull in its well-meaning attempt at inclusion and uplift as all the youth groups I'd ever sat in on. I shouldn't have started uptown by Saks and Rockefeller Center, two other old temples to decorum and money, but I decided it was safe to assume that it would be the same at any church in this city, in any neighborhood, and I wasn't going to look any further. I was too tired of showing up at churches in good faith—it had happened in Baltimore, it had happened in Philadelphia before I moved up here—and feeling incompatible with the people in them to search the Village for a spiritual home. Not even a Catholic one.

There was no way I was going to run into a dark alley, my back against a brick wall, looking to my right and left, clutching my sins—a dirty bundle of the kindnesses I had stolen from the people I loved—to my chest, and slip down into a manhole, creeping on my hands and knees toward a subterranean circus of sex and drugs. The cadences and commands of the Bible sprang to my tongue so often that I thought they would gird my conscience for life. No, I was just taking a walk around the block to get some air. I was still too in love with God to leave him for good, still eager to turn good fortune into a sign that I was a sparrow he had his eye on, that I was still his favorite girl, and he had a surprise for me. I believed he had something to do with the fact that my apartment had yet to excrete vermin the way my boss had yet to explode into cruelty. I would never admit this to anyone but my mother, but I thought he was trying to tell me that I had been right to want to make a life here.

If anyone had asked me what I believed, I would have quoted a line from Frank O'Hara. "I can't even enjoy a blade of grass unless I know there's a subway handy, or a record store or some other sign that people do not totally *regret* life," he wrote. And then a few more from Catherine of Siena. "All I want is love," God told her. "In loving me you will realize love for your neighbors, and if you love your neighbors you have kept the law. If you are bound by this love you will do everything you can to be of service wherever you are." And what did a city have but neighbors? Millions of neighbors. I believed that you didn't have to regret life, didn't have to regret people, and parties, and bars, or the panoramic streams of cabs and pedestrians that turned you heroic when waded in, to love God and your neighbor. But I wasn't going to find a congregation founded on that particular creed, and would have to practice that faith alone and largely in secret. That was fine. I read Catherine of Siena at night so that I wouldn't stray into jealousy, short-temperedness, and despair while I tried to stray into a certain amount of trouble. Men who might be bad for me, maybe, and letting liquor rough me up into someone who would say anything or kiss anyone. This would be my experiment: seeing just how far you could go until freewheeling expansion of mind disintegrated into soul-destroying sin.

Until those opportunities presented themselves, I had Caroline by my side, and sharing an ambition and an apartment with her was adventure enough. Together we fell in love with the city. There were forays into Chinatown for dumplings and cheap haircuts, to Coney Island for the Cyclone and Nathan's. Nights in the East Village listening to music, fried chicken at Junior's, summer Saturdays in Central Park with ice cream for dinner because we were roasting alive in the apartment and could not be bothered to cook. We threw more parties, and, with another young woman, staged readings that filled the back room of a bar around the corner from our apartment. I'd come to Caroline's study after work to talk, leaning in the doorway, the computer whirring, glowing, her aquamarine ashtray full up. From this position she dispensed counsel. *No, you can't tell Joe that you like him. No, I wouldn't date someone with sideburns that look like he has re-created Robert Smithson's spiral jetty on each side of his head, either, and that doesn't make you shallow! No, that's not stalking—and you know I know.* I looked over her shoulder as she wrote. She sat on the edge of my bed, and I gave her advice on the people that she had made up. On the people she wanted to date, who were always disappearing on her. I threw mice we'd trapped in glue out of the kitchen window so she wouldn't have to. We snorted at the things network television, movie studios, publishing houses, and storied general interest periodicals would have us believe. "The melodrama of beset manhood," she'd say to me, referencing an essay by a critic we'd read in college, if some narrative did not feature a sufficiently clever female lead. She would come into my bedroom on weekend mornings trying to cut herself a deal: if I went downstairs and got the ground coffee from the Italian deli up on Flatbush where the cops ate, she'd get the paper. Or if I made us egg and cheese sandwiches, she'd get the paper. And then I'd listen to old soul records on WBGO in the kitchen while I got out the frying pan and she tore through the *Times* on the couch, snorting at what passed for the liberal media.

We didn't care that other girls shared all this with boyfriends. Actually, we pitied those girls. Men would lead you to the stroller-choked Elysian field of adulthood that was Prospect Park. To a descent into rank sensuality, to brunch and dogs and an appalling familiarity with high-end furniture design. To being one half of those couples in baseball caps and sweatpants stuffing restaurants eleven a.m. of a Sunday. The boyfriend: deadweight, hanger-on, cramper of style, distraction at best. If you didn't take our approach, you could end up like Monica Lewinsky, on your knees in your boss's office because you'd forgotten that it was 1998 and feminism had given you other options. Or so we told our friends, who did not have partners either. We could not understand why—they were thoughtful, dry-witted young women who would fall backward into potted palm trees when their excitement in telling a story got the better of them, lest you confuse them for humorless feminists. We were what Henry James knew: our American girl is a thing we can show you. But we were stronger and smarter than Isabel Archer and his other girls—tuberculosis, naïveté, and willingness to be manipulated by rich Europeans having gone out with picture hats.

And just as the Gilded Age had afforded James's untitled young women the ability to run around Europe charming people, so Clinton's economic policies and Giuliani's fascism had afforded us the chance to run around New York perfecting our ideas of freedom without getting mugged. I knew we were cheating, or being cheated, but I reveled in the sun that streamed down Flatbush Avenue into my bedroom windows and over the hardwood floor. I woke up into this light, WNYC coming to me from the top of the World Trade Center, its broadcast as soothing a noise as coffee percolating in the kitchen, thinking: The bomb will never drop. The thought had been creeping up on me for a few years, but now, after years of Clinton and the crippling of Russia after communism, it seemed incontrovertible fact. The Middle East had ceased boiling visibly. The headlines that scrolled around the Fox News building as I entered and exited work caused no palpitations. History—which as a child I'd decided was the progression of the human race toward atomic self-destruction, heaved there by a series of world-shuddering cataclysms in the Middle East—seemed to have stopped.

It seemed safe to come out from fear and worry. A year and a half into my job, I quit. My boss had departed, and I'd been given to the young and accomplished editor to share with another young and accomplished editor. She generated an avalanche of work, and he liked to put his stocking feet up on his desk while talking to me as if he were Howard Hawks trying to get a bang-up scene out of Rosalind Russell. I liked being thought of as an accomplice by a cynical rising star, but the avalanche of work would only lead to more bad books, and while I had a healthy sense of irony, it could only stretch so far. I wanted to find a job that deserved my willingness to work nights and weekends. I walked out into nothing but summer and temp work and interviews, trusting in my diligence.

"You should expect a great deal for yourself," said a magazine editor during a meeting. He had just finished reading my résumé, and looked at me with an open and friendly face. "That's my whole problem," I told him, and he laughed. Isabel Archer could have never made a joke like that.

# CHAPTER 10

## WHAT ARE YOU STUDYING?

In my third year in the city my friend Jordan and I decided to celebrate our departure from the crappy magazine job we shared—and my flight to one I thought would correct my course—by going for a few drinks at the Holiday. At some point I bought a third gin and tonic, and when I began to toss it back, he gave me a warning. "You better slow down there. The bartender's a drunk, and those are eighty percent gin and twenty percent tonic."

"I know, I know," I said. Our hours of badinage had made me feel invincible. But within minutes it was as if I'd been shot from behind, and I dropped my head to the bar. "Oh," I moaned, brow to the wood.

"Oh, Lord." Jordan put his hand on my back. Jordan was a few years younger than me, but had spent his high school years ditching the Philadelphia suburbs for New York City, taking the bus up for weekends so he could hang out in clubs, attending the same parties as members of Sonic Youth, ingratiating himself into a crowd of halfway-to-grizzled punk rockers who were impressed by his pursuit of noise for noise's sake at such a young age. To me, because he had watched New York go from a town scarred by recession and crack to a loading dock for box stores, had seen a whole civilization rise and fall by the time he graduated from NYU, he seemed fifty. Though I could not return his enthusiasm for the music he lived his life by, I let him educate me—let him play me skronk pranks from suburban Maryland in his apartment or go with him to see Japanese psych metal. We were of different faiths, and his refusal to write or play music for any purpose other than his own enjoyment pricked my conscience and made me ashamed of my metaphysical tendencies. Whereas I believed that the Beatles were the holy spirit poured out among teenagers at Shea Stadium that moved them to bring about the sixties, and the Smiths were saints because they continued to give solace to millions of jaundiced young at the time they needed it most, Jordan thought the Beatles were good for nothing, and though he would admit that Johnny Marr was *maybe* responsible for some marginally innovative guitar work, he did not buy into the idea that rock music, or any other artistic endeavor, needed to provide the life-changing charge to the masses found at a tent revival.

But this didn't mean that Jordan felt he could just leave me to die of alcohol poisoning in the East Village and make the front cover of the *Post* the next morning. He set about trying everything. He made me drink water, which I had forgotten to do. Then he put me in my coat, and led me outside for a walk down First Avenue, in the March air, linking his arm in mine. It didn't work.

"I'm so sorry," I said. "I haven't eaten anything all day. I mean— I had a salad." It was two o' clock in the morning.

"Who taught you how to drink?" It was nice of him not to laugh at me. "Let's go to the Kiev and get you some fries to soak this up." I had a feeling that wouldn't work either, but I said nothing, because he was the expert here, and I wanted to believe him. So I ate a few fries. Then I took one last look at the tapeworms on the plate in front of me and announced that I was going to get some more air.

I walked out of the restaurant and straight over to the wire trash can, wondering why the city painted these things a salmon shade of orange, put my hands on either side, leaned over, and evicted it all. When I looked up, there was a short, wiry middle-aged guy walking his bike across the street. "Saying a few novenas, are you?" he said. His joke was accented with Irish. I laughed a weak laugh. "Mmm," I said.

"What are you studying?" he said as he passed. I straightened up and checked the front of my coat and my shoes—how could I have missed everything but the toes of my shoes? Now I was well and alert and fully cognizant of the fact that I had not dreamed I had just vomited on a street corner in Manhattan. "Oh, no," I said. "I'm twenty-six."

It was awful to think that some stranger might mistake me for a sorority girl who hadn't quite figured out that binge drinking was gauche and unnecessary in New York, as there were actually things to do in this town. Just then Jordan came out of the Kiev, in the long gray Swedish army coat, with his hands full of paper towels. With his black fleece hat topping it all off, he looked like a Cossack. "Let's wipe you off," he said. He guided me round a corner and sat me down on a stoop so I could sober up and air out. He toweled off the shoes, and checked me for any other lurking mess.

"Now I have to marry you," I said, and he laughed. He was the only male who had ever seen me in such a foolish and frail position, and, furthermore, had taken it upon himself to get me out of it. This was not out of character. He yelled at me one day when he walked into my cubicle and found me eating Chef Boyardee ravioli, which could fill me up at $1.69 a can, but which he felt was going to rust my entire gastrointestinal tract—for all his punk abstemiousness, he was also a raging gourmand. "Jesus!" he'd said when he saw me lifting a fork full of it to my mouth. "I will buy you some goddamned lunch just so I don't have to see you feeding yourself that shit! You can't be that broke."

"I've been meaning to ask you something," he said, after we had watched a few wasted investment bankers stumble by and had disclosed a few new pieces of our respective romantic histories to each other. This evening I learned that he found pornography occasionally amusing, but not titillating. "A Randolph-Macon Woman's College catalog will do me just fine," he'd said, grinning.

Then the question. "Don't you feel that you would understand more art if you had experienced sex?" he said.

"No," I said. I may have believed most of Freud, I went on, but I couldn't quite believe that sex was the motivating force behind *all* human behavior, and that I was left out of the great cultural conversation because I had not been initiated into the mystery. I did not think, though I could hear Foucault telling me that all my thoughts on the subject were my culture's and not my own, that there was some secret message I wasn't hearing. I was not sure that sex was the only way one could know abandon or connection. I did not think it was the only way to induce the sublime, or understand it. Though I did often wonder, and Jordan was making me wonder it now, I told him, if I was a lesser human being for never having masturbated, or never having had the desire to spank or be spanked. Since the sixties showed us that political action was futile, and it seemed that our mothers had broken through all our glass ceilings for us, the only thing left to do for my generation of feminists was to finish the work of the sexual revolution. So we made it politically correct to achieve self-liberation through self-stimulation, and the movement said that I was not truly liberated because I refused to take up a vibrator in the struggle against the patriarchy. I did not want to be sexually liberated, if sexual liberation consisted of someone stringing pearls through my rear and giving them a golden shower in return, and I did not think porn, having of course never seen any of it, was a delectable hors d'oeuvre to one's own getting it on. Even if you hung it on a narrative and filmed it in the light of rose-colored lightbulbs draped with scarves, you know, for girls.

"So what I mean," I said, "is that I don't think that I need to have whipped a guy in order to understand why *Belle de Jour* is worth seeing, if that's what you're saying."

"That's what I'm saying," he said. He put his hand on my head. "I think you've sobered up."

I had come up with my own version of sexual liberation. It might not have looked very liberated to others, because I did not have sex with the coworkers, bass players, band managers, friends from college, and friends of friends with whom I spent evenings, but I was fairly sure that what I was doing with these young men might dismay and perplex—I wouldn't say shock—the people who I had gone to church with. What I was doing was meaningless, because it would not lead to marriage, and the meaningless, because it could not glorify God, was sinful. The point was to see if I could coax you to sighing—that meant I had natural aptitude. And then to see if I could say good-bye the next morning without guilt or shame impeding my exit—that meant I was Simone de Beauvoir.

My virginity was nightlight and weapon. It put me in the company—well, vicinity—of saints. It was comforting to think of mystics and martyrs, their tears and visions indulged by God and infuriating to those who wrote the rules. I was indeed capable of great feats of perseverance and sacrifice—they just didn't have a byline under them. While riding the subway, I flattered myself in thinking I carried what saints had carried inside them—a quickening ether generated by all they were not living on and swore they did not need—but this notion usually arrived at the end of a day when I'd been too busy at work to eat, and my hunger pangs would evaporate into a headache that not even a burger could cure, while theirs had evaporated into beatitude.

I offered my secret up like an *amuse-bouche* at bars and in bedrooms, and men would tell me that I must be joking. They would be stunned. And I would be, too, when they did not turn repulsed, or overly enthused, and then try to convince me to sleep with them. *I know! Put me in the circus! But before you do that, assure me that you never for a moment would think that I could have ever been anything other than a registered Democrat whose only religion was reading. I'm not saying you can do me a favor, but tell me you can't believe it!* The men didn't mind, because there was never really time for them to mind. I would see them for a few nights or a few weeks, and then they left, or I left, and I didn't care that nothing lasting had come of it, because they had conducted me toward some truths.

I'd been under the impression that men would take and take and then leave you disgruntled, and that the natural state of man in a bedroom was thoughtless cad. I was shocked to discover that they were kind, and anxious too, and figured my sample was skewed—everyone's mother happened to be an English teacher or a librarian. I was also pleasantly surprised to find that strangers could touch you and not leave marks. Used improperly, said church, sex could addle you beyond repair. If someone who didn't love you saw you naked, you would become Natalie Wood in *Splendor in the Grass*, eyes gone wild and trembling, wanting to drown yourself in the bathtub because your awakened appetite could not be satisfied. But the night before slipped from me easily on the subway home, words and gestures still sparking but dimming, and by the time I was home and in the shower I had turned back into myself again: responsible, harried, reluctant to use certain four-letter words. I would land at my desk with a large cup of coffee, ecstatic with secrets—I was desirable, I was amoral.

I was not picky—being picky had cost me experience. Never mind that someone might be ignorant of certain movements in art or play in a derivative band: I was learning a new language, and was eager for practice, no matter how trivial the text—cereal boxes, shampoo bottles, appliance manuals. So I took scraps from Genevieve. Genevieve, of all people, had gone straight, and now that she was practicing monogamy, she wanted me to meet a coworker she had been flirting with but could not touch. Why not? I thought. If only to see what sort of men went to the Citadel and majored in English.

Genevieve's friend was not a misogynist, but he was guilty of a complete lack of interest in literature, and saw nothing wrong with working for a literary agency that only represented celebrities. I didn't like him much, because he seemed too awfully content to make money for a living, but I liked kissing him, and I figured I could endure a couple of dates for that. Another secret revealed: I no longer had pride.

After the date that would be our last, we sat in his living room talking, and his roommate—long straight brown pageboy with bangs, flowered skirt, gold cross, wire-rimmed glasses—came in from her Saturday night and started to chat with us. It turned out that she worked in children's books, and she reminded me of Jane, so we settled into a conversation. I could feel him bristling slightly with boredom, but I kept talking to her, imagining that we'd shut him out with our weakness for Maud Hart Lovelace, until she excused herself and wished us good night.

"She goes to church," he whispered, in a tone that was partly puzzled, partly affectionate, as she closed her door. It made me like him a little more.

"Ah," I said. I wasn't about to put myself in her company, but I wasn't about to mock her, either.

The next morning, on my way out, I passed her at the top of the staircase. I was leaving, having just swabbed my mouth with a fingertip of Colgate, and it seemed that she was returning from church. Overcoat, Bible, knitted hat, purse. And me, standing there on a Sunday morning in fishnets and greasy hair, thinking about how badly I wanted an egg and cheese sandwich and some coffee. Thinking about hot coffee and the burning coals that angels touched to Isaiah's mouth to purify him of his iniquities.

"Hi," I said. Face to face, sensible girl to sensible girl, the party was over. Now she knew I was not as nice as I seemed, because it looked like I had slept with a man who unapologetically declared John Grisham his favorite writer. I knew what I hadn't done, but when standing in front of someone who had spent her morning pre-senting her body a living sacrifice, holy, acceptable unto God, it didn't matter. She must be thinking I was—not a whore, exactly, she seemed too thoughtful for that—someone who was going to find out the hard way that moral dishevelment might look and feel as glamor-ous as a mink stole thrown over a bias-cut satin gown, but over time it would turn into a shabby, impractical costume that would fall to pieces in life's harsher weather. As someone who put herself in a pew on Sunday mornings to put herself out of the reach of all that was lesser, she might feel sorry for me. I did. John Grisham!

"Hi!" his roommate said, smiling. There was no judgment in her eyes. "Have a good day."

"You too," I said, and started down the stairs.

I walked out on to Grand Street, right into the fish market. Jets of water pummeled dead fish in plastic tanks; crates full of Chinese pears covered in red plastic netting sparkled in the sunlight. The day was blinding and freezing cold, morning an irrefutable argument. I started walking to the subway. His roommate and I had ex-changed a sign of peace on the stairs, but the thought of her chased me as I walked. She had seen no reason to exchange her flowered skirts and wire-rimmed glasses for fishnets and heavy tortoiseshell frames. She seemed like someone who knew better than to throw her evenings away to—I didn't like to call people silly, but he had fussily reached for a box of Kleenex at the sight of his own bodily fluids, and that had handed my pride back to me. But I didn't want to know better, either. I could forget what I thought I knew through men. Others took drugs or drank; I preferred the fleeting encoun-ter, Manhattan sprung open like a blue velvet jewelry box, the two of you a small and glittering thing hidden in the middle. I would rather shed an inhibition or two in front of a person and wake up to a bit of news about me, or other people, or the city, and write down what struck me afterward, taking notes, hopefully, for something larger, than dull or heighten the senses in solitude. It might not have mat-tered who I ran around with—only that I was at loose, responsible to no one, not even God, despite my discomfort in the presence of girls who openly carried their Bibles around the city. I liked to think that God viewed what transpired between me and these men as none of his business. "You'll figure it out," my father told me whenever I came to him stuck between decisions, and God would tell me the same if I came to him with any of this. Which I would not.

There was always the possibility that when you pulled out the phrase "God had nothing to do with it," you would sound the self-delusional note of sin: one little white lie won't hurt, the company won't miss this money, I did not have sex with that woman, we'll just be good Germans until the war is over. But I really did not think God minded what I did with men. I was starting to mind. I won-dered at man's infinite capacity to stick his hands in places, as if I was some finger puppet, that I had no business letting him get into, even though he was doing me a favor by telling me things I suspected but could never really confirm, like "You smell really nice," or "You've got the softest skin"—if I planned to hop on a train, limp-haired and rough-lipped, four hours later, with no intention of ever seeing him again. How many apartment buildings would I have to come out of, how many Sunday mornings, until I learned—what? That I did in fact have desire within me and that it could be stirred up for a combination of the merest, stupidest reasons—height, sense of humor, softness of lips, willingness to touch you once the party had cleared out and he remembered you were there?

I thought I had tired of roving about, but if you were a television writer ten years older than me, even if you were a television writer who hated being called a television writer, you might have a hard time convincing me that we could be good for each other. Perhaps I was not sufficiently intimidated by you, because you were light of touch, and lightly colored—you were blond and bearded, which had never figured in my fantasies, bearded and tall like a desert father from Los Angeles who could look down on all my friends from your height of thirty-six years and say, *Suffer the little children to come unto me and I will teach them of the Mekons and of the complete and utter futility of going to graduate school for comparative literature.*

I met him at a party thrown by a writer Caroline knew. By now Caroline and I knew that parties were not always life-affirming triumphs. That could be true if you threw the party yourself. But when you went to other people's parties, your will to live could be crushed—if you weren't bored to death first. It was the risk you took in courting destiny.

"Those glasses are fetching," said a British novelist whose book I had liked, as he passed by me to get a drink. He smiled down at me, and I smiled back. Was he going to stay and talk to me, and find out that my jokes were fetching as well? No, he was just going to pay a compliment and move on. Come back, won't you? Ah. Well then. A pox on you and your long British back and your long British arms, lit by the light of the fridge as you rummage for beer.

Then I got caught in a conversation with an editor who knew Caroline and the hostess, also en route to the fridge but blocked by the crush. *You, please, can certainly pass over me*, I said to him silently. I was afraid of talking to him, because my credentials were meager. So I asked if he'd acquired any books he was excited about. He told me about a young woman whose first novel he was about to publish who had taken up yoga to combat her jitters; if I ever published a book he could highly recommend it. Then the conversation turned to books by young men that his colleagues were editing, and as we talked I felt comfortable enough to hazard a possibly specious, possibly genius generalization.

"I wonder if . . . perhaps women writers tend to . . . lack a certain . . . I feel that they . . . shroud themselves in a high style to defend themselves against accusations of hysteria."

He drew back a little and cocked his head, then said, a bit waspishly, "Where are you getting this from?"

I blushed. I thought we were entering into a spirit of inquiry. Now I felt like he'd caught me trying to fish his wallet out of his pants. I needed to get out more. If I went to more parties—different parties?—I might know how to defend my thoughts against people other than Caroline, who agreed with almost everything I said.

"It's just an impression I have, a highly subjective opinion," I said. "Not worth pursuing."

He asked me what publishing house I'd worked at again, and I told him. I ran it down in a way that made him laugh, to assure him that I knew I was nothing at all, and then I asked him how he got his job.

"I fell into it." I must have looked surprised—which I suppose I was, because to me if you "fell into" a job like his, that intimated incredible amounts of luck and panache, and money, maybe money too?—because then he said, "Well, whoever grows up thinking that editing is something you can do for a living?"

That would be me, I thought. Miraculously, someone clapped the editor on the shoulder in greeting, and he left me alone to recover from his hauteur.

I was no longer shy around men, but I was made shy by the people, like this editor, who could hire me. I could never quite figure out how to befriend people who could help me get where I wanted without looking like a scheming bitch, or how to seize on opportunity, because I was not sure that I could deliver—or if I had any talent to begin with. I knew I should try and try again, that I should wear people out with incessant badgering, but I didn't have it in me. I scurried away at the slightest discouragement, and if I was given a lead, the fear of rejection would keep me from following up on it. Christianity had taught me that reaching out your hand for what you wanted, since it might entail pushing someone else out of the way, was selfish and impolite. When I was younger and wanted to know what to do with my ambition, I went to the Bible. I would page through Psalms and Proverbs and move on to Isaiah, and stop when I heard something so clearly that I thought it might torment me to ignore it. *All men are like grass, and all their glory is like the flowers of the field. The grass withers and the flowers fall, because the breath of the Lord blows on them. Surely the people are grass. The grass withers and the flowers fall, but the word of our God stands forever.* That meant that God did not want me to chase after fleeting fame and honors. That meant that my desire to be very, very good at something and to earn commendation for it had to be watched so that it did not turn into vanity. I still could not reconcile my faith with my ambition—I could not stop thinking that one had to be suppressed for the other—and this left me too muddled to be shrewd. All the jobs I'd taken in New York, I'd taken because they seemed like means to ends, but they were means to ends that I then decided had no value, or ends that never quite materialized. And this was more shameful to me than my virginity—that I had not yet found a job I liked, or written much, and could be easily scared off attempts to do so.

I thought about what my friend Elise said to me at another party. Elise, a painter who wore leopard-print dresses and red suede platforms, was raised in a Detroit suburb, and retained a brusque Midwestern ethos that I found necessary to be around—it was her spiritual gift. Elise had hung a picture of Warner Sallman's luminously severe Jesus, the Wonder Bread Jesus who helped kids build strong bodies twelve ways and helped soldiers beat the crap out of the Germans, over her bed. It was a joke, but then it wasn't—Elise once told me that she believed that Jesus was the risen Lord, and I couldn't even have said that without using qualifiers. "This is what I think," she said. "You have to think, 'I'm gonna take this town!' and believe in it right away and keep living like you believe it. Otherwise you're gonna lose it."

This conversation tonight made me feel that, despite the wisdom of Elise, you could not take this town because the town was run by the suave, mannered, and menacingly self-assured. It was a mistake to think New York City owed me something, and I could wrest whatever it was from its grip—I did not have the skills to execute the wresting smoothly. The editor did. Although I'd bet he never had to wrest anything from anyone, because he'd no doubt come from a long line of academics, psychiatrists, doctors, and lawyers. From the sort of family that assumed you would go to college, and an excellent one at that, so they would not love you just for being a good kid who did not get mixed up in drugs, and they of course would not be as proud as my family, who, while they had on occasion described me as a space cadet who was too smart for her own good, had celebrated my departure for college as if I was setting out for the South Pole. The longer I lived in New York, the more embarrassed I was to be the first person to graduate from college in my family. Where was I getting this from? the editor had wanted to know. Nowhere he'd ever been. Nowhere in particular. My father's father's parents had come out of the Black Forest and over to Philadelphia; they were servants to the family that owned Schmidt's brewery, where my grandfather painted anything that needed it. For the longest time my sister and I told people we were German because our father's father was, and our mother's last name was German, but that wasn't really something you could celebrate, and it wasn't really true. My father's mother, we had been told, was Welsh—but she'd recently informed us she was Irish and English, and my sister and I didn't have the courage to hector our father about that mistake. Our German heritage, in toto: a glazed clay stein with the Löwenbräu lion emblazoned on the front in blue; the copy of *Mein Kampf* my uncle kept shelved under his television set, right next to Churchill's diaries, which always made me wonder if my uncle wasn't secretly sympathetic to the Nazis; a dusty old cuckoo clock hanging in my grandmother's kitchen; my father's love of creamed herring. Hunting around in the burial grounds of my mother's family turned up a few shards of American history: a grandmother four greats behind me was a Lenape Indian, a great-great-grandfather had been patted on the head by Abraham Lincoln as a drummer boy. On my mother's side I was British with a dash of Irish, but how did you express that other than excessive amounts of both drinking and wit, especially when you didn't drink? My grandmother's family had owned a brewery in England, but when her father left for America they told him that by leaving he left behind whatever claim he had on that money, and by the time a food service conglomerate bought it and killed it, it was a purveyor of what someone online had called one of the worst beers in Britain. My mother's father, the son of an Irish cop from Camden who had one kid too many, was adopted by a man who had bastardized his own family name—it was originally Pfeiffer, but when he ran away from home to enlist in the army, he was so nervous that he didn't bother to correct the officer who was writing it down as Phifer. I was a Germanic Anglo-Celt whose family history was full of erasures, silences, misspellings, and illegitimacies. I knew exactly what a car lot in winter sounded like when the wind kicked up and the plastic flags snapped. I knew that hot peppers on cheesesteak hoagies perked up the lettuce and tomato gone soggy in all the grease. That there was nothing more beautiful, sometimes, than to watch cornstalks flicker yellow and green in the sunset as you drove back from a day at the shore.

But all this was useless information in New York. There were no astounding yarns to spin, no charm in these regionalisms, and neither class anxiety nor Christianity were considered real, or fashionable, torments. I had only myself here. And Caroline, and all the other girls we knew who had come to New York without money or connections, and we were no help to each other at all—yet. I worried that we never would be. We had to depend on the kindness of relative strangers phoning other strangers on our behalf. And strangers had been kind. But when they weren't, I had nothing to beat them off with. Caroline might be able to stand up for herself by walking away and saying, to herself and to anyone else who would listen, "That guy's an asshole." But even she had started coming home from work and drinks saying, "You know, it does matter where you went to school," and I was reminded again tonight that she was right.

Then Caroline returned from wherever she had been, grabbing my arm and whispering in my ear.

"I put a huge hole in Fran's window screen," she said.

"What?" I pulled myself away from her to get a look at her face to try to gauge if this was comedy or tragedy. "How'd you do that?"

"I was trying to smoke out the window and I lost my balance when I was trying to settle myself in and my elbow poked through it."

"Oh, man." I shook my head. You couldn't take either of us anywhere. We were chorus girls who'd snuck onto a millionaire's yacht, snapping our gum and screeching while we popped open ancient bottles of champagne. Someone was going to toss us over the side for sure.

"I think Fran's okay. But I'm freaking out! I looked like a total fucking idiot!"

I borrowed a line from my father that hardly ever worked on me: "Ten years from now, who's gonna care?"

She looked at me.

"Yeah, okay, I know. I know!" This party was making me claustrophobic and testy.

"I need a drink," she said. And then we pushed ourselves through to the refrigerator.

That, Roger said later, was when he noticed me. Standing with Caroline and laughing in the light of the fridge while we tried to find beer. We had a few more beers and stayed until the rooms emptied. Just when Caroline and I thought we might really leave, the person who would become Roger took a seat in the folding chair next to mine. Caroline nudged me while she talked with another guest to let me know she knew someone had cast his line in my direction. His manners and curiosity were a relief at the end of this evening. He asked me where I worked, where I was from, what I listened to. He even asked permission to tell me a story.

"May I briefly describe it to you?" he said before he began.

"I think I bored someone earlier," I said to him at one point. He asked me who, and I told him a little of what I had felt.

"Well," he said, "that guy does seem rather patrician." He smiled. "You're not boring me in the least."

I let him take me out, and discovered I liked listening to him. His words were fleet and agile, graceful and attuned, reflecting the flash and ripple of his mind. He sounded like no one else I'd ever met. He sounded like music, and that was hard to come by. That I wanted. And so I dragged him in a doorway under some scaffolding by the West Side Highway one night when we went out walking by the water and commanded him to kiss me because he was taking too long in getting around to it.

And then I shrugged his arm off my shoulders in a movie theater, just to make sure he knew that I could not be had so easily.

"Oh, so aloof. Why so aloof?" he said. But he seemed to take delight in my resistance. He had a smile he would turn on me while I answered his many questions about why I loved God, or who I'd kissed before he met me, or if I wrote a novel what would I write about—a smile that expressed sly anticipation. *Here, let me help you out of that straitjacket,* he said when he smiled, *and together we'll figure out who you might be when you're not wound up so tight. It'll be fun. Yes, fun, a concept that you have no word for in your language.*

I would not tell him that he had revealed all the dark, pale boys slouching in the back of the room at shows and readings to be fronds of wilted lettuce lying underneath hardened cubes of toothpicked Swiss on the buffet table that was romance. I am on to you, and I am *over* you, Messrs. Neurasthenic and Eunuchoid, I thought when I stood browsing next to them in record stores. I have no time for your parsimonious hearts. I hope you find that seven-inch import flexidisc you're looking for. I have a feeling that by the time you do, you'll also have developed a discriminating nose for the underwear of Japanese schoolgirls.

But I was just as cold.

"Oh, you," he said. "Why won't you let me?"

I buried my head in his chest. I wondered that myself, sitting on the subway in the mornings thinking of him and his deft, expert tenderness. I could not come up with ends to the sentences I started when I tried to find the answer to his question. What would happen if I—if we—if I just let him—would he still—could I ever—would I die I mean not die but who would I be if—

It occurred to me, sitting on the subway thinking of his hands and his mouth, that I might not press charges if he ever dropped something in my vodka tonic.

And then, another night: "Pardon my vulgarity, but I wish to fuck the living daylights out of you."

"Oh my God!" I said, and laughed, and then he laughed, and I turned on my side away from him. Speaking his pleasure and frustration aloud satisfied me in a way I understood—in a way that giving him the pleasure he sought might not. He had given me words I could repeat to myself—it was a review of my performance that I could carry around like a press clipping in a wallet—and I could go a good long while on words.

"I will woo you until you marry me," he said. We laughed some more. I might want you to, I thought. I think I might.

Not very long after, he met someone his age who wanted to get married immediately, and not eventually, and then he and I began to put each other away in archival drawers marked Summer 1999.

"What are you up to?" he asked me one night, after having donned the role of friend. It was his idea to meet for a drink.

"Oh, trying to figure out what I want to be," I said. Irony: a self-pitying girl's best friend.

"What do you want to be?" he said. Oh, stop it, please, I thought. You are no longer responsible for coaxing me free of myself! I almost said: "Joan of Arc!" But I imagined that even he would not forgive me for such a declaration, even if it was—partially—a joke. Or that might have been the point—to remind him that he was right in getting away from me. He was an atheist, and should be with an atheist. That was one way I had been looking at it.

"I want to be brave," I said. I wanted to say to him also that I had realized his beauty too late, that I had made a mistake, and I was in pain, which made it impossible to sit and listen to him talk about his new life.

"You give off this immense strength," he said. I shook my head. Caroline did. Genevieve did. My sister, Elise—everyone else I knew did. Not me. And if I did, it was what ruined what we had. I didn't want his decency and concern here in some bar if they could not be mine alone.

We said good-bye on the street. He gave me a kiss on the cheek, and right before he did I saw a look on his face blaze up and then fade and I thought the look said, *Oh you I am sorry I wish for more time and another world.* In return I gave him a look that said, *Please come back I was so stupid.* Then I watched him walk east on Bleecker, and when I was sure he was gone I started down Broadway and let myself cry.


"Don't do it," said Caroline. I was standing in the doorway of her study, arms crossed over my chest, listening. "Don't get involved with someone who could give you work."

But I had come to New York expressly to fall in love with people who could give me work!

"Yes," I said. "Remind me again what the problem would be."

"It doesn't work out, and you don't have work. And you feel like crap."

"Right," I said. But I had read *The Company She Keeps*, and I knew how these things worked: it was a foxtrot you did, one hand at the small of someone's back, the other holding a gin and tonic, and I wanted on to the dance floor.

Aaron had not read that book. I'd read more than he had, but he'd written much more than I ever would. A friend told me to send him my writing. I did, and he sent it back with a note that described it as unpolished, but promising. Sentences from the note needled me while I waited for the subway or sat in front of my computer screen. And yet this did not stop me from mouthing off to him in great detail about the writers I admired when we first met in person. He smirked, nodded, drank up. "It's clear you take your work very seriously," he said.

Aaron had codes. When he wrote pieces that he termed "whoring," he asked that his name not run beneath them. He believed in hard work and loyalty to employers and in setting up and abiding by systems, because systems would help you reap the harvest sown by your hard work. He too had been sent to Christian school, and though he no longer believed, his parents, like mine, still attended a very large suburban church.

"Do you think there's been a complete breakdown in critical thought?" he asked that night. Did he have seven hours? He did. And then at three in the morning we parted at the 14th Street station.

He did give me work, and we went along as if he didn't want anything more from me than clean and lively copy, and I didn't want anything more from him than a few good clips. But he kept asking me to talk to him. He asked me questions over e-mail, in bars, at shows. Let's talk, he kept saying, let's talk, and I could not resist. So I would talk, not looking at him anymore, looking off around wherever we were because it was easier to say what I thought when

I wasn't facing people who intimidated me, and then when I came in for a landing, he was there, grinning, saying, "Go on, go on." I liked the way he looked at me over his glasses—sometimes skeptical, sometimes amused, sometimes impressed. With his long nose and black hair that pointed down into a slight widow's peak, there was the sense of him presiding over a reference desk, that he was someone you had to get past in order to get the information. He made a habit of calling me on what he thought was disingenuous—a word I never used, because I could not imagine that I was wise enough to divine anyone's true motives. If I complained that a young artist might not deserve the overwhelming success being heaped upon him, he felt obliged to point out that he suspected my criticism was purely subjective and motivated by envy. If I made a crack about the sprawling middles of suburban tourists, he felt obliged to point out that I came off as sweet, but I was actually very mean. He had spotted her—my real, scared, snot-nosed fifteen-year-old self, who shadowed me everywhere, who I had been trying to shake.

He asked me to see a band. We shouted at each other in the concert hall, his mouth on my skin, my comprehension the excuse. There was a hole in the elbow of my cardigan, and I'd scrunched up the sleeves so that it wouldn't be noticeable, but in the line for the coat check he touched it and smiled.

In the bar he told me that he was waiting for someone else to come back to town while also caught in the middle of a fling that, as he said, had gotten a little out of hand. I put my hands over my face. Oh, here's where I get off, I thought. At the stop for Latent Attraction That Will Heretofore Express Itself As Nothing But The Highest Respect And Admiration. Please don't make me get off there. I've made others get off there, and it's no good.

"Take your hands away from your face," he said, as if urging Saltines and ginger ale on a sour stomach. I did.

"I think—I think we should just throw ourselves into something," I said, looking down at the floor, speaking quickly. "And if being to-gether is terrible, then it's terrible, but at least we'll know for sure, and we'll live. We'll live." I thought everyone had come to this city to have life, and have it more abundantly, and his codes and systems baffled me, because they were defending him against abundance.

"What would you do if you were me?" he asked. It was a pro-posal and a dare.

What did I have to lose? He wasn't going to change his mind. "I would kiss me."

He came right at me. Flushed, laughing, our tangled legs knock-ing over empty bottles. We kissed until I began to unbutton his shirt. "Oh, no," he said. "I'm taking you home." He hailed us a cab, and in the cab said that the driver couldn't go fast enough. In his apartment, under his old man's clothes, I would find a conspirator, someone eager to see what the two of us could come up with.

I would never know why exactly he decided what he decided, but he told me after a few weeks that he just couldn't. I guessed he could see that the girl coming back to town was steadier than I'd ever be. She was some sort of scientist, so I imagined she did not have feel-ings. Or at least the kind of feelings that could get you confused for a fifteen-year-old girl—envious, defensive, garrulous, outraged by bad writing and bad bands.

A lunch with Joe made me think I'd guessed right. I told him that I was glad that we'd been able to meet, because it had been a while. He explained why.

"I think," he said, "when we get together we wallow in bitter-ness, and that's not good."

Bitterness, my bête noire. Joe didn't seem to notice that he'd de-livered a blow. Was it bad form to speak honestly about work and life to someone other than Caroline? Was I something calamitous, inadvertently wreckful? I couldn't see that Joe and Aaron, who were both enjoying some success, might be made uncomfortable by someone who didn't keep their crankiness close; that perhaps I was doing other people some violence.

Joe and I walked toward Sixth Avenue. "Are you reading anything you like?" he asked.

"Oh, this biography of the Brontës."

"What exactly is the difference again between reading literary biography and self-help?"

"You'd rather I actually read Tony Robbins?"

"Touché." He laughed. "How's your beau?" he asked, meaning Aaron.

"I seem to be the other woman," I said. My father would have said I was trying to get a rise out of Joe. He would be right. I had no professional success to brag about. It seemed that I still didn't know what my aim was here in the city, and had started to think that most of it was probably just to get here and not get evicted from an apartment—so I thought I might make myself look like I was having a time as a girl about town.

Tourists and lunch breakers ebbed and flowed around us. Joe stood looking ahead, in khakis and white cotton as always, patiently waiting for the light to change, poised for the rest of his life to unfold smoothly and without unsightly emotional mess. Possessed of one of the best jobs you could have in this city. Possessed of someone he loved, and had loved for years.

He refused to take me up on my ironic tone. "That's sad," he said. But I wasn't sure we'd all grown up enough to pretend that we'd never drawn puzzlement and censure from others—or ourselves.

---

I took a trip and came back to find that a barstool flirtation of Caroline's had turned serious. "He's never what I would have dreamed for myself," she told me as I unpacked. She was sitting on my bed. "You know I like them dark and strong. But I like him more than I've ever liked anyone." I remembered one night when we first came to the city, when we were out for the evening and she'd come to tell me that she was cutting out because someone had come to find her and take her away. She wore a long black coat and skirt and boots, my scarf wrapped around her, looking like something out of a Russian novel. I had rarely seen her face that undisturbed by cynicism or boredom. It was pure red-curled prettiness. She had the same look now. She had spied the person she might spend the rest of her life with, and, unlike the Lady of Shalott, she was going to live. There was a catch, however. "You're not going to get what you dreamed you would," she intoned.

When she wasn't spending nights at his place, she was going from the kitchen to her bedroom and back again in a hooded sweatshirt and jeans, phone cradled on her shoulder, holding a bowl with a pot holder under it, talking to him in a voice shaded with confidences. When I did get a chance to talk to her, the phone would inevitably ring, with me in the middle of some story about work, and she'd ask if she could call him back in fifteen minutes. One night, having had to wait one too many times for her to get off the phone, I broke. "What could you possibly have to say to him?" I said. "You talk to him five times a day and then hours at home." But it was as if she had not heard me.

It looked like the age of kindred spirits—see L. M. Montgomery—was past, and it was foolish to look for some other female friend who didn't already have some better half to confess everything to. We were all getting older, about to leave our twenties, and the circle of girls who could continue to take up the flag of spinster loyalty was dwindling. Everyone was falling in true, boring love.

It would not do to go out and find someone for myself. But sitting alone at a party riled me up into revenge against my state. I saw someone across a room telling someone else he had gone to school in Baltimore, giving me reason to set myself down beside him when I spotted him sitting alone. When I sat down, I realized I had found the answer to all my problems—a moral philosopher whose father had been a priest. His name was Eric. He didn't seem to notice that I was throwing myself at him by interviewing him about what he was studying and teaching.

"Let's go make out," I said. This had never failed.

"What?" He really had not heard me. I repeated myself. "Oh, I don't think that's a good idea," he said. He'd just been left by someone, but thought I was a nice person and didn't want to drag me into the unstable morass she'd left him in.

Usually an inclination for doing the right thing would please me a great deal, but not tonight. "I'm not asking you to marry me," I said.

That seemed to make some sense to him. "All right," he said, and stood up.

We walked home in the snow, and then climbed the stairs to my apartment. "You're telling me a girl lives here?" he said after looking in on the mess and the paper in my dark bedroom, and I could tell he was amused, and I liked him even more. Then we began. But he stopped it. I listened, trying not to be annoyed, as he explained and apologized.

"It's okay," I kept saying. I put my hand on his back. "It's okay." I had no idea that men could be this overcome by guilt and shame. It sounded like my own shame and guilt, the kind that twisted you up and then nailed you down and kept you from doing anything ever.

But he asked for my telephone number, and while giving him a look that I hoped said, *Why go through this charade?* I wrote it down.

In bed, unable to sleep, I decided that God—or something similarly omniscient and insistent on people getting a hold of themselves—was punishing me for imposing my erotic will on another. Something was trying to teach me that there were better things than getting felt up on a flea-bitten sixty-year-old couch— like pure-hearted platonic friendship between the sexes—to be aspired to.

When Caroline came into the kitchen the next morning and asked how the party had been, I laid it all out for her. "And then he ran out!" I said as we messed about with pots and pans. "Can you believe it?"

"Wouldn't you rather be doing that with someone who cared about you?" she said. I stared at her. I thought of Joe: *That's sad.* Caroline had become another person, one who spoke patronizingly of what she herself had been no stranger to. It was a little unnerving to me, too, to think that this was all I was accomplishing in New York. That the only stories I had to show for myself, the only narratives that had beginnings, middles, and ends, with memorable dialogue and striking scenes, were because of whatever I'd gotten up to with men. But they weren't stories. They were a pile of false starts.

The night before Caroline moved into his apartment, we were sitting on her bed, talking. She was fighting a fever, so I'd helped her finish sweeping and cleaning out her room. Before I left for my own she asked me how I was doing.

"I'm a little lonely," I said. "But I'm fine."

"I'm sorry," she said. But she was grinning the grin of the sated.

After she moved out we would meet for lunch, but I did not enjoy it. "He and I are so happy," she would say. She had floated away, never to return, content to sink under and drift to the silted, seaweeded bottom with her love. I'd nod and keep quiet, wondering what to say that didn't sound inane or false. Love, I saw, was the thing you kept to yourself, the thing that transpired away from everyone you knew, the one experience that could not be translated to your closest friends.

There was a moment where I thought she'd come to. "And then they want to become your *boyfriend*," she whispered, across a table at McDonald's, as if it were a thing to be avoided, a disease, a deplorable state. "They want to crawl inside you and spend every waking moment with you." Oh, here she was! Yes, this was it! Our new adventure would be to be women *with* men. We would be female D. H. Lawrences, mapping our own star equilibriums, armed with protractors and telescopes, decorated in jet-beaded necklaces and jewel-colored stockings.

No. That story had ended.

"I don't need a best friend," I told the orderly girl who moved in. "Just a roommate."

"Absolutely," she said, with the finality of a briefcase snapping shut.

# CHAPTER 11

## WHERE ARE THE YOUNG SISTERS?

I had the chance to go to England for a few weeks in the summer, so I did. In London, I told a cabdriver that I had been an English major.

"Novels!" he said as we sped from Heathrow. "I'm sorry, but I could never read fiction. It's a waste of time." The sun was out, filling the black cab. The cabbie, who wore a Hawaiian shirt and a gold hoop earring, had a shaved red head and the face of a young-verging-on-middle-age Alec Guinness. He continued in a tone that made it clear he meant no offense to me, he personally just didn't go in for that mess.

"I mean, what the fuck do I care about someone's made-up life?" he said, making a very smooth left. "I do collect books about boxers, though, as some of them had very interesting lives." He'd grown up in the house in which Jack the Ripper murdered Annie Chapman, he told me. I saw his point. When you had lived that close to danger, even though the danger had taken place a hundred years ago, why would you need to plunge yourself over and over again into other people's predicaments?

In Oxford I wandered around, humbled by the yellow spires. As I walked by University College, I heard a young American tourist asking a student if he could smuggle her into the Shelley memorial inside its gates. I stopped to listen. The guard, with a crew cut and Ken doll physique, told her she couldn't go in—University College being off-limits to tourists. The student offered to sneak me in with them.

"Isn't it perfectly awful?" he whispered to me, hanging back, as the girl had public raptures in front of the altarlike setup. And it was: a lurid red cupola three shades deeper than the color of port wine Wispride snack cheese, bordered at the top by an inscription painted in gold. And then in the middle, on a marble pedestal, lay a marble Shelley, curled up as in death or sleep or swoon, nearly naked except for a piece of fabric twined round him so as to obscure the naughty bits—which, the student informed me, had reportedly been sanded down. The display returned me to the position I held in college: that the Romantics were useless unless they were writing pointed meditations on London, urns, and nightingales. As the young woman circled and sighed, the student told me that Oxford had kicked Shelley out for writing a pamphlet championing atheism. But they'd taken him back, and here he was, still causing trouble, still troubling female hearts.

A flash went off, and the bulldog towered over her, snatching the camera and shaking the film out of it. "There's a reason why we don't let tourists in here!" he said. The student and I made an exit while the girl yapped up in her defense—"I'm not hurting anyone!"—and then caught up to us outside the gate to thank him for smuggling her in.

"Shelley's my hero," she said. "I don't care that I got yelled at—I'm a defiant spirit, just like he was." We smiled. Though I was mortified on her behalf. And then my own: I wasn't so different from this girl, hand over her heart on the street, identifying strongly with a dead person. I was going to Haworth next, to visit the Brontë parsonage. This girl just wasn't trying to hide the fact that she knew her soul was as sentimental and emphatic as a sampler, stitched neatly in the front and knotted cleanly in the back, allegiances uncomplicated and defended to the last.

In Haworth, I prayed to Charlotte in her father's church. *Tell me how to make something of my life,* I said. *Assure me that I'm right never to have tried to make money. Assure me that it is not a sin to walk around feeling wind and rain whipping up inside you, black branches clawing at you, when you are confused and lonely.*

In my room at night I read what John Ruskin wrote of the Gothic novels that had enthralled masses of young Victorian women. "But the best romance becomes dangerous, if, by its excitement, it renders the ordinary course of life uninteresting and increases the morbid thirst for useless acquaintance with scenes in which we shall never be called upon to act." I shut the book and tried to go to sleep, telling myself I had no such morbid thirst, when I knew that I did. I dismissed the Romantics' poetry, but hoped for tempests, shipwrecks, and near-drownings to make my life apparent to myself. I thought of the Gothic novels Jane Austen read and sent up, and her suspicion of unchecked sensibility, of Marianne Dashwood crying out to Willoughby in a way that made you fear for her, and then of Charlotte Brontë, who, in an epistolary snit to the editor she loved but who could not love her back, said of Austen that "the passions are perfectly unknown to her." This question again: of feeling, and what to do with it. In writing, and in life. I had no editor to confess them to, no romance to serve as a fitting receptacle. My feelings, because they were not gainfully employed, had been experienced by others as sudden and unjustified ugliness, my envy and curdled pride striking out like a lizard's tongue in the middle of an otherwise agreeable conversation—conversation being the only outlet for their expression. My feelings were too intense and large in number. I wanted to exterminate them.

When I returned home, a collection of Iris Murdoch's writings showed up on the free book table at work. Back at my desk, I began turning the pages. "Love is the extremely uncomfortable realization that something other than oneself is real," she wrote. My face burned. *Love is the extremely uncomfortable realization that something other than oneself is real.*

I looked up from the book and around the office. High noon. Phones ringing, the copier shuttling back and forth, people walking up and down the hallway talking. I was having a revelation in my cubicle, I was sure of it. *This is the truth,* I heard God saying. *This is your answer.* I read on. And if you have love, she said, you write disinterestedly, unclouded by narcissistic imaginings or noxious emotions. Murdoch's idea of fiction was that it should be an open, airy house, full of rooms in which the characters could move about freely—a house in which the characters lived independently of the author, unable to be confused with the personality who had created them. Which I took to mean, even though I'd learn that Murdoch herself would wreak havoc with her own, that you shouldn't have imaginings and emotions at all.

I could not write a novel, but sitting in the sanctuary at the Catholic church Genevieve and I had started attending, looking at all the faces around me, I thought I should try to pledge myself to an open, airy house in which we all might try to rid ourselves of selfishness—in which I might try to calm myself into wanting only peace and quiet, and, once that was taken care of, justice for others. I thought I could learn how to love there. I did not think I was very good at love. I was very good at being polite, inoffensive, and a good listener, but that wasn't love.

One Sunday at Mass, a young woman stepped up to the lectern to tell us why she was converting. This was something they asked those converting—the catechumens—to do if they had the stomach for public speaking. "I thought I could live a spiritual life on my own, just by going through the required reading," she said. "*The Imitation of Christ*, *The Dark Night of the Soul*, and so on. But then I realized that Christianity was intended to be lived in a community. And I needed to be a part of a community. I could not live the Christian life in my head."

God was speaking to me again. I'd been getting by on dipping into Catherine of Siena, *The Dark Night of the Soul*, and Saint Thérèse's autobiography. Pretending. Consuming the homily but not the host. Giving up chocolate and swearing for Lent. I was sitting in a church whose dark wood and marble floors reminded me of the chapel at college, but all the things they'd taught me there had started to fade. That Jesuit motto—"Men and women for others"— I'd taken it seriously. Now there was nothing to show for it. Had I only volunteered back then because they'd made it easy? Probably. Even Caroline had done some volunteer work for a local political party's office in Brooklyn. I just came home from work, exhausted, and then worked some more. To what end? I read too much and thought too much. I needed to stop asking Charlotte Brontë to permit my florid pessimisms. I wanted out of my head.

That summer, I signed up to participate in the Rite of Christian Initiation for Adults. From summer to Easter, when we would be confirmed, we would meet once, then twice a week with our sponsors—randomly assigned godparents who would help with our questions or problems as we progressed—and some church staff.

The first RCIA meeting was held after Mass, in a linoleum-floored room behind the sanctuary. There was a sofa crowded with stuffed animals. Karen, the woman who was in charge of the program—she didn't seem that much older than me—laughed as she cleared them out of the way so there would be places for us to sit. There were six of us: a few members of the financial sector, me, and then a woman who lived at the Catholic Worker. Three of us were quixotics. Three were marrying into the church, but they seemed no less serious about the process because they were fulfilling a requirement.

The stuffed animals, colored in highly flammable hues of orange, white, and purple, gave me pause. I wondered if they were used in role-playing exercises—for AA? Marriage Encounter? Pre-Cana?—and I feared for a moment that one day we would be forced to use them for the same thing. I feared that this was going to end the way most of my attempts at group spirituality had: in boredom, judgment, and despair. I stopped myself—there would be no more judgments made on the lives and tastes of those in charge and those around me. I was going to sit on the couch among these fellow New Yorkers for eight months and just take whatever this church had in mind for us.

When I told my mother, over the phone, there was a silence. "You know I don't agree with this," she said. "I don't understand it."

"I think this is something I need to do," I told her. "I think this is going to help me." It might make me show more kindness to her. Could she be against that?

There were several more conversations like this. "I just want to understand," she would say whenever we got on the phone. "I just want to understand." So I would say things like, "The pope has nothing to do with this," and "The Catholic churches I've attended don't mention Mary at all." My mother's silence in response to those statements shamed me. I thought I knew what I was talking about. But when my words hit the air, they turned dumb and convenient. Evangelicals had a term for people like me—grocery-store Catholics—and it was the worst sort of Christian you could be. A grocery-store Catholic picked and chose what she was going to believe in, and I was concentrating on what satisfied my liberal sensibilities. When I tried to explain what I liked about the Catholic Church, I wasn't very persuasive either. I kept thinking of the books in the church library, small signs that said much to me, but would not mean anything to my mother: *Earthing the Gospel. Socialism and Christianity. Peacemaking.* These were not self-help books. They were gardening manuals, directions for beating swords into plough-shares. Handbooks for tending to the world outside the building. For doing justice, loving mercy, and walking humbly with your God. The Catholic Church had turned that line from the book of Micah into a hymn, and made it into a commandment—one that evangelicals did not seem familiar with.

"But what does it say about your faith that you're converting just because this religion presents God in a way that is pleasing to you? You're making God in your own image," my mother said to me. I did not think I was doing that at all.

My father weighed in once over the phone. My father, after years of spending Sunday morning fertilizing the lawn, had started going to church with my mother. My sister and I had no idea how this had happened. We didn't want to think about it, because it meant my father, who had survived two bypasses and only cried in front of us once, at his brother's funeral, was not the mighty German fortress we believed him to be. We kept forgetting that he could be a bit of a sentimental Irishman, which we should have remembered from the period in high school when he struck up a relationship with the soundtrack to *The Phantom of the Opera*. My sister and I would get in his car to go somewhere, start it up, and be assailed by a blast of "Masquerade" or "The Music of the Night," the album blaring just as he'd left it. That was a lapse into emotionalism we could understand.

"I'm not as torn up about this as your mother is," he said. "But I still think you're crazy. It's a dead religion." Fair enough. I'd rather my mother call me crazy once over the phone and then just let me get on with it. He never said anything about it to me again. But soon in the mail there arrived a set of xeroxed pages from an unnamed book outlining the church's shortcomings. Aside from a postcard he'd mailed home from a St. Louis sales training session in 1985, it was the only piece of mail my father had ever sent me.

I did get one family blessing—from my father's mother. One Sunday afternoon my father took us to visit my grandmother, who did not leave the house much after my uncle died. We sat, as we usually did, in the living room where my father and uncle had wrestled and watched television, and my grandmother served us coffee. She liked my sister and me to have the couch and my father the easy chair with her rosary draped over the arm. She would then ask us all about New York, where she had lived for a year in her teens and then left, homesick for Philadelphia. But she listened to WOR all day long, and liked to talk to us about Giuliani and crime.

Whenever I thought of my grandmother, I thought of the hydrangea bushes flanking her house. She was as careful about those flowers as she was about herself. She kept her nails painted a deep Revlon pink, her white hair curled and soft, and she never wore polyester—always cotton, linen, and wool. It was never clear to us how much we took after our grandmother. In my mother's family, everyone was always letting you know the ways in which you looked and behaved like someone else. The seemingly sui generis had precedents: not only was I the spitting image of my Aunt Susan, but whenever I had a cold I left my tissues all over the house just like she did when she was a kid. My sister had my grandmother's face, which was my father's. I was freckled and white like my grandmother—a rash of them on my forearms, my shoulders, some creeping onto the backs of my hands. But we had no idea how much of our temperament or behavior could be traced back to her. She and our father never said, which gave us the feeling that we couldn't ask.

I wanted her to know I was taking up the religion everyone she'd ever known believed in. When I told her, she smiled.

"Your uncle would be pleased," she said.

"Really?" I said. I had never really talked with my uncle about going to Mass.

"He liked that you were a religious girl," she added. "He thought you might one day be a nun."

I didn't know why he would think that—other than I'd never had a boyfriend, much in the way that he had never had a wife—but I was glad to hear it.

"Oh jeez," said my father. My sister was my mother's, and I was his, but once in a while he was reminded that his daughter also belonged to his brother: two people donning confirmation names and cassocks and thinking that was going to solve something.

My sponsor and I often met at a diner around the corner from church. She was fifty-two to my twenty-eight. Jan, who just that year cut her long blond-going-gray hair to her chin, lived in Chelsea, still bought pierogies and kielbasa from the last remaining Polish butcher in the East Village, occasionally taped *All My Children* to watch after work, and ten years earlier had lost her closest friend to AIDS. I would ask her questions about her friend. She had been angry at God, she said, and stopped going to church for a while. We would talk about the place of suffering in faith. I didn't think I had experienced any true suffering. I told her I often wondered when God was going to lower the boom.

"Don't you think," she said, "that maybe the cross that God has given you to bear is living in New York? Living on the salary you do, doing without, trying to live your dream, and having your job?"

I didn't. Living in New York was a cross that I could put off any time I wanted. God hadn't given this to me—I chose it, my evangelical self reminded me, and if I chose something, my evangelical self went on, it could not be of God, because God would never give you what you thought you wanted. If New York frustrated me that much, I could move to Philadelphia, Baltimore, or Chicago. Or take off for Mexico to build houses. If you could shrug off your suffering, it didn't seem like suffering to me.

"I don't know," I said. "I never thought about it that way."

"Maybe you should," she said. "It's hard to live here. There'll be other struggles, but maybe this is your struggle now."

But there was no struggle. There was just misunderstanding and fumbling. And that was just comedy—the distance between what was hoped for and what actually transpired.

Margaret, a friend of mine, asked me out for some drinks. There was a member of the group who gave me pause: a loud gesticulator who made comments about women, gay men, and Chinatown residents in a way that at some parties, I could see, had served to heat things up a notch before the flame died out. I laughed a few times in spite of myself—in between wondering when I could leave because this guy was hoovering all the pleasant out of this room and wondering how long it would be until he turned his mockery on me the way crazy people on the subway turned their monologue on you when they caught you staring at them.

The conversation flagged, so I took the opportunity to excuse myself, grabbed my bag, kissed Margaret goodbye, and walked down the steps to the street, wondering which subway I should take.

It was a Thursday, winter, ten thirty, Greene Street full of laughing groups percolating with the clip of stilettos on pavement.

"Hey!" someone said. I turned around. It was the boor, standing on the steps of the restaurant. Had I forgotten something?

"I just wanted to let you know—I know we didn't talk much—but I think what you're doing, you know, how you're single and still waiting to, you know, I think it's great."

I knew he was referring to the fact that I had never had sex. Margaret had exposed me as severely retarded of heart to a stranger, and here he was exposing it to a street full of revelers.

"Thank you," I said. Whatever it was that roused little old ladies to beat muggers—and this man had mugged us both of some decency out here—over the head with purses, I did not have it.

"Nobody sticks to their guns anymore, especially in this city," he said. It wasn't clear what he was after—he had to know this was not the suavest of overtures—but anyone who wanted to share his hunger for moral courage with a stranger couldn't be that bad. Again they had been wrong in the churches I'd grown up in. They never imagined we would turn our back on church, and so never counted on us learning that we had been warned off the world for no good reason. Here I was, holding fast—admittedly, holding fast with a little more ambivalence than conviction—to desires that made sense only to God. And yet this person had left his seat to commend me for remaining chaste. It wouldn't do to correct him and say that I was starting to think my situation was something of an accident, not just the result of an overdeveloped conscience. I couldn't tell him that I thought my resolve had begun to resemble the cheap bravery of the virgin martyrs, who cut off their hair and plucked out their eyes without first knowing what a gorgeous thing it was to be handled by men.

"Well, thanks," I said, and then walked away.

This guy didn't bother me, really. What I hadn't done yet didn't bother me either. What bothered me was that I had not yet been in love. Someone had yet to look at me and say *You, you, you.* Four years here, and not one true love with whom to swashbuckle through life, but bouquets of weird and invasive compliments thrown from the possibly racist and sexist in the middle of Soho. New York, you son of a—

Well, that wasn't exactly true. Roger, I thought. And others, too. I just hadn't returned their look. I descended down to the train and saw teenagers snaking themselves around each other all over the subway platform. The girls straining the seams of their jeans, the boys swimming in theirs, strung out on each other's every pimple, eyelash, and breath, lapping each other up, cutting their eyes at everyone who passed by. I could be tempted to say that loneliness was suffering, standing there wishing that I had learned when they had what abandoning yourself to another felt like, and how to want it so much that you'd snatch it, shamelessly, in public.

In February, we went on an overnight retreat to a college in North Jersey. "In the sixties, this used to be a house of studies for the young sisters finishing up their degrees," said the elf-nun who welcomed us. She paused, smiling, tilting her head, honoring the ghosts of those girls. "But where are the young sisters?" She went on to tell us that in the early 1970s, with the drying up of young sisters, the college had been turned into a retreat center. Elf-nun: Boston accent, neat pilled cable-knit sweater, her measured speech a sign of God's grace and peace being upon her. I wanted to be an elf-nun.

That weekend, I practiced being a young sister. There was prayer in a stained-glass chapel, prayer by morning and late afternoon light. There was snow on a sloping graveyard, where the young sisters who had become old sisters were buried, and which I wandered off to whenever possible. Clean planes of snow like sheets of paper to be written on, sheets of white wiping out all the mistakes I had made. There were cinder-blocked dorm rooms with wooden night tables and bedside lamps. In the communal shower, I dreamed that I was naked of men and money. Wait, I thought. I *am* naked of men and money. I could live like this—twin bed, notebook, pen, graveyard, institutional eggs and coffee served up in thick white dinnerware—for months. Maybe for the rest of my life. Would they let lay people hide out here? Would they let us pretend that we were at McLean for a weekend here and there, even if we weren't bipolar, just a little weary and depressive and searching? If this was another decade, another century, another millennium, I could have put my celibacy to good use. There would be an acceptable framework for it called the convent, and through it you would express your intellect and independence; through its rigors you would summon an incarnation of female wisdom and strength that could rival wife and mother.

But I could not be cloistered. When I went to hear two Colombian political prisoners speak at the Catholic Worker house in the East Village with Melinda, I saw the room she shared with another woman—a dim, joyless shoe box stuffed with a couple of faded batik bedspreads and spiked with dying plants. However much I had been taken with this experiment in college, and admired Melinda for her commitment even as I questioned it, I couldn't help thinking that there was something of suicide in allowing oneself to be mired in a losing battle against power and wealth. I didn't want power and wealth. I didn't mind living with a roommate and subsisting mainly on salad and toasted cheese sandwiches, my crowded bookcases the only thing I'd be sad to lose in a fire. But I could not give up my privacy for the greater good, or give up the hope that one day I might be able to possess what my grandmothers would call nice things—

several pairs of unscuffed shoes, three or four uncommon, intriguing dresses, a few sets of crisply patterned sheets, colorful cookware. And I still wanted to perform for the city—more and more I felt that I could stand firm against its plagues—and for the city to take notice. I wanted to kill the parts of myself that had brought me grief, but I also wanted to discover how, and with whom, to let other parts flourish and grow over the rot.

Saturday morning in the chapel I read of Saint Scholastica. It was her saint day, said the missal. She had a brother, Saint Benedict, he of the rule, who would travel with his disciples from his monastery to visit her every year so that they might talk for hours about the soul and God. Night came, and they were still at the table talking when Benedict said he'd have to start back. Scholastica couldn't bear it. She wanted to talk until morning. Rules were rules, said Benedict, and he couldn't spend a night outside his cell. Scholastica said nothing. She put her head down on the table, began to cry, and her tears drew rain to the heavens, so much rain and thunder that there was no way Benedict could travel back home. "May God have mercy on you, my sister. Why have you done this?" he said. She told him why. "See, I asked you, and you would not listen to me," she said. "So I asked my Lord, and he has listened to me. Now then, go, if you can. Leave me, and go back to the monastery." But he had to stay, and his annoyance gave way to pleasure as they picked up where they had left off. Scholastica, contented, died the next morning, her soul traveling up to heaven in the form of a dove. That's when I would rest, too, I thought. When I found a willing partner for a long conversation.

That night we cut loose with a board game that required us to divide into teams and use our skills at trivia, sketching, bluffing, and charades. There was a cheese and wine spread, some crackers and salami. Lila, a short, fiery girl my age with silky black hair and

French manicured nails that sparkled as she gestured wildly, was up at bat for charades. Though she had been gesturing wildly to us, we weren't getting it. She rolled her eyes, then began to make the universal sign for sexual congress: fists upturned, pumping back and forth at hip level while her pelvis rocked back and forth. Everyone laughed. "Lila!" someone said. The timer went off, and she stopped.

"Oh, my God!" she said, out of breath. "It was the Immaculate Conception!" she shouted at us. Even Paula, Lila's sponsor, a reserved West Indian woman who was a member of the Legion of Mary, was laughing.

Karen, who had gone off for a few minutes, came back into the room. "Hey guys, guess what?" she said. "I think we've been drinking some other retreat group's wine." She sat down in a folding chair and leaned back against it. "Whoops," she said, taking a drink from a full cup someone passed her. "I paid them back, though." Catholics! They were not afraid to incorporate a modest amount of alcohol into social-spiritual gatherings. They embraced the madcap and possibly vulgar, which meant that they embraced life, in all its silliness and expanse and color! They knew from wry and rue. And I was going to be one of them.

On Sunday morning we each had a meeting with Karen in a small conference room. "I do have a question," I said. "How are we supposed to understand the role of the pope? I can't accept the teachings on birth control and homosexuality, and while I can keep my faith separate from the Vatican, how can I explain to anyone who asks how so many Catholics can live ignoring what the pope says about those things?"

"Well," she said, "those are good questions." She thought for a moment before answering. "The way I think of it is this. We live in the United States, governed by the president. We won't always agree with the government or the president, but that doesn't mean that we're going to leave the country. We're still Americans. It's the same with the pope. He governs this body, but not everyone is going to agree with him, or do what he thinks is right. And that doesn't mean we're not Catholic."

I was disappointed. I was looking for something airtight and irrefutable from a person in charge, preferably bolstered by a quote from someone dead. What I had received was more of a rationalization than a reasoned stance. Though it was an attractive rationalization, one that made a lot of sense if you decided not to think too hard about it.

She looked at me. "What would you think about waiting until next year to convert?"

"Why?"

"Well"—she tilted her head to the side, spreading her hands out on the table—"I feel that you aren't enjoying the process, and so I'm not sure that you're certain that this is the path you want to be on. Listening to you in our discussions, I hear a lot of guilt coming through, and so I wonder if you're in a free enough place to know that this is what you want for sure." Her voice was soft, apologetic. "Have I said anything that you disagree with?"

"Oh, no!" I said. "I really want to do this. I'm sure I want to do this. I don't want to wait." I could say these words—*I want, I'm sure, I don't want to wait*—and say them quickly and firmly because Karen did not have the power to give me a job and would never inform me that what seemed like predestination had actually been a one-night stand. "The guilt—that's—I mean, people have always joked that I should have been Catholic because of my guilt. That's always been there, my whole life. And I'm just not a very demonstrative or animated person. I've never been."

I had never failed out of anything, and I was not about to get left behind a year in Catholic class. She needed to have called me on my real failure: not having forged lifelong friendships with the disparate crew of Christians—of New Yorkers—that this parish had put in my life. I had gone to the Catholic Worker with Melinda, rode home from a meeting with Paula back to Bergen Street on the 2/3 train once, laughing and talking, and I always looked forward to my dinners with Jan, but that was as far as I was willing to go in weaving myself into a community. I was afraid that to go any further would be at some level a self-gratifying sham, not unlike screenwriters hanging out with cops or strippers for material and street cred.

"I'm sorry I gave the impression that I wasn't enjoying this. Or learning, or changing. I feel that I have," I said.

"You're sure?" She tilted her head to the other side. I thought she believed me.

"Yes," I said. "Yes."

Spring came, and I visited Eric in Baltimore. Eric did not believe, but was sympathetic to those who did, and his sympathy to my search had taken the form of old rosaries at Christmastime and a heavy set of old books encased in a red and gilt box labeled "The Library of Catholic Devotion" for my birthday. "With the words of our Lord in red, just how we like 'em," he'd said, hands behind his back, as he watched me examine the volumes.

His sympathy could also take the form of gentle mockery. I told him about a black Labrador that came occasionally to five o'clock Mass—a seeing eye dog that lay down at the feet of its owner with patience in a way that made me think that it was getting something out of Mass, too.

"It's almost," I said, "as if the Holy Spirit—"

"Holy Spirit my ass," he said. "It's well trained!"

He also liked to remind me of the time we were walking around the city, and when some street evangelizer tried to serve us with a tract, I blurted out, "I'm Catholic," to let the guy know he should save his breath and printed matter. "I'm Catholic," he liked to say, shaking his head in the way that I knew meant, *You, my friend, are a piece of work.*

The sun was going down in Fells Point. We'd been talking for hours. He was trying to finish his dissertation; I was trying to live up to my potential. He asked how the retreat was. I told him. And then I stopped. "Am I making any sense? Am I being articulate?" He could make me feel that my mind was a bowl full of egg yolks and whites, sloshing and staring up at whoever was holding it, awaiting and accepting of its fate, whatever it might be: omelettes, poaching, sunny-side up.

"I think you're quite articulate," he said. And then added: "Giggles."

It was his fault that I giggled. He could make me laugh so hard I had to stop walking and catch my breath. He, however, was carved out of somber, so whenever I managed to make him laugh I was happy. We sat down on a bench by the water.

"When is it exactly that the pope is infallible?" he asked, feigning confusion. "When he puts on the funny hat or sits on the throne? Or does the throne make him invisible?"

When we settled down, I asked him a question. "Do you think it's intellectually irresponsible of me not to be reading every single thing I can get my hands on about Catholic doctrine?"

He looked out at the water and smiled. "You've already done something intellectually irresponsible by converting," he said.

But there was something else other than my mind at work here, whether I liked it or not. I could not find the words to say this to Eric. It was something I had trouble admitting to myself. Remembering Kierkegaard and his knight of faith—someone who believed in spite of the evidence against it, who believed because she had subjectively experienced, not deductively reasoned her way to, the truth of God's existence—was no comfort. If I told Eric about that day in Florence to try to explain myself, would he tell me that I was just as well trained as that seeing eye dog?

A few summers before, my sister and I had taken ourselves to Europe, and when in Florence, we visited the baptistry. We stood under the dome, under a bearded, dark-eyed Christ looking down on us from the ceiling, seated in judgment, surrounded by angels, saints, evangelists, and prophets. His face gave me a start. I recognized this face, although it had never been made visible to me. This was the Jesus who had looked out at a city and longed for it. *O Jerusalem, Jerusalem, thou that killest the prophets, and stonest them which are sent unto thee, how often would I have gathered thy children together, even as a hen gathereth her chickens under her wings, and ye would not!* This was the Jesus of the lover's sigh. Of the mother's sigh. Receiving who would be received. The Jesus I had been praying to all my life, whose open hands offered infinite mercy. There he was suspended above us, arms outstretched, suffering everyone to come unto him, whether indifferent, curious, hostile, or humble. He had been sitting there for centuries, wanting really only a few things from us while people came and went below him, arguing about just what it was he wanted, and how much of it. Come unto me, if you want to, everyone down there flipping through guidebooks, taking pictures, arguing about where to have lunch, tugging your children on to the next sight.

That day I saw that I could not be anything other than a Christian. I could not be a Buddhist. That seemed faddish—what you did when you wanted to be spiritual without having to subscribe to a religion that was unpopular for the way most of its adherents practiced it, it was what hippies and vegetarians did, and I wanted no part of it. If the Beats embraced it, with their sloppy rhapsodies, I wanted no part of it. I was too much a lover of Christ and his words to leave him behind for Judaism or the Unitarians. He had come alive to me—for me?—in that baptistry in such a way that I knew it would be impossible to follow anyone else. If you walked into a building and, upon Christ's looming, you felt that you should drop to your knees, even though you had spent your life arranging things so that you would never be in such a supplicating position, you had to give up: he was yours, and you were his.

On the first Sunday of Lent, on a damp, cloudy morning, we met at St. Patrick's Cathedral to attend the Rite of Election, a ceremony in which all the catechumens in the New York City diocese declared their intentions before God and Cardinal Egan. Once our names were called and we stood before the altar receiving a blessing, there was apparently no turning back. There were hundreds of people there, faces of many colors. But then the priests before us: corpulent, white, pink, reminding me of all the stories I'd heard about the princely class that lived like kept women in their rectories. Fat white men lording it over the faithful. Here was the other church, the church that I'd been suppressing my knowledge of. I wouldn't ever say that it was the true church, but it was the church most people thought of when they thought of the Catholic Church, the one that turned a blind eye to the sexual abuse of its children, that would not let women become priests or let their priests marry, that castigated its liberation theologians. The moneyed, secretive, inflexible machine. How many people would I have to climb over to run down the aisle and out onto Fifth Avenue? This really was intellectually irresponsible. The pope, Mary, Padre Pio, Pope Pius, Opus Dei, the sexual abuse, the forbidding of birth control, the official stance on homosexuality. I wouldn't marry someone if I had to ignore this much sin and dysfunction. Or would I? But think: Why had

I come all this way? And who had led me here? Dorothy Day had submitted. And if it was the church of Dorothy Day, it was the church of Catherine of Siena, Teresa of Avila, Gerard Manley Hopkins, Thomas Merton, Walker Percy, Graham Greene, and Flannery O'Connor. A church of dissenters and mystics.

Karen called at the office to say that she'd received the copy of my baptismal certificate. Those of us who had been christened in the church had to obtain them to prove we didn't have to get dunked in a pool in front of the church during the Easter vigil. I'd phoned St. Aloysius—St. Al's, my father and grandmother called it—in Oaklyn to send me one. It certified that, according to the records of the church, I had been baptized there on April 8, 1973, by the Reverend John Lubicky. Msgr. Thomas M. Flynn had signed and said so.

"Did you know that St. Aloysius is a Jesuit parish?" she asked. As was the church I was converting in. And the college I had attended. "And according to this, you'll be confirmed almost twenty-eight years later to the date." She paused. "There are a lot of essences at work." Essences? I smiled. I would never use the word *essences*, but who was I kidding? It was just another word for what Karen and I both believed in: fate, and God in control of it.

At Mass, in the last few weeks before Easter, the readings reminded us that Jesus healed the blind. As Paul wrote to the Ephesians, quoting an early Christian hymn:

> *But everything exposed by the light becomes visible, for it is light that makes everything visible. This is why it is said:*
> *Wake up, O sleeper,*
> *Rise from the dead,*
> *And Christ will shine on you.*

We were also reminded that Jesus called Lazarus forth from the tomb—and perhaps I wasn't as deadened by fear and anxiety. I had independent confirmation of that from my sister, who'd told me, impressed, that she'd noticed I'd stopped yelling at her to get off my back and quit acting like our mother. I took it as proof that my heart was airier and open. I was no longer frightened of God; I no longer believed that his plan for my life was to extract grudging submission from me until I died. I had signed up to teach English as a second language through the church. And at rush hour in the morning it was possible to feel what my father used to try to get me and my sister to feel when we sat at the kitchen table putting off driving to school, which was that "Today is another day of wonderful opportunity!" In the morning I had my limbs and a job and could walk around the city staring up at the buildings and the sky. I had the city, I had these buildings. I had mornings, and the train humming with purpose, everyone snapping their papers in half into the straphanger origami needed to read them standing up, squat cups of coffee like whiskeys ordered neat, intently consuming news of the world—what to eat, who to see, what to wear. Tapping their feet to whatever was in their headphones, breakfasting steadfastly, sheep may safely graze, on Gideon New Testaments or the Torah, fortified, ready to go, the train and its riders vibrating with that line from Longfellow: "Let us then be up and doing, with a heart for any fate." Leaving the train like leaving Mass, bolstered by thinking of the last line in the liturgy: Go in peace to love and serve the Lord. Or mammon, whichever you preferred. I no longer cared.

Good Friday, and Genevieve was beside me. We had freed ourselves from work, slipping into a pew together as the church filled up with anticipation and bustle. Just before I left the office, I had gotten an invitation to go to a party with a bon vivant who knew people who knew people. I would have to go home and put a dress on and come back into the city.

"Nice work," said Genevieve. "A hot date on Good Friday."

Thomas took me to a party on a roof in Manhattan. The hostess, an actress, complimented me on my dress when I was presented to her. An editor laughed at what I was saying and said, "Stop! Go home and write it up and turn it in on Monday!" Numbers were exchanged. The city was asking me to open myself up to it. It meant me no harm. Now I could see. Just circulate, it was saying. Just be yourself. Wait. Was it God or New York? Who was on the line?

"Tell me again where you're from?" said Thomas.

"New Jersey," I said, and took a drink of champagne.

"New Jersey?" he said. "Come on. No way. I could have sworn you were from Ohio or Massachusetts or something. There's nothing identifiably New Jersey about you! Nothing."

I wasn't sure exactly what it meant to be from Ohio or Massachusetts or something, only that it meant that I must not come off like the progeny of a construction don who operated a pizza chain named after his grandmother on the side. Like someone who knew how to show you a good time under the boardwalk. Who would, if you crossed her, take you under a turnpike overpass and kick your teeth in while macing you with a can of Aqua Net. A Jersey girl. She would have an accent—chlorine in the water supply—and it would be redolent of hoagies, tanning salons, leather jackets, hair gel, Jets and Eagles jerseys. I took what Thomas said as a supreme compliment.

He suggested that we walk over to a fancy new hotel. I ordered some dumb pink drink because the occasion seemed to call for something a little more dressed up and ludicrous than a vodka tonic.

I drank two drinks too fast and my lips felt like rubber, as if they were bouncing against each other making that noise that kickballs made when they hit blacktop, and that was all he was hearing when I opened my mouth to ask him questions about who he was and where he had come from. I kept eating nuts. The bar filled up.

"I used to think I wanted to be Carl Bernstein," he said. "So I pretended to be him for a while, and then of course got burned out on politics and thought maybe I should be a rock journalist. Capital *R*, capital *J*." We chortled. Rock journalism last mattering, of course, in the mid-nineties.

The bartender brought a third round. "Do you want to run a tab or charge it to your room?"

"Charge it to the room."

I looked at him. He really couldn't have gotten us a room. A room. I looked down at the bar. Where was he getting the money for this? He had just told me about eating peanut butter sandwiches for dinner, and I was wearing a coat I had bought at Strawberry on a lunch hour. And what did he want with me? He seemed like a kind person, but he also seemed to have a facility with famous people, seemed to want to know them, and that made me suspicious. I would not say he was an operator, but if he spent a night with me, he might be shocked at my naïveté. With him, everything was talked over and then laughed at, there was a constant exchange of opinion on books as if they were horses to bet on, there was patter, lots of patter, and maybe it wouldn't hold both of us up. I did not see us twining our souls together like Benedict and Scholastica.

"I'm not that kind of girl!" I said.

He laughed. He took a drink, and looked at me, and it was the look of an older brother watching a younger sister lose it for the thousandth time because she never could tell when he was just kidding. "You're hilarious."

The next morning, we stood by his car. "When are we going to do this again?" He was leaning against the passenger side.

"Well," I said, "when do you want to?"

"Tonight?"

"I would, but I'm becoming Catholic." He might as well know why I had to get home. And why I would not sleep with him. He laughed. I could feel the joke coming. Some joke about how I was blowing him off because I had a date with Jesus.

"So you'll be making out with Jesus." He smirked.

"Not quite." I laughed just to show I wasn't one of those humorless Christians, I wasn't an unbreakable column of ivory. Really, I was more like Teresa of Avila, who said she could be bribed by a sardine.

I showed up to the meeting the morning of the vigil puffy-lipped and bleary-eyed, my hair in a greasy, runty ponytail because I hadn't showered, pawing my way to the coffee and doughnuts. Could people tell what I had been up to? Did I care? As I greeted everyone and poured some coffee, I decided that I could not. Now I really was a Catholic, and perhaps did not need a public ceremony to confirm it, because I was as cavalier about the responsibility of body to soul as the kids in college, Catholic from birth, who'd chased Saturday night Mass with benders. They had swallowed so much host that they had a lime of the body of Christ crusted up on their insides, absolving them of most low-level sins of the flesh. And I did not feel guilty for sleepwalking into church and trailing my own behind me.

That night, we waited in the back of the church in the dark, standing behind Father N and the Eucharistic ministers. The only light in the church came from the fire in the bowl of the baptistry. "May the light of Christ's rising dispel the darkness of hearts and minds," said Father N as he touched a candle to the bowl, and we exchanged smiles as we hovered. I could see my sister and Genevieve in the crowd. There was a feeling of waiting in the wings and walking out into the glare of expectant faces—a feeling I last had in junior high, before piano recitals and choral concerts, before you took to the stage to do your part, a feeling I had never experienced just by standing in a church. After the candle was lit, the procession traveled up the aisle, the large candle lighting pew by pew the small ones held by the congregants.

For a large part of the service we stood in a line up front, facing the congregation and submitting to a series of questions and proclamations. Some of us would be baptized; all of us would take communion for the first time.

"God does not give up on us," said Father N. "God always brings us out of the place of death and into the place of life."

We were asked to renounce our sin and make a profession of faith. "Do you reject the glamour of evil and refuse to be mastered by sin?" he asked.

"I do," we said. The glamour of evil. This city. I no longer wanted to walk its streets thinking of what I didn't have and how I'd never have it.

"Give them the spirit of right judgment and courage, of wonder and awe," said Father N. "Be sealed with the gift of the Holy Spirit," he told us, anointing our foreheads with oil, confirming us.

We then took places in the aisles of the church with our sponsors, and people began to file out of the pews. I seized up, shoulders tensing, vowing that only a few friends of mine would ever know that I'd stood in a church with my eyes closed, letting strange people lay their hands on me in a gesture of blessing. Because it sounded, out of the context of this Catholic ceremony, disturbingly Pentecostal.

But we were in a house of *miserere*, I remembered, which meant a house of mercy, which meant a house of mystery. Here are strangers of all sorts, strangers of kind face. They keep coming. They're singing "Veni Sancte Spiritus." I hear piano and voices. They're passing their hands over me, patting my shoulders, grazing my bare arms with their fingers. A little girl, her gold hoops glinting, led by her father, touches my hand, and I'm a stone dropped down into a stream, disappearing from the world as I know it.

# CHAPTER 12

## IMAGINE THEM DEAD

It was eight in the evening. It was August, and it had just rained. The humidity had been cleared away, leaving the smell of trees and sky behind. I was standing on a corner, waiting for a light to change so that I could cross the street to a date. I had not taken pains. I was wearing a cheap and much-laundered blouse over a skirt, feeling washed out and like I needed to be quarantined.

I stood on the corner thinking of Elise. Earlier in the week she and I had met for breakfast at a diner on Ninth Avenue, eating eggs in a booth before we headed to work, and she declared that she was going to be celibate for a while. My father often told us that he knew he couldn't get married until he knew for sure who he was and that he liked who he was. Which was why he married my mother at twenty-nine—ancient, we knew, for the early seventies. Maybe I should keep away from men until I figured out who I was and what I wanted.

Thomas had excused himself, not so politely, from the conversation we'd been having. He had told me, in so many words, with an e-mail, that I was aloof and insane. I couldn't argue with him. Perhaps being around me when I wanted you but you didn't want me—or you wanted me but I didn't want you—was like riding past a solid old house, and you stop to check it out, because how could it be abandoned it is so quaint and well kept, but why is the door unlocked? So you walk in and look around and then you start to hear faint disembodied screams from an upper room or booming footfalls on stairs and then you don't feel so at home and so you run right out the door and back into your car and drive away with the tires squealing.

"It isn't that you're not pretty," someone once said to me. But what was it? One night, in the middle of a dinner that straddled the line between date and friendly outing, I swore I saw the person seated opposite exchange his flirtatious manner for a probationary one when I announced I wished I knew more about Kant. Did I know too little? Was I too insistent on turning dates into seminars on the subjects I'd missed while majoring in English? Did they look at me and see a sexually naive succubus with a Metrocard? Did they think I would cling, and demand, and ask for more than they might be able to give?

I could call them up for exit interviews, but who needed to know what people were really thinking about you? Whatever I had turned men away for I would never disclose to them if pressed—because it would reflect poorly on me and might make them paranoid. Too fond of drinking, too sloppy a kisser, too lacking in love of novels, too dismissive of the spiritual, too old, too conservative, too short. My mother used to tell me that if you noticed someone had a run in their stocking, or a dip in their hem, and it was clear that there would be no way for them to fix it, you shouldn't let them know, because it bordered on cruelty to tell someone they were in disarray when they were nowhere near a bottle of clear nail polish or a needle and thread. I had a feeling that these men had turned from what I could do nothing about, and I thanked them for not mentioning it.

"You don't know what you want," I had been told. I thought I did. At the end of it all, I would have a marriage like the ones my professors did—I would marry someone full of love for poems and good Letterman stunts, someone who would pour wine for the friends we'd gather around our table to get them all telling stories, yes, stories, even though he himself was professionally suspicious of narrative, someone who would bring out an old photo album when he got a little drunk to demonstrate how beautiful I had been on our wedding day, at which point I would head for the kitchen, plates in hand, in embarrassment and in protest of sentimentality.

My father knew he wanted my mother. I thought about this, too, as I waited for the light to change.

The story was that he knew he would marry her the first time he saw her in the bookkeeping office at the dealership. At the time my mother was engaged to an Italian guy who liked to go drag racing on the weekends.

"Why are you with that guy?" my father wanted to know.

"I'm with him until someone else sweeps me off my feet," my mother told him. I imagined her delivering that line while shuffling papers, not looking at my father, sending him packing with brisk ponytailed indifference. The Catherine Deneuve of the back office.

Whenever my mother came to this part of the story, my sister and I also wanted to know what on earth she was doing with this guy. My grandmother had said the same thing to her: *What are you doing with him? You could do better.* We could not understand how she could spend her weekend afternoons at a drag strip in the Pine Barrens with an Italian guy. Good Lord. My sister and I could have ended up as girls who wore Cavariccis and had guidos for cousins.

"At the time, he was the best thing going," she told us.

At the time, my mother hated my father. She and my aunt had been working for him for nearly three years. The girls in the office called him Little Hitler, and Little Hitler at one point made my aunt cry at her desk. An older woman named Florette, a confidante to them both, stepped in on my father's behalf and told my mother that really, my father wasn't as bad as all that, and if he asked her out, she should say yes. Three months later they were engaged, and my father's mother wore black to the wedding. The moral of the story was that you could never tell whom you would fall in love with. You could not count anyone out.

A tall young man, laced with brashness, and possessed of an intolerance for horseshit because he, like Elise, came from the Midwest, waited in the bar. I had written a piece for him a few years before, into which he inserted a joke about Monica Lewinsky diddling with a cigar. I called him up and politely asked him to take it out, as I would never say or write a thing like that, and he did, and apologized, though not without some bemusement.

A few hours passed in the bar. It was very easy to talk to him. He was telling me about some thoughts he had about his work, and I came up with a few suggestions and offers of help.

"Oh, it's okay," he said. "We don't have to spend time talking about it. My life will be all right."

*My life will be all right.* Who thought like that? Or, if they did, who would admit it out loud? In New York!

He asked me to come with him to a party for a friend the next week. So I did. He didn't say anything that made me want to talk to him for hours. Our sentences got shorter, came slower. He grew nervous as we talked. He did not wear his intelligence, which there was a great deal of, like something you were supposed to notice for its color and cut and expense. If he had it, what was he doing with it? If he had it, he needed to throw it around like cash to buy my respect.

"I wonder if I'm too earnest," he said. We had been talking about some recent books. "Am I too earnest?"

"If you have to ask, you probably are." He needed to be punished for boring me while I wore a pretty dress and sipped a cocktail.

Later, when he got out of the cab we were sharing, he slammed the door behind him. I realized that I had said a terrible thing; it made my mother gasp when I told her about it. I wanted to try again. I called him up. He said that he was indeed angry with me, but relieved that I had called.

He walked me home at the end of another night. There was some hesitation. "Well, you could either go home or come up," I said.

A few evenings passed in my twin bed. He didn't like films with subtitles, I learned. He had never been to the Museum of Modern Art. I couldn't tell if these statements were the truth, or statements he made because he knew you could provoke New Yorkers by cheerfully declaring you had no real desire to avail yourself of the cultural buffet the city had laid out for you. And as we talked in the bed over the next few nights, I couldn't tell whether it mattered. I sat up in the bed, arms around my knees, while he lay next to me, propping himself up on an elbow. He had made himself at home. Men seemed to do this. To decide on you—to decide things about you before you had even noticed their eye color.

I watched him play softball one Sunday in Prospect Park with his friends. I watched him back up, up, up, to catch a fly ball, and then whip his arm out in front to toss it to whatever base needed it. Calling out directions with a fist in his glove. As he jogged into home plate, changing sides, sending a joke to another player, his voice carried across the field and it seemed as sure as his throws. I decided that he could have been a major-league baseball player, a comedian, a lawyer, a front man, a lead guitarist. It was a little unfair, I thought, for one human to be loaded up with all that grace and beauty going nowhere but toward close friends and family members. He was Gregory Peck and Cary Grant. Tall and laughing, quick to goof and crow, like my grandfather. Dark curls, decent, sturdy, with impeccable comic timing.

Then came the blue sky that seemed the sort of joke only a God could make. The instantaneous disappearance of two buildings and thousands of lives, people gone missing without a trace. An obliterating cloud had come, just as I'd feared it would, but it came as a cloud billowing out from crumbling buildings.

The television had been an electronic snow globe for months, so I walked a few blocks to Margaret's apartment. We sat in the heat in her living room on her Salvation Army furniture and watched men in khakis and women in suits run again and again from the white clouds flooding the streets. The very fact that I was sitting by Margaret, who had spent some time in Sunday school but did not think the disappearance of two buildings and thousands of lives was the prelude to Armageddon, meant that this might not be the end of the world. We waited, for hours, for the Brooklyn and Manhattan bridges to sink simultaneously or the Empire State and Chrysler buildings to implode, until Margaret said, "I guess that's enough for now," which seemed right, and she shut off the television.

At home I kept the radio on. All day and all night, even when I left the house. Wars could be declared while I slept, but I did not want silence and then a click of a knob releasing news of war or rumors of war. What must all the seven-year-olds be thinking? Children. What lies were their parents telling them so that they could sleep at night, or eat, or go to school? That was one relief—there was no other consciousness but my own to settle.

In the days that followed I walked around with my sister, with Caroline, with Elise, with him, waiting for planes to fly over us dropping bombs. My sister and I went to a service at a Catholic church in the neighborhood. We walked up the stairs and into the sanctuary, and the warm light gave calm: there was still light, still an electric company churning it out, still grids and circuits and the will to gather. But how long would we have electricity, how long before we started eating out of the cans in the back of the cupboard, until everything went gray and white?

My sister and I sat next to each other in the pew. It was as if we were sitting waiting for a plane to take off into the fog and thunder that had grounded it on the runway for hours. She put her hand over mine. When we stood up to sing, I couldn't open my mouth. I couldn't sing the hymns. I couldn't pray. I would be a fool if I opened my mouth to ask God to watch over us or give us peace after he had taken it away for thousands of people and might be preparing to end the happiness of everyone within this church and without. I could not seek consolation from him. I was ashamed that I had ever thought I could, and that death had to come within blocks to finally convince me otherwise.

"Did that make you feel any better?" I asked my sister when we were out on the street.

"Sort of," she said. She took my hand and we walked down Sixth Avenue. There was only my sister, the two of us still able to talk to each other and eat with each other, and there would always be my sister. That was all I was able to hope for.

I went to Mass in the city alone a few weeks later. An imam and a rabbi had come to speak, and I listened to their words about peace and brotherhood from a seat in the back of the church. The words were pieces of art on display—something beautiful from another time that I could sit and appreciate but not be expected to get caught up in or do anything about.

Faith in any incarnation was troubling. I could not look at the posters of the missing in Union Square. The missing were not missing, they were dead.

I kept going to Mass, thinking that belief might come back to me, even though I knew it would not. I quit it easily—so easily it made me wonder if I had been headed there all along. The Christian life now seemed like a set of calisthenics that I had done since birth and would have to do until death. There was no transcendence, only calisthenics. You had to get in vans. You had to sing the songs. You had to read the Bible and pray every day, in the morning and at night. You had to play piano during offertory. You had to help the church secretary collate notes on index cards for the pastor's sermons. You had to help out in the nursery. You had to teach Sunday school. You had to lead Bible study. You had to show up for meetings to mix with other Christians. Go on retreats. Bite your tongue when you felt anger or selfishness surging to the tip of it. Train yourself to discount several voices at once—your own, reason's, and the voice of God as it had been rendered by various powers over the centuries—in order to fix on something that felt like truth. I had done all these things. I had never expected fiery signs to tell me I was on the right path. I most often thought I heard God speaking in the still, small voice the Bible said he used. But God's voice had only been the sound of my own idea of him echoing back to me—an idea that had never really differed from the one I'd been handed in childhood, in that basement.

I let myself give in to the doubts that had always been there. I let myself give in to facts. Stories unearthing the widespread abuse of children by priests were everywhere that winter, and I could not sit in a Catholic church without wondering if the priest in front of us had ever abused a child, or thought about abusing a child, or kept silent if he knew a child had been abused. I could not sit in a Catholic church without thinking it was a corrupt institution that cared more for its princes than its faithful. Sitting there would be tacit approval. I stopped going. Doubt now claimed me. Mystery was unacceptable.

If you took God away, it left you with people. What you expected from them was up to you. Whatever you withstood or expected—you wrote your own law, and you gathered the people around you who withstood and expected the same. After that—I was tired of thinking about it.

The person I loved had been raised with Christianity, and though he had stopped believing at twelve, he was glad that he had been taught what it taught early on. If anyone needed proof that you did not need to live with God to live in kindness and patience, he was it. I believed him: his life *would* be all right. It was good to stand next to him, and tilt my head up to his face when we walked down the street. I did not need Christianity to practice how to love. I needed only to love him.

At night, in his apartment, I would lie in the dark under the covers, watching him stand in the bathroom brushing his teeth, the water running, while I waited for him, feeling expectant, protected, my limbs too heavy to move toward anyone else but him. It seemed that you did not fall in love so much as drift, edge, and creep. For the first time in my life my mouth had fallen silent. I had turned into a cat that liked to drop itself down next to him wherever he was—the couch, the bed, the movies, the subway—and doze in contentment next to his goodness, height, and laughter. It made me suspicious. He could tell.

"You're going to run away, aren't you?" he said. We were walking around his neighborhood at ten o'clock at night, because I wanted to visit an outlandish display of Christmas lights. I was eating a sandwich, which was the first thing I'd eaten all day.

"You're going to have to untie my knots if you want me," I said.

"You're a head case," he said, watching me throw the sandwich papers away. "A nutjob."

My father had once or twice used those words to describe me, also shaking his head and smiling. They were the words of men who had no time for pretension, for equivocation, for dithering, for thinking when thinking was useless. I needed to stop hesitating. I had not done well at deciding what would make a satisfying day job or who would make a suitable companion. Converting hadn't cured me of lust for the unattainable—it might even have been a symptom of that sickness. I needed to let him stop me from thinking and wanting; all my thinking and wanting had done no good.

"Are you in love?" Caroline asked. She and I were looking at each other across some bar stools one evening while a young Russian man played a Billy Ocean song on a piano.

Was I in love? I thought so. He seemed to be in love. There were flowers sent unexpectedly to work. There were gleaming appliances that plugged into computers and televisions. Dinners and dinners. Money had been laid out—an amount of money that seemed foolish to me, given that neither of us made very much of it. That must be love.

It did not matter that, more than occasionally, video game gunshots and a pile of green bottles and pizza boxes greeted me when I entered his apartment. That the one time I took him to Mass, he shuddered at having to hold strangers' hands during the Lord's Prayer and the way he went on about how creepy it was, you'd think I'd taken him to a key party or a séance. That on Sunday afternoons his living room could be fogged over with the static of televised sports, a Sunday-afternoon sound that had depressed me when I'd come upon it at other houses as a kid, a sound that my father had never forced on us, a sound that meant you couldn't come up with anything better to do. That one night, in a pizza place, when I was in the middle of what I thought was an impassioned and informed diatribe against the media, he leaned across the table and said, "Shut up!"

"Why?" I said. "What did I say?"

He lowered his voice. There was no malice, just desperation to get me under control. "You're really loud, and people are looking over here."

I lowered my voice. "I wasn't that loud!"

"You were! And you were going on about things that none of us can change, and I don't see what the point is in getting so upset over things we can't change."

I stared at him. It was one thing to not believe in God, but another thing entirely to not believe in conversation as sport and catharsis. It was as if he'd stopped me mid-kiss to tell me he couldn't stand the taste of my mouth. I wanted to tell him that, but he might think that I was overreacting. I might have been. I ran in the direction of the adolescent retort. "So if we can't talk about the things we can't change, I guess this means we won't ever be talking about the Israeli-Palestinian conflict, or—"

"I get it," he said, shifting in his seat. "I'm sorry."

I guessed I was in love, because I had been able to push this incident, and other troubling attitudes and habits, to the back of my mind.

"Well," Caroline said. "Imagine them dead. Imagine them dying. Then how do you feel? If the thought of it scares you, then you probably are."

The exercise had light-as-a-feather-stiff-as-a-board overtones, but Caroline was Caroline, and I closed my eyes. I saw his long body in the coffin, mouth set, hands over his chest. Still pink. Lilies at the altar. Like on Good Friday. I thought of the way contemplating the crucifixion had always called up sorrow, unworthiness, faith, and resolve. Those were the things I felt when I imagined him dead. Unworthiness and resolve. When I thought of him dead, I thought of how I wanted to make him happy, how I wanted to become less cramped of heart for him. I wanted to stop being late, being sloppy, being cold and unyielding.

Caroline asked me that question only once, but I poked myself with it constantly. People in love should be able to produce a ledger showing that expenditure had led to gain. If asked, I could run a sharpened pencil down the side of a page, ticking off all the ways my life had changed for the better: improved audiovisual arrangements, miles of California desert, sexual creaturehood, relative sanity. But what did he have to show for being in love with me? What would his ledger say?

"What do I give you?" I would ask him. I was good at the commemorative collage: origami paper, clippings, and text for his birthday or Valentine's Day. And he thought he had a good in-house editor. But the refurbished old record player ordered from far away broke shortly after he received it. Months would go by before blinds would be hung like he asked. Months would go by before we actually slept together. Four years would go by before he got the new belt he kept asking me for.

"I just like being around you," he would answer. "Being around you makes me happy." One more thing I had to take on faith.

I knew I was in love because he had revealed that I was indeed female. I was crying, I was cooking, I could get pregnant if we weren't careful. The bras that had seen me through college and most of New York had been retired. Sleepy's took my twin bed away and left me a queen-size mattress with a bed frame, and to celebrate we ordered Thai food and had a picnic on top of it. He was showing me I was more than a mind. Sometimes it made me hate him.

If he looked back on us years later, perhaps all he would see would be a triptych of me bursting into tears—in cars, in airports, on subway platforms—while he stood watching. We'd be out, talking of nothing, and then he'd be standing next to a small rumpled weeping heap. Or he would drop me off at my apartment after a weekend away, or put me on a plane while he stayed on in a city for work, and I would be paralyzed at the thought of hours or days without him. He might be driving, and then there would be crumpling, and he would pull over so that he could figure out what was under the small rumpled weeping heap, to see who was in there. I didn't know who was in there—apparently it was an inconsolable five-year-old who needed him like she used to need her mother. But I'd never been that kind of child. I couldn't explain to myself why I needed him near me and why there were no words for it, and if he could take words away from me and leave me in a soundless, incoherent ache, then I must be in love.

Realizing that I enjoyed pleasing someone I loved by cooking—more than realizing I could acquit myself at sex—this was also how I knew that I had become what you might call a *woman*. In that MayaAngelouArethaFranklinCelestialSeasoningslunarphasefolicacidrunwiththewolvesDemeterandPersephonediffusewheretheyarelinearhipsandmakersthiswoman'sworkputalittlebitofsugarinmybowl way. With a new apartment came a new refrigerator and a new stove—my landlord had parked two big white metal boxes from Sears in my kitchen—and I started poring over *The Joy of Cooking* the way I'd pored over my Girl Scout handbook in childhood, which is to say exhaustively, and in complete and total fascination. I prowled *Martha Stewart Living* for intricate but satisfying dishes, and lowered foil pans loaded with cheese, noodles, and an afternoon of chopping and calibration down onto the table in front of him. Each time he bloomed into happiness at their arrival, and I saw why Sylvia Plath, Mary McCarthy, and Joan Didion had been fanatical cookers and entertainers: it was one more arrow in their quiver. I might not ever have a job that I believed in, but I could stun and delight one man by producing pots of complicated sauces and plates of untough meat, and do something for him that he could never do for himself. It made me feel a little less guilty for having given up teaching English as a second language after work. If a feminist who had previously lived out of a toaster oven, partly on principle, but mostly from laziness, was moved to take up the household arts with relish and pride, simmering in sentiments she'd last seen stitched on her grandmother's potholders, then that was love.

But I had to consult books to be sure. To me he was the kind of man Jane Austen always wrote about, the sort who made the heroine feel that she should speak kinder words and give less disparaging looks. Emma Woodhouse, Catherine Morland, Fanny Price, Elizabeth Bennet, Marianne Dashwood. All those women falling in love with men who showed them to be too myopic, too judgmental, too suggestible, too rigid. How Austen corrected them in the form of a spouse.

*Middlemarch*. Dorothea Brooke had made the tragic mistake of acting on the belief that the really wonderful marriage must be one in which your husband taught you Hebrew. This city was filled with Casaubons, dried stalks of young men castrating themselves with ambition and self-seriousness before you could do it for them, who at parties saw only a black hole dropping down to a womb when you opened your mouth to make a joke or a point. Except they were much worse than Casaubon because they actually produced. And produced and produced. He could not teach me Hebrew, but he told me, whenever it surfaced, that I had to take every bit of self-deprecation out of what I wrote and said, and the more I followed his direction, the stronger and less easily wounded I became. I swore as a matter of course now—fuck those Casaubons!—and he often blamed himself for that.

*Jane Eyre*. Rochester mistook a stormy, stiff-backed girl for a bird, for a fairy, for an imp—flittering things that went where the wind did. He gave her nicknames that were wide of the mark, names that showed he was blind even before he lost his sight. But when he gave me nicknames, they fit warm and snug. He sketched quickly but thoroughly in his mind before he spoke them aloud, and at just the right moment.

Mary Wollstonecraft had died so that women and men might live in friendship, and he and I gave it to each other. "Were women more rationally educated," she wrote, "could they take a more comprehensive view of things, they would be contented to love but once in their lives; and after marriage calmly let passion subside into friendship—into that tender intimacy, which is the best refuge from care; yet is built on such pure, still affections, that idle jealousies would not be allowed to disturb the discharge of the sober duties of life, nor to engross the thoughts that ought to be otherwise employed. This is a state in which many men live; but few, very few women." This was what I required of love: an equality in which no one accused the other of being an irrational female, or an oblivious male. We both understood that we shared the burden of being flawed.

And that we had to make each other laugh. And get the other a doughnut if doughnuts were wanted, though it was agreed upon that he had the right to take a much larger bite out of my doughnut than I would ever take out of his, because he had a boyish, indiscriminate appetite, and I liked to watch it flare up. It meant he could do anything and go anywhere if we decided to. So there was tender intimacy of the sort Mary Wollstonecraft demanded, and there were often doughnuts and coffee in a car with David Bowie playing, with the feeling that we were kids on the lam from juvie hall, but also as placid and fused as those old Russian couples airing themselves out in Prospect Park, and if you told me that passion, having been kindled and fired into sex, eventually subsided into years of such pure, still affection, and that this was love, I wouldn't mind one bit.

# CHAPTER 13

## LIKE DISASTER

After hopping from one job to the next, I found one I liked. I checked facts for a magazine. No one threw things or made me come in before ten, and in return for my hard work I received a regular paycheck that allowed me to eat overpriced chicken salad sandwiches on a daily basis, and write the occasional article because I wanted to, or had been asked to, not because I had to pay a bill. My bosses were generous and sympathetic, so I stayed put.

Three years passed, and I moved to a desk that gave me a view of the Empire State Building. Looking at it made me want to cross myself. When I stayed late to write, I liked to stand in front of the window and look down on Times Square and across to the Hudson, committing the colors of the sky to memory. In those moments it was enough to know that I had that view behind me as I tapped at a keyboard. Even if it was unclear where the writing would go, it was the attempt, and the setting of the attempt, that counted, and if the attempts never added up to anything as grand as the view, I could console myself by thinking I had at least done what I'd said I wanted to do in my high school yearbook —"live and write in NYC." But my high school self would have none of it. She reminded me of our

position: Since when have we ever been fulfilled by merely satisfying the minimum requirements?

On the forty-seventh floor I could see the traffic but not hear
it; I could hear the city move, but those who steered it were invisible. After seven years in New York, the influential were still as
distant as the lights of New Jersey. I could stand at the window re-
joicing in my innocence—I had not dirtied my hands! No one had
crushed me, because *no one knew where I was!*—but I also pined for
a way down into the action, imagining the flirting, the banter, the
sizing up and putting off taking place on the streets below, wondering how many of the taxis moving down Broadway were carrying young women to advantageous assignations or professionally
fruitful dinner parties. I heard how the city worked from friends
who were bold enough to mingle in circles where the insincere often
descended—plummeted—into the cruel, and their gossip brought
me as close as I could stand to be. Backstabbing, freeze-outs, flagrant theft of intellectual property—it made my heart lurch to hear
of it, when it didn't entertain me immensely.

The friends I'd made at work would call me to the window to
watch the sky bruise and flame as the sun went down, and it seemed
a miracle, here in New York, to be alerted to sunsets by coworkers; it spoke of cordiality, of civility, of friendship untainted by
ulterior motives. We holed up in each other's offices with coffee,
jokes, and grievances, trading notes on books and movies, telling
the ongoing stories of families and boyfriends—and careers, such
as they were. When mired in a triumph of stupidity, the women I
worked with sighed and said, "It's hard to remember that there's
a whole other level of discourse," or when confronted with a
Barbara Kingsolver novel, said, "Life's too short." They coined
memorable, hilarious phrases that allowed us all to diagnose, and
then dismiss, trying people and situations. They stayed late. They

edited each other's work. They bought each other lunch, drinks, or flowers as needed. They stood down lazy journalists. They also knew their limits—which might have been our downfall. We knew too well what we would never do to get ahead. But it made me proud to know them. My business card might not impress certain people at certain parties, but I'd found the office camaraderie I'd been searching for, and if I had to hide out in a skyscraper to have it, I would.

With these women I felt comfortable enough to pull out the words *mind* and *soul* in the middle of the day. Or *Jesus*. For that I would seek out my friend Amy, who once said to me that she sometimes thought that the moment you mentioned you believed in God out loud in New York, people would look at you as if you'd instantly sprouted stirrup pants and a Scünci. We were the daughters of prayer warriors who had enrolled us in dance school and men who sold cars. We were perhaps the only two women in that building—on that block, in the city—so blessed.

"Amy," I would say before I got up to go back to my desk, putting my hand on her knee, "God has laid a burden on my heart for you."

Amy had wanted to be an actress, so she could keep a straight face. "I'll lift you up and remember you in prayer," she'd say to me, her hand on my knee, all Tennessee Methodist sincerity. And then we'd crack up, Amy's laugh ringing out like gunfire let loose by Loretta Lynn above the cubicles. Sometimes Amy would close it out by exclaiming, "Praise!" or its variant, "Praise Jah!" This way we said to each other, *I know, I know.* But when your mother still prayed for you, throwing her voice was a hard trick to pull off. I would walk back to my desk, thinking I could hear God—no, our mothers—telling us that we might be big-city big shots snickering away in our tall buildings, but the last laugh would be on us. In hell.

Down on the street at lunch, walking among the out-of-town girls streaming up Broadway, trapped in the mob of vacant eyes rimmed in smudged liner swarming Times Square at noon, hell could sometimes feel closer than our mothers imagined. Blond, tan, plump, square-faced girls trussed into khaki jackets and billowing cotton skirts. Girls squat and iced in pastels like petits fours, sipping pink and yellow drinks as they trudge through Times Square clutching bags from the MTV store, Hershey's, Virgin Records, and Planet Hollywood. The anxieties and complacencies of the mothers written on the faces of the daughters as they shout, "Mom!" over their shoulders to get them to shut up or hurry up. In the elevator back up to the office someone's *New York Post* tells me that there's more squabbling over the plans for Ground Zero. New York, you'll make a mall out of a mass grave. New York. And here are the show ponies with their copies of *Us Weekly* and *Star*, turning off their pink and blue iPods and then dropping them into their bags like packs of gum. We get off on the same floor and they always stride purposefully—officiously?—in this season's heels from Barneys in the direction of the magazine's marketing and publicity department, but I might never know for sure what they do at the company because we studiously ignore each other in the reception area while waiting for the ride down, my eyes fixed on framed covers of the magazine, their thumbs scrolling away at their BlackBerries. What music could they possibly need that badly? I strain to listen, but one of them is snapping her gum. It's their city, too. It's their city entirely. They're why the Howard Johnson's on 46th Street will close, why new condominiums proliferate, why money has been steadily wiping away what looks like grime but is only just history, why the Associated Food in my neighborhood ripped up the linoleum and put in faux hardwood floors, and while I am not against renovation, I'm not sure it's worth spiffing the place up if you can't keep your produce from rotting. Elevators all over Manhattan are full of these women: blond hair bright in ponytails, bodies without an extra ounce of fat. Or plump and self-satisfied with the correctness of their accessories. Handbags like lapdogs, lapdogs bedecked with buckles, trailing long strips of leather—Orthodox boys trail tzitzit under their untucked dress shirts, and these girls are as marked by their superfluous leather. Coats and shirts and pants never rumpled, never stained. Shoes pointing forward, never cracked. Boots shining and taut. Hair pulled back, hair straightened, hair highlighted. They have no problem in giving themselves over to the law, and don't strain to fulfill it. They willingly eat nothing but salads and drink nothing but Crystal Light in the service of perfection. They keep bouncing on the treadmill, faces free of expression or sweat. They're as scared of their own smells and hair as we all were in seventh grade. Which makes me as enraged as I was back then at the lies still circulating that make us curb our appetites and smooth ourselves down into sheets of acetate satin. How is it that I am standing here and they are standing there? Love of sex, learned early on behind the bleachers? Why else the Brazilian waxes? I do not want their jobs or their lives, but sometimes I would like to have their shoes, and in order to buy those shoes in good conscience, one must take up those jobs and those lives. I wonder if they are looking at my shoes and thinking anything about them. Doubtful. Can they tell that I burst out of things, my shoes scuff up, my tights run, and I sweat from drinking too much coffee because I manage a staff and find, to quote Kierkegaard, being an authority the most boring thing in the world? I may look at them, but the women in my elevator don't look at me. In another building, blocks away, women in elevators had forced Caroline, just by standing next to her and barely flicking their eyes her way, to shove her feet into expensive pointed-toe heels so she could rise above the feeling that she was merely a member of their retinue. These women might force us to change, but we could not force them to do anything. It looked like we had won a few years ago, what with the Doc Martens and Alanis Morissette, but these women would win in the end. They wanted the things the world rewarded us for wanting: money and sex. They did not get mixed up in God and books—*Bor*-ing!— and instead ran straight for whatever would please themselves, like greedy, canny squirrels. They made me think that if I had lived solely as a body, not minding God or books, my sleep would now be untroubled.

Back on the forty-seventh floor in a conference room of women, I felt no safer. Sitting at the bottom of the long table at meetings reminded me of sitting at the adults' table at Thanksgiving—but instead of being forced to face the existence of gout and cancer, I was forced to face the existence of infertility, infidelity, nannies, and contractors. At thirty-one, I had no money, no baby, no real estate, and no real desire for any of those things. Should I ever decide to wake up and remember I had fallopian tubes, I was banking on my genes to pull me through to late-in-life motherhood—my great-grandmother had given birth to my grandmother, the last of seven, at forty-three. But listening to my older colleagues could start me thinking I'd been irresponsible in not rapidly succeeding to my specifications—if I had, I might not be so reluctant to give my life over to a child—and in failing to consider a man's earning potential when I considered his worth.

"Well," a woman said one day at a meeting, "I certainly never expected to marry my soul mate."

Another one laughed. "Tell me about it," she said.

A third colleague was as startled and confused as I was, and she spoke up. "But Bill is *my* soul mate! What are you guys talking about?"

There was laughter, but no one answered the question. I took the laughter to mean that if you married someone for their intelligence and imagination, you were condemning yourself to unkempt houses, money troubles, the quicksand generated when two people were depressed and anxious and ambitious at once. They were laughing, I thought, at women like me, who had been known to tear up at footage of the young Joan Baez singing with the young Bob Dylan. But my father thought my mother was his soul mate. What would they say to my father, who was as hard-nosed as they came? Perhaps when I got back to my desk, I should call and tell him that here in New York we have discovered that the marriage of true minds is a lie, and he could laugh and tell me how dumb we all were up in our skyscrapers.

On Saturday night, at parties thrown by the girls from work, I could believe again that the war between men and women might be over, and that it was right to persist in living by what we'd read in college. I watched these girls and their men move through the night, and watched how these boys, these men, stood on watch as their girls stalked success. These men talked straight, wore sneakers, were birds of dun plumage. Their women were feathered with bright chatter, withering one-liners, ambition, desire, neuroses. In their sparkling vintage dresses and shoes the women were the stars, generating heat and light. And the men were content to bask in it, reaching out to touch the hair, the shoulders, the backs of their beautiful, willful, brilliant girls.

I watched my friend as he made people laugh and then laughed himself, beer in hand, at their stories. It was a point of pride, that he and I could spend a party apart—see how we are not crutches for each other? And then the relief of returning to him at the end, full of anecdotes and impressions, comparing notes as we walked to the subway.

Sunday mornings we sat on the couch drinking coffee and handing sections of the paper to each other. We took walks together around the neighborhood, and as we walked he would say that it was a shame that I had never lived in Manhattan. But I didn't care. You could *smell* things in Brooklyn. The ammonia from cleaned school hallways leaking out on to the street, childhood wafting back to us. Roses. You could smell the sour, tangy scent of boxwoods planted earlier in the century—the smell of my grandmother's yard. There were sounds other than traffic. You could hear the trickling of the fountain in St. Augustine's churchyard and its bells ringing on the hour. When the sun went down, you could smell dinner being prepared. Steak. I could always smell steak. Peering into basement apartments, into first-floor windows, watching families gather. Imagining all the daughters in their bedrooms with books, lying there stuffing themselves with just a few more pages before their mother's voice, calling up the stairs once more, turned insistent.

But on Sunday nights, he could seem like nothing more than a body docked next to mine in bed, only something creaking and rolling in the night. When I was small and waiting for sleep, the thought of heaven—the unending chore of singing God's praises in an unending stretch of white—bored and terrified me. Now it was marriage that appalled in the middle of the night, and there was no God to call on to quiet the static of worry. Were we each the end of the other's life?

He was my first, and I thought it meant we were going to marry, because I'd known several girls who stopped at the one they started with—some with lovely men, but some with inexplicable men, and it was the inexplicable ones who made me think this was a fate to be avoided at all costs. I wanted to marry, and I might want to marry my friend, but—I could not think clearly on that point, and on many points, because my mind was in rebellion against both God and the world as lived, and having no faith in either, it pinwheeled with resentment, panic, and regret. There was the girl who stayed up all night writing and proofreading her sentences, and then there was the girl who fantasized about breaking a leg and having a doctor write a note excusing her from capitalism so that she could lie around and read all day. The girl who could stay up all night writing and proofreading had not yet found her calling, but she could stay up all night scouring her life for missed opportunity.

I would stay up listening to phantom reproach. My two daughters—I wanted two so that they would have each other to snack and chortle with—would not be satisfied with stories of the Empire State Building standing at a forbidding yet tantalizingly intimate remove. *Mother!* they would say. *You were born in 1973, in the year of the zipless fuck—the birthright of your generation!—and you somehow never, ever availed yourself of its pleasures! You never studied abroad in London, your spiritual birthplace, or charmed an Englishman to follow you back across the pond. You were living in New York City among nonfinanciers but never once found yourself as the muse of a painter, a singer, or a poet, even after you pushed God to one side. What souvenirs do you have piled up to show us that you were not your mother, after all? That shy Scottish man in the Glasgow club who sat on some stairs chatting with you about the Talking Heads while Caroline made out with his redheaded friend, who seemed to be a combination of soccer thug and East End gangster? Please! We'll be writing novels entirely in Mandarin and marrying French presidents before we're twenty-one, you'll see.*

If we slept in his bedroom, I would stare at his bookcase, which contained more personal effects than books, and was empty in spots, and wonder if he had been sent to teach me that there were more important things than books. I'd thought that the person you

loved should be the one with whom you lost your way—the one
with whom you estranged yourself from the familial. But with him
I felt the same way I'd felt around my family—a little bookworm
lost in her own world, praised for it, thought amusing for it, but
never joined in it. My mother would drop me off at the library while
she did errands, and I'd walk through the doors, anticipating an
hour spent in no noise but footsteps and creaking floors. I'd kneel
on the carpet to look through the books on bottom shelves, creeping around the aisles, a calm growing inside me as the pile of books
on the floor grew taller—a calm like that of church, but better than
church, because here I was free to roam and circle back among pos-
sibilities, to choose and reject as I liked. Kneeling in the aisles exam-
ining jackets and copyright pages, transfixed by even the addresses
of publishers as I paused to think of the snappily dressed people who
must have been streaming in and out of those Manhattan buildings
that very minute. And then coming out in the sun to my mother in
the car, keeping all that I'd thought to myself—Kerouac's poems
were terrible, what was the big deal, where was the book I'd read
about in the paper, why did I look at *Absalom, Absalom* and then
walk away from it back toward *Bright Lights, Big City*, was that a
failure of taste or was it just summer, I guess I should want to read
Anne Sexton but her poems seem glib and gossipy and since loyalty
to one suicidal lady poet was probably one loyalty too many, it was
going to Sylvia, was it shallow to check out a book because of its
cover, or lose interest in it because of its cover, was it silly to visit
the juvenile section to make sure the books I'd checked out years
ago were still there, taking them down off the shelves to feel the
grain of the mid-century paper, run my fingers over the grooves of
the ink-and-pen illustrations, and sniff them the way you'd sniff a
baby's head when I thought no one was looking? And then back to
our house, which had only one bookshelf, filled with study guides to

the Bible and the unread biographies I'd given my parents, and up to my bedroom to splay myself out under some author's spell until dinner.

The plan had been to turn those hours in the library from secretive pleasure to vocation—to avoid becoming an adult who would look back fondly on those hours as nothing more than a childhood idyll. I was still struggling to make good on those hours, still struggling to convince myself it was going to be worth it, and it was lonely, while struggling, to love someone for whom books no longer mattered like they once had in childhood and college; that part of his life, he admitted, had ended when he started working in New York. To his credit, I kept reminding myself. To his credit! But the loneliness remained. How could it be that books were left behind, largely, in our conversations, that the hours spent reading were still a secretive pleasure, that I felt as if I were still not yet fully known, as if part of me was in storage, waiting to come out—and how to even allow myself to say that this was disappointing, and sad?

He did listen when I couldn't help but talk about it. In the car on the way back from a trip to visit my aunt in Maine, I had to tell him of the awful things that had happened to the subject of a biography I'd been reading—had to tell him as if she were someone we knew personally and wished the best for, and he exclaimed over the story and laughed at my retelling. I was grateful and happy for his indulgence, but I wanted him to share passions with me too— passions different than his own, ones that proved his mind had traveled to out-of-the-way places, ones I'd heard of but never made it to. It wasn't enough that he let me talk of dead people as if they were alive; I wanted him to have some imaginary realm he liked to climb into that didn't involve tabulating box scores or ranking record albums, a realm we could visit together on equal footing of enthusiasm and wonder.

It was asking too much, I thought, to have both love and intellectual companionship. If I was loved, and so well, I had no business trying to get out of it. And if I felt like Alice Kramden sometimes, shaking my head whenever he proved that boys would be boys by grumbling about having to go to dinner with friends on the night of a playoff, and resented him for turning me into Alice Kramden, that was my problem, for ever having thought men and women had evolved past that comic strip.

I made my longing his problem, too. It was the only thing we argued about—and he indulged me there, as well, because I was always the one bringing it up, thinking that if we talked about it, we would somehow find a way to bring about the intellectual companionship I wanted, thinking that honesty was a form of faithfulness, and talking was indeed a cure. Or I would learn that I didn't really need it, or he would live up to his potential, or a compromise between the two would emerge, and then we'd get married. Or then he'd make me laugh, and I'd forget all about it, because when he made me laugh I saw his mind at work—bounding over all the usual images, rolling around in wordplay, making a break for the lunatic—and when I laughed, breathless, helpless, I fell in love. Sex bound people, but so did laughing. When we made each other laugh—building on each other's jokes, piling on unlikely scenarios and acting out parts—I thought that was collaboration enough.

But wasn't it my responsibility, now that it was not God's, to arrange my own happiness? I could not trust my gut or my mind to lead me there. I had never learned to trust either of them; Christianity taught that wisdom lay beyond you, not within you. People who had never known God walked around on the street secure in their judgment, letting their own powers of reason serve as their compass, considering that compass a fairly stable mechanism to set store by, and I envied them for their ignorance. I was cursed: I had been given a very specific and detailed description of love, and it was impossible for me to dismiss it and proceed as if whatever I'd found true or useful from literature was as dependable. Especially if, when I turned to literature the way I used to turn to the Bible, the joke was on me. I read *Anna Karenina* because I wanted to know what Tolstoy would have to say about a woman torn, and finished it feeling exhilarated but more than a little ripped off—not because Anna saw death as the only solution to her struggle, but because Levin bowed finally to Christ. Eight hundred pages on marriage and yearning, and Tolstoy wanted us to know that Jesus was the way, the truth, and the life? "Are you kidding me?" I cried aloud when the final passages came into view. Oh, and Dostoyevsky, too! Both of those swindlers, reeling me in with their sympathy for the tortured conscience—only to wrap it up neatly with a commercial for Jesus! If I tried to live by words other than his, God wanted me to know, he would scoop me up like the prodigal daughter I was and lock me back up in his care, where I would never again take issue with that verse from Jeremiah: *the heart is deceitful above all things.*

To have love that was predicated on a shared belief in what you'd both read in books seemed like a luxury, a fantasy, the sort of thing only people who had not been raised in the suburbs by a family constitutionally unable to get above their station, and with a God who demanded self-sacrifice, could get away with. To walk away from someone because his heart impressed me more than his mind—this was the whim of a sexual epicurean or the shortsighted snobbery of a teenager. But didn't some people have a long-running, highly arousing dialogue that lasted until death? Yes, and they were the people of fiction. But didn't many of my friends have this? Yes, and they were not cursed. I didn't feel comfortable being the only authority I had to answer to, because I saw my mind as diseased, flighty, untested. If I had to write my own version of love, it would not be legitimate. It would hurt someone.

Who needed bad dreams, I thought, when this was what I put myself through while lying awake?

In the mornings I told myself—as my mother used to tell me whenever she saw me moping—to snap out of it. I took spiritual classics with me on the subway. *The Seven Storey Mountain*, *Gravity and Grace*. I knew no other way to remind myself that the self was nothing and the other everything. If you lived your life according to that principle, I thought, even if you did not believe in God, you could not help but be happy and quiet at heart. You could stop yourself from sinning against another. I would renounce all my worry and desire and stay with the one who loved me.

I went out to a party with Elise, reluctantly, and someone approached me. His name was Mark. He decided what was going to happen to us. First, he announced that I would accompany him down the stairs and out on the street while he smoked. I followed him down and then back up. There was loud gregariousness. There were booming, declarative statements. At six foot three, he seemed to be the only thing in that small room. *You there*, his look said, and I excused myself to find Elise. Elise, who had introduced us, had smoked pot for the first time that evening, and was lying flat on her back on the carpet under a table. I crawled under the table to lie next to my murmuring friend, whom I loved because she threw herself into life, thinking, What is going on? How long can we go on pretending we are still seventeen? What do our parents think of us? My sister and I, still unmarried, while our cousins had three children between them, children that my mother and father doted on as if they had been ours, which filled us with shame, even though my mother and father repeatedly assured us that they did not want us to hurry up and find husbands just to give them grandchildren. And then all of us here tonight, in our late twenties and early thirties, roaming around someone's apartment getting high and drunk and boasting about concerts we'd seen. Mark found us under the table, rounded the rest of the girls up and got us all home. It was late. Elise was struggling to appear well and lucid in the cab, apologizing even as she vomited out of the open door. After everyone had emptied out of the car, he announced that we would go for a drink, just the two of us.

At the bar, he put some songs on the jukebox. One of them was "Down in the Tube Station at Midnight." And then he told me what the song was about—I'd never realized Paul Weller was singing about a mugging. It was a small thing, maybe a stupid thing, to seize on, but I liked being told something I didn't know about subjects I thought I had covered. He talked about England, socialism, the seventies, Thatcher. He was neither pompous nor hesitant; he knew a lot, but didn't want to oppress me with his knowledge. I talked about kitchen sink dramas, angry young men, *Billy Liar*, the domestic novel. He smiled. And then he kissed me in the bar, midsentence. I had always been the one telling people to shut up and start kissing, and this seemed like a meaningful reversal. This was what I had been waiting for—for someone to fall out of the sky and knock me down. For someone to make it look like an accident—like my departure was nothing I could help.

I thought and thought, and my friend receded. If I stayed with him, it would be in deference to rules drawn up by the God of my childhood, and that was cowardice. Look around, I told myself, look at the evidence—all your friends have lived their lives without God's guidance, and they have yet to blindly pitch into sloughs. Take responsibility for your desires—don't stifle them under superstition.

*That* was maturity. To stay would make me feel that I'd been gagged and bound by the old ideas, and that was not fair to either of us. That was going to be even uglier and unhappier than leaving.

He thought we had a story, but it wasn't the story I wanted. My imagination had failed in that regard. But I could no longer listen to God, or Thomas Merton, or Kierkegaard, or Iris Murdoch, or anyone else who I'd let talk me into thinking that what I thought would make me happy was nothing more than vanity and inexperience. I needed to prove myself wrong.

"The imagination, filler up of the void, is essentially a liar," Simone Weil wrote. But how much of our lives were spent imagining? And how different was imagination from hope, when in summer the world existed to give you what you had never been given before?

On the trees the leaves rustled and quieted like birds settling themselves down in nests. We sat on a hill in the park.

He understood what I felt—he'd started late himself—but he pleaded.

"Can't you give in?" he said. "Can't you just forget all your questions?"

I'd stopped believing in God because I had too many questions, I told him. If I had to love someone the way I had to love God, I would have to leave.

Mark had abandoned a PhD in philosophy to work with computers. He made three times as much as I did but wore faded navy blue T-shirts with holes and unraveling seams that he had worn as a teenage clerk in a record store. I thought I might be in love because I'd started to decorate him with metaphors. His mind was an attic full of the best that had been known and thought in the world, full of thoughts piled up like skulls inside him. His mind was a dark, icy ocean of code and logic that I would never cross. And then he would drop down to his knees on a sidewalk to go nose to nose with a stranger's golden retriever, as if he and the animal were old friends having a chance meeting, old friends with the same strong, heedless heart.

With him I thumbed my nose at conscientiousness. While other people were becoming famous, I was leaving the house at ten at night to sit with him in bars and pump jukeboxes full of dollars. There was romance in this to me—the romance of pure hanging out, of making a date for the languorous exchange of opinion. Hanging out had never been fully experienced—it had always been skipped over or fraught with someone's impending disappearance, but with Mark, I felt that I was young, and properly so; in New York, and properly so. Better late than never. One night in the favorite bar he'd put on a live Otis Redding song that, according to him, went into such a frenzy at the end it was not soul but punk. "Here it comes," he said, touching my arm, looking at the ceiling toward the speakers, and then looked back at me, smiling. *What did I tell you?* said his look. It was like being caught in sudden rain together, sitting there under that noise. It seemed that he was often showing me something I'd never seen or heard. And then we'd stay up even later because I'd learned that while there was probably no such thing as mind-blowing illicit sex—illicit because I felt as if I was on the run from two people, those people being God and my friend—there was such a thing as sex that was quietly, alluringly different. That was dangerous enough, because related to that finding was a realization that sex was really just a slightly more complicated way to have a conversation. And now I wanted to talk to anyone who'd listen.

Everywhere I turned there were delights behind apartment doors and in bars and the backyards of friends; the city was a radio that gave me "Wouldn't It Be Nice" every which way I turned the dial.

The Empire State Building was still standing, no one had come for that yet, the white dust had blown away, and here was summer, green coming back to us again and again. Hymns came to mind as I walked under trees.

> *Praise to the Lord, who o'er all things*
> *So wondrously reigneth,*
> *Shelters thee under His wings,*
> *Yea, so gently sustaineth!*
> *Hast thou not seen*
> *How thy desires e'er have been*
> *Granted in what He ordaineth?*

You could try to leave church behind, but the only way to articulate joy would be through hymns. I wouldn't admit this to Mark, even though he was the kind of atheist who had affection for the bearded old coot of William Blake's paintings, and had encouraged me to remain a believer. "Many of the world's greatest minds have believed in Jesus!" he said, one night on the way to the favorite bar. "Even Wittgenstein felt his pull!"

He told me that he had memorized some of "Dover Beach" after coming across it again on a subway poster. He recited it once. Carefully, not looking at me, and it sounded as if he'd memorized this for the same reason I'd memorized certain psalms: as something to hang on to in an anguish. I'd forgotten—if I'd ever known—how beautiful the poem was. His voice came slow and steady like lava scalding its way to the sea, telling me that

> *the world, which seems*
> *To lie before us like a land of dreams,*
> *So various, so beautiful, so new,*

*Hath really neither joy, nor love, nor light,*
*Nor certitude, nor peace, nor help for pain;*
*And we are here as on a darkling plain*
*Swept with confused alarms of struggle and flight,*
*Where ignorant armies clash by night.*

That summer I threw a party, and the apartment filled up quickly. Mark arrived in the holey T-shirt, which dismayed me, as I dismayed myself for caring what he wore. He arrived drunk. Drunk and loud. He must have been nervous. I stood in the living room having a conversation while his voice towered over the crowd. "Dick Cheney is Satan!" I moved to the kitchen, and it came at me again. "It is abundantly clear that the Beatles suck, and you must admit that I am right!"

Then I sat down with a friend whose opinion on matters aesthetic I respected, and out of nowhere she pointed to him and said, "That tall young man has a rather . . . distinctive face, don't you think?"

"Mmmm," I said, and changed the subject. I did not have the strength to tell her that when he wasn't drunkenly, haphazardly opinionated, I thought he had a rather distinguished face, all horn-rims and woodcut planes, and topped as it was with a bristle of light brown hair, it called to mind atomic scientists or English professors of the late 1950s. Right now he was looking as if he had more over-grown only child in him than previously detected.

Caroline came up to me later by the table of drink and food. "Is that the new guy you're seeing?" she said. She sounded skeptical but amused. "Brian Eno!" I heard Mark tell someone. "Brian Eno!"

"No," I said.

Near the end of the evening, my friend called, asking to come over. I agreed, thinking everyone in attendance was an adult, and a New Yorker, and as such, knew how to handle complicated situations. It was in this city that Cole Porter composed his songs of valedictory sangfroid. Discernment, empathy, and urbanity would prevail. But a woman I hardly knew, for reasons I could not guess, heard me on the phone and told Mark who was coming before I could. Mark cornered me in the bathroom. What was I doing? he wanted to know. Why was the other guy coming over? I had never learned how to fight anger, and his was throbbing, maybe violent, so I asked him to leave. I followed him out to the steps and watched him walk to the corner, fury pitching his lope into the wind. To think he would throw a punch was to err on the side of hysteria and smelling salts, but trusting in cool heads and better natures had not worked out too well this evening. Here I was at a party with a scene on my hands because I had thought too highly of myself and my desires. With friends and strangers watching me have words in corners. I appreciated scenes in novels, but it turned out that I could not handle them in real life.

"It's tough to be you," a guest said, not unkindly, one brow arched, as he shook my hand on his way out. It wasn't tough. It was fucking embarrassing.

My friend arrived. He slipped into the dark kitchen and started emptying bottles into the sink while I took a call from Mark. I could hear the glass and running water while I talked. Gentle, constant. The sound of it chastened me.

At a party on the Fourth of July, when impractical shoes were making it hard for me to climb up a fire escape to a roof where, we'd been told, we could see the whole of the city, Mark took both my arms and pulled me right up through the hole, heaving so hard the skin on my arms burned. I took his hand and we walked over to the edge of the building to watch water and lights shimmer all around us. Elise had been saying that she was looking for a man who would kill to save her life. We laughed about it, but I thought she was onto something. Years of feminism, and yet an offhand show of physical strength, offered not to impress but to solve a problem, could make me wish Mark and I were at the end of the evening already, alone.

Back downstairs at the party, I found myself talking to a man whose clothes and hair were absolutely correct, but also a little rumpled, as if he'd just landed on tarmac in the desert. He held himself like someone who knew his worth, which I could tell he thought was considerable—chin tilting up, eyes darting around the crowd, voice modulated and leached of enthusiasm. The voice of vetted New York, which was still hard for me to hear without hoping it would vet me, too, and take me home. He dropped some names, I made him laugh. I tried to make him laugh some more, to see if I could keep his eyes on me. Just to be able to say no. Or consider the offer.

Flames of appetite and vanity licking at me, rising higher, obscuring my sight, fueling foolishness—this was what sin felt like. An altered state in which good sense was seared from me and I forgot that other people might be watching, that other people existed, that anything existed other than my need for an attachment that would confer singularity upon me. *Who will be enough for you?* My friend had asked me this once, and what I knew he heard in my silence was, *No one*. And then a cautious demand for reparation: *I fear that only a rotating cast of a dozen men will be enough, and no one, not even New Yorkers, will let me get away with that.* I thought about my grandmother, who left her fiancé for his best friend, who became my grandfather, and my mother, who broke off her engagement, and my sister, who had scampered from man to man with a gleam in her eye, dispassionately noting just how much they would bear to be near her. There seemed to be some family tendency toward making chumps, and growing up I believed I could never be the sort of woman who did those things—that I must not have it in me. Yet

I did—leaving one person for another, only to entertain thoughts, however brief, of leaving that person for yet one more, knowing he wouldn't be the end of it either. My grandmother, mother, and sister never wavered after they got what they wanted—and this was what I might not have in me.

In a film from the forties, I'd be slapped in the face for my antics, but people didn't keep each other in line like that anymore. They just excused themselves politely to get a drink because you'd bored them. I got another beer and stood by myself, leaning against the building, drinking and looking at all the Williamsburg types.

Mark walked up and wrapped his arms around me from behind. With his mouth on my ear like a lion nosing some kill or his cub, he said, "Do you want to sleep with that guy?"

"No!" I said, laughing. I made a start but he held me to him. A flush ripped through me. Something else feminism had neglected to mention: sexual jealousy as powerful aphrodisiac.

"Hmm," he said, and let me go.

"What are we doing?" Mark asked me one night.

"I don't know," I said.

He stiffened. I sensed rage being summoned. "Okay," he said, "I can't do this." He climbed over me and started to put on his clothes.

"You don't have to go," I said. But maybe he did. He didn't have to wait around for me to decide whether or not I was in love with him. I thought I was, but his anger came and went too often, and there was petulance in it. Maybe even a will to possess in it. And his silences could be deep and long, leaving me wondering what to say to start the conversation back to life, feeling panicked, as if I were standing outside a locked house after midnight, wondering should I throw stones, is there a light on, did someone leave a key under the welcome mat, is there a welcome mat?

I missed my friend. I missed talking to him, telling him every single thing I did or ate or saw or heard. And I missed his running commentary. I missed his crankiness and his laugh. I wanted to make him laugh and I missed laughing. In the end we were goofballs in arms. I didn't care about what wasn't on his bookshelves anymore.

I decided to tell Mark that I thought I should leave him. I didn't want to go on uncertainly, hurting him. I walked to his apartment, climbed up the brownstone stoop, and rang the doorbell. I thought I might vomit.

"Hey!" he said, smiling to find me on his doorstep unexpectedly.

"Can I talk to you?" I said.

The smile fell. "Are you coming here to tell me that you don't think you can see me anymore?"

I was too frightened to answer. He had been walked away from recently, and here I was, about to do the same. But I was also trying to be honest and clear.

He slammed the heavy carved wooden door to his building shut. The rattle of the glass in the door's window echoed. I sat down on the stoop. Maybe he would come back down. He didn't.

I got off the stoop and walked up Sixth Avenue and then turned onto Fifth. Should I go tell my friend that it was over, that I was coming back to him? Couples were walking home from dinner out, from work, from bars. Fluorescent light shone through the windows of the bodegas and car services, bleaching the sidewalk and everyone on it. I walked around the neighborhood until I could tell myself that things were in order, that nothing was lost. The world was ticking away, and everything would be all right.

On a visit home, my father and I walked in the backyard, talking. I took off my shoes and followed him around the lawn in bare feet as he took the hose to his various trees and flowers. I told him all that had happened. The leaving, the waffling, the going from one to another and back.

He looked at me. "I didn't know you were like that," he said.

"I didn't either."

"Are you going to church?"

"Nope."

"He'll get you in the end," my father said to me. I said nothing. I stared at a rhododendron bush. I didn't want to drag out all the things that I felt I'd settled or get in the sort of useless conversation that involved explaining your position to someone who might not want to understand you so much as convince you.

"I've exhausted it all," I said. "I've got nothing left to give him."

Standing next to my father and his belief, I knew for sure that I had none. Then alone in bed, at night, I would drift back to thinking that maybe Augustine was right. *You have made us for yourself, O Lord, and our hearts are restless until they rest in you.* Praying but not praying to God to show me what to do to end my restlessness. I'd left my friend to search for shocks and charges—for what my father called sparks. My father thought that sparks were necessary, but it seemed to me that you encountered them only through great upheaval or timely accident, and I could not endure or wait for either. I wanted to stay by the side of the person who had seen me clearly and who had made me laugh. I wanted to be good—stable, faithful, intelligible to myself and others—more than I wanted to wreck lives looking for what I might never find. That was what now appalled in the middle of the night—not marriage, but the idea of a future without one friend forever by my side. And a fear that you could end up like Isabel Archer, married to a vampire because you had waited too long for the arrival of the perfect decorative complement to you the exquisite *objet*. Love was not anything that pleased your conception of it, I told myself, or embodied the images you'd fed on, cherished, and burnished. If you dreamt of it at desks, while looking up from books, and then it came to you, you should run. Electricity hummed with sign and symbol, sound and gesture. But those things would not pull you through to death.

My friend kept appearing to me on the street. In grocery stores. Coming out of subway stations. *You can't play around anymore*, he said. *We're getting old. We're all running out of time.* I had asked for a sign and received it. I gave up my questions and returned to him.

# CHAPTER 14

# THEY PAID HIM NO MIND

When you no longer talk to God, it doesn't mean that you don't think he might be trying to talk to anyone else who will listen. The city—my neighborhood—is full of his messengers. Mormons up by Prospect Park, two by two in ties. Old ladies in hats and hose marching with young ladies in rayon skirts and blouses, accosting me in the Key Food parking lot with their copies of *Awake!* Tracts pushed into the iron railings of my doorstep from the Baptist church on Sixth Avenue, study guides to Romans and John slipped in plastic bags as if they were toothbrushes and mouthwash coupons from the dentist: spiritual hygiene. God did not need me to love him. When you passed the Brooklyn Word Church on Fifth Avenue, its red carpet and stained Plexiglas cut to fit the cross-shaped windows in the wooden doors, enjoyed now only, occasionally, by an old black man in a suit watching a television full of static, it might look as if God was nowhere to be found. And the gated and padlocked Assemblée Pentecostal de la Foi Apostolique, its doors falling off their hinges and toward each other to make a pietà suggesting that sometimes the church is Christ needing us to help him carry his cross. But God lives.

God lives on the subway, and he loves to take us all hostage. God is most often a short West Indian woman wearing sturdy shoes and a crushed velvet hat with the brim folded up who uses her ear-splitting voice to curdle your goodwill first thing in the morning. Who makes girls in stylish outfits stamp their feet as they get off at the next stop, tossing their long hair, finger in a book, saying, "I haven't even had my fucking coffee yet!" to their fellow refugees. At night God is a tall West Indian man in pressed jeans and sneakers who favors a fierce look and a neat beard. "Fear God," he begins. "Fear *God.*" He stands in the middle of the car, by a pole, laying down his sermon like he's laying brick. Word after word after word. Then troweling on silence. Then word after word after word. Word after word that I want to hurl back at him because we are all sadder and wearier than we were in the morning, all of us wrung out like dishrags, everyone huddled into themselves, the fluorescent light in the 2 train harsher and brighter at night.

"If you die in your sins, you will go to hell. No if, no but, no maybe. That is as sure as the breath that you breathe. Except a man be born of the Holy Spirit. So seek the loving God while you still have this breath in you." People turn their music up. The young Orthodox Jewish guy next to me starts up a retaliatory incantation, eyes half shut, head back against the subway map. "We are very close to the end of times. And the Lord is no longer in the churches. For those of you outside the churches, for those of you who have lightly esteemed the words of the Lord, he will not be mocked. For those of you who stiffen your necks or harden your hearts at the provocation of the Lord, he will not be mocked. He is going to come like a thief in the night. It will be just like the days of Sodom and Gomorrah. And the days of Noah. They paid him no mind. No mind. It will be business as usual. But then every eye shall see and every ear shall hear and every knee shall bow and every tongue confess that Jesus Christ is Lord."

People move down the car. They exit at the next stop. "Read the Word every day. His words are true. Tell the Lord that you don't know anythin' because we don't know anythin'. We. Don't. Know. Anythin'." Everyone else has headphones, but I only have a book, which I can't concentrate on because the man's voice is a bass drum. I know he can tell that I am someone who loved God before I hardened my heart, that he can see a mark on me, and knows I am using a novel to do what, I imagine he'd tell me if he caught my eye, only the Bible can do for me. I suspect he also knows that I use people, and music, and this city to do what only church can do for me. And that I prefer to not know anything. I prefer not to know whom I should marry and why I should marry him, or how the world will end, or if we'll ever figure out the most perfect way to write ourselves lives of contentment. If I were going to die on the subway, let me die on the subway. I would not have died having done anything much with my life, but I could pretend that by planting myself on a subway seat for years I died defending everyone's right to live as they see fit, to escape whatever towns or families or churches told them otherwise and live in a utopia of their own creation. Thinking you know anything makes it impossible to say that God is light. It makes Korean cabdrivers tell me they think God sent a tsunami to Indonesia because it is a country of Muslim infidels. It makes voters convinced that legalizing gay marriage will result in domestic partnerships between dogs and humans. It makes young Muslim men think their sisters' sexuality is poison, and stone them because of it. I prefer novels. For the same reason I prefer this city. Both teem with particulars and offer no one truth.

The conductor comes into the car. People stare: since when do transit workers mete out justice? Stout, strong, gentle, wearing the calm but authoritative blues of the MTA, ready to clean up anthrax, blood, or Snapple in her industrial goggles. Whoever has her for a mother is lucky. "Sir," she says, "I'm going to have to ask you to stop." He says something we can't hear. "Sir," she says, "I don't have anything against what you're saying but the customers have complained, and when they complain it's my job as a transit worker to take action." He repeats himself, and she repeats herself. He gets off at the next stop. It would probably be a fantasy to imagine that God lives in the conductor, and cringes when his followers think harangues are the most effective nets with which to go fishing for men. But when you have loved God, you will never stop wondering what's coincidence and what's not.

God lives in the music and shouts spilling out of the Spanish Pentecostal church around the corner from my apartment when I walk home from the train. They keep the doors cracked wide, and I sometimes stand outside listening to the drums and tambourine and clapping. I look to see if there are any kids who seem bored, but there aren't any. It always seems like a party in there rather than a service, especially with everyone trickling out on to the street afterward to laugh and make plans, parents marching the kids in their dress shoes and shirts over to the bodega for brightly colored food and drink. I wonder what the kids will think about this scene when they grow up, and what their parents need this night for. "Come on in!" a man says to me when he sees me standing on the street with bags of groceries in both hands, looking in, listening to the music, studying joy and abandon, listening to the love songs I can't sing. He's smiling. "Come on in!" he says. I smile back, just to let him know I appreciate the offer, and keep walking.

# ACKNOWLEDGMENTS

The following readers have my undying gratitude: Paige Arthur, Meghan Falvey, Christopher Grau, Tavia Kowalchuk, Amy Maclin, Jordan Mamone, Miranda Purves, Lauren Sandler, Apollinaire Scherr, Deborah Shapiro, and Emily Votruba. I owe more than I can say to John Williams and Dawn Bauer.

Thanks also to Roberta Myers, Laurie Abraham, Alex Postman, Ben Dickinson, and Anne Slowey for their editing and encouragement.

I am especially grateful for the enthusiasm of Gail Winston and Alison Callahan, who edited this book.

Finally: these pages would not have been written without the support and wisdom of Mary Ann Naples, a friend who just happens to be my agent.

# PERMISSIONS